T0265750

The Master's Tools

The Master's Tools

How Finance Wrecked Democracy
(and a Radical Plan to Rebuild It)

Michael A. McCarthy

VERSO

London • New York

First published by Verso 2025
© Michael A. McCarthy 2025

1 3 5 7 9 10 8 6 4 2

Verso
UK: 6 Meard Street, London W1F 0EG
US: 207 East 32nd Street, New York, NY 10016
versobooks.com

Verso is the imprint of New Left Books

ISBN-13: 978-1-78873-066-2
ISBN-13: 978-1-78873-064-8 (UK EBK)
ISBN-13: 978-1-78873-065-5 (US EBK)

British Library Cataloguing in Publication Data
A catalogue record for this book is available from the British Library

Library of Congress Cataloging-in-Publication Data
A catalog record for this book is available from the Library of Congress

Typeset in Sabon by Biblichor Ltd, Scotland
Printed and bound by CPI Group (UK) Ltd, Croydon CR0 4YY

For Ellen, Thorne, and Wren
On to new adventures

Contents

Preface: Deckard on Skid Row

In 1953 the architectural critic Esther McCoy described the Bradbury Building in downtown Los Angeles for *Arts & Architecture* magazine as a "fairy tale of mathematics." According to McCoy, its exterior was "hardly distinguishable from the general drabness of the neighborhood," but once inside one's senses were overwhelmed by intricate wrought iron railing, weighted bird-cage elevators rising and falling, and the wash of Southern California light that bathed the foyer as it flowed in from the otherworldly glass ceiling.

This marvel, now a landmark, was built in 1893 by the architect George Wyman, who noted that a key source of his own inspiration for the designs were ideas found in the 1887 utopian novel, *Looking Backward: 2000–1887.* Written by Edward Bellamy, the book makes a case for democratic planning through a first-person account of a man from 1887 who wakes up in a utopian society in the distant year of 2000. Wyman was inspired by its description of public buildings of the future, "great distributing establishments" located in each city ward where people did their shopping.[1] Upon seeing them, the nineteenth-century man in the novel says,

> It was the first interior of a twentieth-century public building that I had ever beheld . . . I was in a vast hall of light, received not alone from windows on all sides, but from the dome, the point of which was a hundred feet above.[2]

What the character found himself in was a large, and quite beautiful, socialist distribution center where domestically produced or imported goods were made directly available to any resident in need.

Though Wyman's own atrium was inspired by lofty egalitarian principles, the Bradbury Building was not constructed as a public works project and never functioned as a public space like the one in *Looking Backward: 2000–1887*. Instead, well past the year 2000, the building's financing and actual operation followed the vein of another logic, that of finance capital.

The late–Victorian Era landmark was the project of millionaire mining entrepreneur and real estate developer Lewis Bradbury. It was built, as historian Jessica Kim writes, as "a paean" to the city-empires dominated by financiers and industrialists whose extractive supply and investment chains crossed national borders.[3] Though originally from Maine, Bradbury settled in the Mexican state of Sinaloa and built a personal fortune there by investing in mining companies. He then turned the precious metals he claimed as his own into a luxurious life on California's golden coast. As with all successful imperial adventures, Bradbury used his Mexican spoils to invest back into his own projects in Los Angeles, including one of the largest mansions in the city at the time and his namesake, the Bradbury Building. His wealth did not stay where it was exploited but instead flowed back across the Mexican border into Southern California. The natural wealth, dug out by Mexican workers from deep within mountains, was reinvested in private projects in Los Angeles, which could—on their own—turn a profit.[4]

Over a century later, the Bradbury hosts tourists who tiptoe through the foyer to catch a look at the famous landmark and its glass ceiling. Many come to see the location of the pivotal scenes in the cyberpunk film *Blade Runner*, where Rick Deckard (played by Harrison Ford) is stalked by the Nexus-6 combat model replicant Roy Batty (played by Rutger Hauer). For fans of the film, Batty's final monologue drips through the space,

I've seen things you people wouldn't believe . . . Attack ships on
fire off the shoulder of Orion. I watched C-beams glitter in the
dark near the Tannhäuser Gate. All those moments will be lost
in time, like tears in rain. Time to die.

But behind the Hollywood sparkle that draws in onlookers is a
speculative investment overseen for returns.

Its management by a shadowy asset manager unaccountable
to any public is typical of the broader political logic of finance
itself. The property is owned by a Hong Kong–based private
equity fund, Gaw Capital Partners, and is managed by an
asset management company, Downtown Properties. Both are
largely owned by the same person, financier and real estate
investor Goodwin Gaw. The regular income from tenants and
the film crews that rent out its space flows back to him and
his partners as returns. The building is one of the most desirable addresses in the city. Space there has been rented out by
the California Southern Railroad Company and the Los Angeles Police Department's internal investigations unit. Current
tenants include an exclusive membership-only shared work-
space, a luxurious Japanese clothing brand that sells pairs of
sneakers for over a thousand dollars, a contractor that designs
and fabricates facades for skyscrapers, and the Berggruen
Institute and its holding company, whose large global portfolio consists of financial investments heavily skewed toward
real estate and private equity. It is also where I wrote most of
this book.

For two years as a fellow at the Berggruen Institute and the
University of Southern California's Center for Science, Technology and Public Life, I was fortunate enough to call a small nook
in this fairy tale of mathematics my office. The imperial history
of the building, from the encaustic tiles, shipped from Mexico
when it was first built, that line the foyer to its juxtaposition with
the surrounding neighborhood, which includes America's most
infamous open-air slum Skid Row, encapsulates the core problem
that this book takes on.

Why has finance capitalism left people worse off and further wrecked democracy along the way? Why are our lives and politics increasingly determined by the financial sector, whose players Tom Wolfe described as the "Masters of the Universe" in *The Bonfire of the Vanities*? And how might an alternative to investment for profit leave people better off, reinvigorate the demos, and rebuild democracy? We live in a world where the vast bulk of investment decisions are concentrated in the hands of a small class of capitalists located all around the world, like Goodwin Gaw, whose capacity to invest is a result of the fact that they already have vast swathes of money. And yet so many outside that group feel themselves bound up in the system of asset speculation because of the retirement and personal accounts they have tied to it. This book considers this politically. It argues that this arrangement has led to a major decomposition of the fabric of democracy over the last half century. Finance capital is a giant moth eating through a coat we all share for warmth. The result is that our institutions remain democratic in theory but oligarchic in practice.

But this book is not all doom and gloom; there is a silver lining. If investment got us into an oligarchic mess, democratized financial institutions can get us out of it. In this sense, the title implies an inversion of the poet Audre Lorde's famous phrase "the master's tools will never dismantle the master's house."[5] In the case of finance, the means by which the masters plunder the universe—the pooled funds, retirement accounts, asset management firms and banks that enrich them by dismantling democracy—are the tools necessary to rebuild democracy. But I will argue that they must be transformed and democratized by a demos already differentiated within itself along lines such as race, gender, geography, political affiliation, industry, and occupation. Only then can finance be wielded in a new, deliberative way, by the demos and for the demos. As Lorde writes, "Difference must be not merely tolerated, but seen as a fund of necessary polarities between which our creativity can spark like a dialectic." This book argues for political organizations that are extended into the economy that are built on the spirit of this collaborative difference.

Regarding collaboration, the book was not written alone but rather through and with myriad community activists and policymakers working to transform finance capitalism as it exists into something deliberative so that it might serve the interests of the demos. It was inspired and shaped by the work of grassroots movements such as the San Francisco Public Bank Coalition and Public Bank Los Angeles, as well as by think tanks reimagining corporate ownership, such as Common Wealth in the UK and the Democracy Collaborative in the US. With researchers at the Berggruen Institute and the Jain Family Institute, I collaborated with Public Bank LA to produce a series of public-facing policy briefs on what a democratic public bank might do for the people of Los Angeles. Our briefs focused on housing, green infrastructure, financial justice, and democratic governing mechanisms. As a result of these reports receiving some media attention in the public banking fight in Los Angeles, I consulted with the staff of Congresswoman Rashida Tlaib (MI-12) on the Public Banking Act of 2023, which she introduced with Congresswoman Alexandria Ocasio-Cortez (NY-14) to the US Congress in December. My own contribution to the democratic governance of public banks relies heavily on the ancient democratic use of the lot, an approach that has greatly benefitted from discussions with Claudia Chwalisz at the Paris-based think tank DemocracyNext. It is, to my knowledge, the first time in US history such a lottocratic provision for allocating public finance has been included in a bill.

Many people have given me feedback on these ideas, in all likelihood many more than I have remembered. (A good piece of advice to authors: keep a record.) I owe thanks to Aaron Benanav, Robin Blackburn, Ben Braun, Charmaine Chua, Anya Degenshein, Mathieu Hikaru Desan, Devika Dutt, Yakov Feygin, Isabelle Ferreras, Nils Gilman, Kevan Harris, Pete Ikeler, Nic Johnson, Rafael Katchaturian, Martijn Konings, Leila Lorenzo, Steve Maher, Chris Muller, Saule Omarova, Mark Paul, Dylan Riley, Charlotte Robertson, Keeanga-Yamahtta Taylor, Camila Vergara, and Gabriel Winant. Gilad Wenig and my partner, Ellen Wagner, helped me with the graphs, tables, and illustrations. A special thanks to Asher Dupuy-Spencer, my editor at Verso Books, who read and gave feedback on multiple versions. The book also benefitted from discussions at the Democratizing Finance Workshop at the University of Madison-Wisconsin, the Future of Capitalism Group at the Berggruen Institute, the Democratic Socialism in Global Perspective Workshop at the Havens Wright Center for Social Justice, the Structural Power of Finance Workshop at the London School of Economics, and the Economic and Political Sociology group. Both intellectually and politically, it is a result of collaboration though the faults are mine alone, and I hope that it is read as a political project in progress—one the reader will join in building themselves.

Some of the chapters in this book develop arguments I have made elsewhere. Parts of Chapter 2 are drawn from "Beyond Abstractionism: Notes on Conjunctural State Theory," in *Marxism and the Capitalist State: Toward a New Debate* (2023), edited by Rob Hunter, Rafael Khachaturian, and Eva Nanopoulos. Parts of Chapter 3 are drawn from "The Monetary Hawks" (2016), published in *Jacobin Magazine*. Parts of Chapter 4 are drawn from "Our First 100 Days Could Be a Nightmare" (2020), also published in *Jacobin Magazine*. Parts of Chapter 7 are drawn from "The Politics of Democratizing Finance: A Radical View" (2019) published in *Politics and Society*. And finally, parts of Chapter 8 were published in collaboration with the Jain Family Institute and the Berggruen Institute in a report for Public Bank LA titled "Municipal Bank of LA: Democratic Governance Frameworks" (2023).

PART I

STRUCTURE

A Theory of Democratic Rupture

1

Mother of Antagonism

A book which does not include its opposite, or "counter-book,"
is considered incomplete.
Jorge Louis Borges, "Tlön, Ukbar, Orbis Tertius"

A Utopic Vignette

This book contains two even smaller ones. One about our current
conjuncture of finance capitalism and another about that conjuncture radically ruptured. A book and a counter-book, to use the
idea of Borges. Let's begin with the second, the counterfactual.

Imagine that capitalism were to suffer a democratic rupture
and you found yourself living through its effects. It's a sunny
Friday morning in 2045, and you're running late for a meeting
to deliberate over and agree on the priorities of the city. You're
riding Los Angeles' electric speed rail instead of driving on
congested freeways like you would have a few decades ago
because a new democratic process for allocating funds has completely reshaped city life. You step off the train in the Public
Finance District, where the streets were converted into pedes-
trian zones after huge investments in transportation eliminated
the need for cars downtown. The smog has nearly vanished,
and emissions are significantly down. The cleanliness of the
sidewalks would have come as a shock even ten years ago. Gone
are the days when residents of the city's mega slum, Skid Row,
lived in clusters of tents with nowhere else to go or slept alone
flat on the gum-and-stain-encrusted concrete. Instead, the city
has allocated finance for public housing and health projects

that have gone a long way toward solving the problems of the worst off.

Today, you will participate in the process that helped these changes come about. You pull out your phone to check the message you received months ago: "Minipublic Duty Notification: You have been selected at random to participate in the general assembly for the People's Bank of Los Angeles in its Green Planetary Futures Division. Your role will be on the standing commission of workers, to ensure the needs of the workers of Los Angeles are met. The assembly will make decisions about financing that will determine which green public goods our city will invest in in the next four years. Your voice, deliberation, and judgement are essential."

In the past three decades, financial institutions have undergone a profound change. Where they were once institutions designed with private-wealth gain and preservation as their core ambition, today they are mainly governed with the public interest in mind. Private financiers and their institutions were once the masters of the universe, the kings and queens in bespoke garb whose boardroom courts were the arena in which governments around the world would come pleading for special favors. Today, however, those with expertise in financial matters play a neutral consultant role to people's assemblies—what are called minipublics— a repurposed way of governing through small bodies of residents selected by lot. Guided by the principal of subsidiarity, mini-publics now decide how public credit and investment is allocated in the city.

Just a few decades ago, the ownership society divided people with common causes into atomized investor-selves who ambitiously outcompeted each other on social media accounts and in labor markets. But today the standing commissions and people's assemblies governing finance have helped to reconstitute the body politic to empower the working-class majority and to ensure that public finance is allocated in ways that reflect our shared social values and protect planetary durability. The organized voice of workers, for instance, now has permanent power, not only on the boards of trustees of public pension funds but on a wide range of investment funds and public banks that redirect flows of credit and investment into the greening economy. The green commission similarly ensures that decisions in public finance are consistent with the broader strategic goals for zero carbon emissions and the promotion of environmental flourishing. There are other standing commissions as well. Finance has become an inversion of its former self, both serving shared social goals and planetary ecological needs. The master's tools have been repurposed.

And you are paid to deliberate. Fridays have been converted to days set aside specifically for the work of democracy—holidays from production and for the governance of investment. And through support from federal legislation, which provides a governing and financing framework for democratic finance, minipublics governing flows of credit have flourished at a wide range of scales: communities and tribal lands, municipalities, regions, states, countries, and beyond. There are even planetary investment boards. With the work of economic democracy guaranteed, financial flows follow a new democratic logic informed by an ancient technology: the lot.

Financial Dilemmas

This is science fiction. But as in the best of utopian fantasy, we can see traces of it inverted in our own time. The allocation of finance is not decided upon democratically, and it is allocated principally for the profits of the few not for the social good. Even over their own pools of finance, such as pension funds, workers largely have no voice at all about where their assets are invested. And when they do, as in the case of 401(k) retirement plans, workers are encouraged to approach their accounts like atomized profit maximizers, if they manage their accounts at all (which they rarely do). All that matters in today's global financial system is returns, increasingly at the cost of everything else. This is the time of finance capitalism, where financial instruments are used in the service of extraction and exploitation of both nature and labor. But the place of finance is not an iron cage in which our histories are imprisoned. The contradiction of finance is that it offers paths not only toward deeper disorder but also toward emancipatory social projects.

In a letter to his friend Ludwig Kugelmann, dated July 1, 1868, Karl Marx wrote, "I represent large-scale industry not only as the mother of antagonism, but also as the creator of the material and spiritual conditions necessary for the solution to this antagonism." In the richest capitalist democracies and around the planet, it is not large-scale industry that plays the role of chief antagonist, it is the financial sector. And similarly, it is finance itself that can create the conditions that not only redress its damages but also realize more flourishing forms of social, and therefore also natural, life.

Though the financial sector continues to occupy a dominant position in business, there are cracks in its ruling edifice. Shifts in popular opinion, for instance, have done away with any hint of finance's moral legitimacy. We are witnessing the throes of what German critical theorists once termed a legitimation crisis, this time with finance at the center. The banks, hedge funds, asset managers and insurance companies that dominate Wall Street in the US and the City in the UK are widely viewed as sources of human suffering by populist insurgencies on both the left and the right. And for good reason. With its growth, the financial sector has generated a litany of social ills: tremendous upward redistribution, stagnant wages, and increased worker precarity. It has made political economies more prone to economic volatility and hastened the ecological crisis. When we look at capitalism's failings today, finance seems to always be right there, holding the smoking gun—or financing its sale and the pulling of its trigger.

But despite its loss of legitimacy, since the 2008 financial crash, the power of large financial institutions has remained undeterred precisely because these same institutions have also eroded democracy. Simply put, the formal democratic institutions that are the principal conduits of public policymaking are less responsive to the needs of ordinary people and planetary ecological sustainability because the voice of the public is increasingly made silent by financial power. Finance has come to occupy the driver's seat in the economies of advanced capitalist democracies like the US and UK, and their financial logic radiates outward to the peripheries. They put finance at the very heart of global capitalism. The corresponding importance of credit allocation and the growth of the value of financial assets in generating income and economic activity has bent the will of politicians in its direction, with the demos rarely noticing. And this structural power is only one source of leverage. Hedging their bets, so to speak, financiers flood capitalist democracies with money and influence to corrupt and undermine the democratic process and keep popular opinions and proposals off the political agenda. Since the 2008 financial downturn, the private power of finance has become entangled with the public power of the state.

On the other hand, the civic orientation to finance has undergone a profound shift since the eruption of Occupy Wall Street. Among the Young Turks taking on finance are the coalition behind the People's Bank in Los Angeles and Common Wealth in London and the architects of Jeremy Corbyn's inclusive ownership fund plan—financial activists now fighting for emancipatory alternatives. Since the 2008 financial crash, both activists and policymakers have moved from defensive criticism to the offense and now propose a bundle of alternative institutions of finance to replace and crowd out existing ones. The occupiers of Zuccotti Park gave voice to a simmering dissatisfaction that long predated the housing collapse and clarified, in populist terms, what its target was: the skyrocketed wealth and disproportionate political power of "the 1 percent." Yet the alternatives to finance capitalism that it gestured toward, such as reducing income inequality and returning to New Deal–era regulations, failed to *reimagine* finance itself. They were, like many liberal proposals, a nostalgic politics premised upon a return to a mythological golden age of capitalism. They left the *political* problem of reconstructing finance for the social good unaddressed.

The great public policy debates have taken place quite some distance outside the renowned public policy schools housed in the world's elite universities. Instead, a hodgepodge of scholars, independent think tanks, politicians, cryptographers, socialist magazine writers, leftist podcasters, and grassroot activists have delved into the thorny utopian project of reimagining what the institutions of finance might look like were they to serve the social good and promote democratic and ecological principles rather than undermine them in the service of wealth extraction. When it comes to plans, a thousand flowers are beginning bloom. The crisis of legitimacy of finance's neoliberal era has ushered in a new intellectual moment ripe for innovative thinking and reimagining, even if finance's rule remains largely intact. A wide range of alternative institutions and experiments have been put to paper and the digital airwaves, ranging from quite marginal changes that tinker with investment norms to ones that are deeply transformative, aiming to control investment flows itself. The plans include environmental, social, and governance investing (ESG); widening access to financial markets through brokerage apps; blockchain-based decentralized finance (DeFi); breaking up banking monopolies; sovereign wealth funds; inclusive ownership funds; public banking; public asset managers; democratizing central banks; industrial planning and a national investment authority; and bank nationalization (or, more euphemistically: state recapitalization).

This marks a profound cultural shift across the advanced capitalist world, the likes of which have not been seen in at least two generations. The horizon of radical possibilities prior to the 2008 meltdown was short-term; principally defensive and oriented against elite grabs, both domestic and abroad, it clung to besieged working-class institutions that to this day remain hobbled. Especially in America, it mirrored the conservative worldview in its inability to articulate a coherent vision for something beyond the reigning norms and institutions of capitalist democracy. And the so-called Washington Consensus, which was locked in place after the Volker Shocks that marked the governing shift from

Keynes to Friedman, made alternatives nearly unimaginable. The best many social critics could muster, which is as far as many still go, was a return to something akin to the postwar labor-capital accord, which is itself more a fantasy than a historical reality. But the onset of a legitimacy crisis for market capitalism has contributed to a wild flowering of new ideas and proposals that cut a middle-ground. We have witnessed the emergence of popular political demands that are more deeply transformative in their scope and that are even plausible as medium-term goals for a well-organized political movement.

Yet those that tinker with radical policies for the future often pay little attention to the politics of the proposals that they advance. Alternative experiments and models, including efforts to democratize finance through phone apps such as Robinhood and through blockchain projects such as Ethereum, are typically celebrated for their capacity to correct market failures, generate income and wealth for Wall Street outsiders, counter procyclical trends, and redirect dead speculative liquidity and hoarded wealth into socially useful production. But policies and institutions are not installed simply because they are efficient or egalitarian. Their desirability, in economic terms, is a question entirely separate from their feasibility in political terms.

In other words, in contributing to a project that imagines alternative futures, many of today's utopians, including the cryptopian variant, ignore the problems of power and democracy. This book aims to redress that. Its main goal is to understand how democratizing finance might transform the one-sided power relations that define the corporate sector's place in contemporary democracy. It makes a simple claim: either people democratically control finance or finance controls government. The more difficult task this book confronts is showing why and suggesting how.

To take up this problem, this book develops an approach to emancipatory transformations called *democratic ruptures*. At heart in these ruptures is the urgent need to democratize the most significant realms of life that lie outside the bounds of liberal democracy, such as our major economic institutions. The public versus private separation that courses through our political rhetoric and legal code is an illusion that needs to be shattered. Democratic ruptures do this by subjecting capitalist production, distribution, and investment to robust processes of popular participation and deliberation, making formal democracy itself more dynamic in the process. They are ruptural in so far as they wrest this decision-making power over investment away from capitalists and political elites and transfer the power to ordinary working people, the demos.[1]

In the 1967 book *Strategy for Labor*, the polyonymous philosopher André Gorz wrote about his key concept, "non-reformist reforms," which, he argued, lead to a "modification of the relations of power." Gorz pleaded that "to fight for alternative solutions and for structural reforms (that is to say, for intermediate objectives) is not to fight for improvements in the capitalist system; it is rather to break it up, to restrict it, to create counterpowers which, instead of creating a new equilibrium, undermine its very foundations."[2] This book will concretize Gorz. It examines the *forms of power* that capitalists wield and considers the *modes of reform* available to the demos to take their business sectors on. Capitalist power itself varies across time in both *form* and *degree*. And the sector of capital whose interests dominate politics rises and falls alongside the combined and uneven rhythms of capitalist development. To address this political complexity, this book asks two key questions. First, how might we develop a general framework for understanding how to democratize the economic spheres beyond the confines of formal political institutions? Second, how might we then apply that framework to our current period of crises to democratize finance?

To provide compelling answers, this book takes on three nested tasks. The first is to understand the capitalist politics in the geographic centers of finance capitalism at this conjuncture. Here, I explore the relationship between financial institutions and democracy, arguing that to understand capital's political power we must analyze it at a conjunctural level of abstraction. We must understand the powers of business that are given in the unique institutional arrangements of a society at a particular time in history. It is not enough to point to invariable abstract laws true of capitalism across all of its conjunctural configurations. Such claims, I argue, reproduce a static view of politics that understands them as driven by necessities merely functional to the reproduction of capitalism itself. These "laws," however, are qualified in profoundly important ways by institutional variation, the concrete expression of history, and human action. I will demonstrate that the mobility and liquidity of income-producing assets under management by various kinds of asset managers forms the basis of their political power. It anchors their three main forms of political leverage: engagement in the policy-making process, their growing prominence in the economy as a whole, and their logistical entanglement with state institutions and nonfinancial corporations. I refer to this as the *asset power* of finance. It is the principal source of hegemony for the financial sector in the advanced capitalist world. In theory we live in a liberal democracy, but in practice it functions more like an oligarchy of finance.

The second task will be to analyze broad modes of financial reform that, in some combination, we might deem important for subverting the power of finance and subjecting it to democratic processes. I do not consider reform alternatives principally from the perspective of their economic desirability or the degree to which they can solve market failures and redistribute income. Though the desirability of alternatives is a fundamental concern—we shouldn't support alternatives that leave us materially poorer—this is the primary preoccupation of today's policy planners and wonks of the future and not a debate that I have much to add to. Instead, this book addresses an equally as important but far less discussed concern: *power*. It asks, to what possible extent would the reform projects on offer weaken and upend the political power of finance and its adjacent corporate actors?

As I argue in this book, there are also distinct levers of capitalist political power to which finance in particular enjoys access to a far greater extent than any other sector in the countries that host the hubs of global money circulation. The political capacities these levers generate offer distinct ways for the masters of finance to remake formal political institutions in their image; they are part and parcel of the financial sector's planetary dominance and help explain its durable place in capital's coalition. But I will leave it to later to give actual definitions of each of the levers of power at the disposal of finance and the reform paths available.

This book explores ways to transform the capitalist institutions of our society not as they are in theory but as they currently exist—the stuff of a democratic rupture. It should be taken as a given that capitalist society is always knotted with contradictions. Therefore the possibility is always left open to what fantasy author China Miéville has called "distinct roads to rupture, of various and unforeseen shapes."[3] My account does not discount other possible roads and known unknowns but rather explores, in book-length detail, one plausible rupture with respect to the circuits of finance. For the sake of depth and focus, I necessarily take a partial view.

A large part of our failure of imagination is due to the left's rigid conceptualization of socialism, which some take as the all or nothing reward of mass insurgent struggle culminating in something that resembles the smashing of capital's citadel, the capitalist state. This is a demobilizing and nearly fatalistic view. On the one hand, it makes the goal for those aiming for something more humane than contemporary capitalism so far out of reach that it appears impossible, which in fact *it is* in any short- or medium-term sense. On the other, it makes the more feasible transformations that we might work toward appear trivial and hopelessly timid, which leads to inaction and ultimately reproduces the capitalist relations that hardliners seek to upturn. Not only are these strategic views demobilizing, they are also inaccurate.

Transformations in the character of policies, state institutions, and the organization of work and production either empower or disempower the working class within a capitalist context, *within the limits of that context*. I will show that the financial reform agendas that dominate the imaginative landscape of alternatives are undergirded by distinct class logics: normative projects aim to *reproduce* finance capitalism; regulatory projects aim to *restore* a finance capitalism of the postwar period; supplemental projects aim to *redistribute* financial assets to create a fairer finance capitalism; and control proposals are part of a *hegemonic* alternative to finance capitalism itself. I will argue that only hegemonic projects can contribute to democratic human and ecological flourishing in the longer term.

Finally, this book adjudicates between the possibility of different kinds of democratic participation in alternative financial institutions as a means of building up the power of ordinary people in general, the demos, and the working class in particular. If our aim is to reconsider the actual role financial institutions might play in a society oriented toward producing social goods rather than private ones, we need a political apparatus to do so. We know that finance capitalism underinvests in socially and ecologically needed goods and services. But we have yet to think through the conditions under which financial institutions might. I argue that we need to devise new modes of democratic engagement that might put that institution into action and to renew it in both good and bad times. We need, in other words, a theory of the social reproduction of emancipatory institutions. The critical factor is democracy.

I explore three distinct modes of democratizing finance: *representative*, *direct*, and *minipublics*, which use the participant selection mechanism of random selection, known as sortition or lot. I argue that when it comes to popular control over the allocation of financial investments and credit, minipublics are much more desirable than either representative or direct forms of democracy. Finally, I build on the promise of lottocratic governance to lay out the concrete design of a democratized pool of finance, in this case a democratic bank, built on a combination of class- and issue-based commissions and randomly selected people's assemblies.

The argument moves from the general, how we make sense of capitalist politics at the conjunctural level, to the contemporary, the ways in which finance exerts its power in particular, to concrete alternatives, how we might reconstruct finance to transform financial and social power relations, empower workers and the dispossessed, ensure a green transition, and move toward a more socially inclusive model of growth. Social and political theorists often fail to combine their theoretical critiques with realizable transformative visions that are also technically detailed and feasible. But while criticism has long been a beacon of critical social theory, alone it fails to give clear insight into even the most proximate steps on an emancipatory path. We don't just want critical theory; we also want constructive theory. This is the ambition of this book. It aims to walk the fine line between criticism and construction.

This book is built on five distinct theses that together make up my argument about democratic ruptures broadly and democratizing finance specifically. I present them here in simplified terms to indicate to the reader the broader shifts in the argument that will follow.

The Argument in Five Theses

Thesis 1. Capitalist politics are not static, ahistorical constraints on human flourishing but are constituted historically and change over time and across place. It is only with an examination of the present conjunctural character of capitalist politics that we can meaningfully envision the concrete alternatives that are most desirable not only in terms of their capacity to resolve our economic, social, and ecological crises but also with respect to their distributional effects on decision-making power.

Thesis 2. The global financial sector, centered in Wall Street and the City, has emerged as the dominant fraction of planetary capital. Because of the dilemmas that it imposes on democracies and its hegemonic position, finance capital is the principal obstacle to emancipatory transformations and a viable green transition. But, somewhat counter intuitively, the profound investment capacity that it has generated and the pools of investment capital it manages are also the key to achieving these transformations.

Thesis 3. The financial sector uses three forms of leverage to disrupt and shape formal politics in order to stymie efforts to reform it and to achieve a green transition: *engagement* (in formal policymaking), *prominence* (in the economy more broadly), and *entanglements* (with both state institutions and nonfinancial corporations). Underlying each lever is the fact that the character of the income-producing assets in finance capitalism are both increasingly mobile and liquid, that is, easily convertible to cash, and are often controlled by those who don't own them, asset managers. As a result, finance capitalism has eroded democratic institutions and made them substantively oligarchic, turning them into their own tools. Undermining these sources of power is key to building durable democratic institutions on solidaristic lines.

Thesis 4. Today financial activists and policy planners have four broad modes of policy reform available to them, and they advance projects and proposals in each. These are: *normative, regulatory, supplemental* and *control.* While each is rhetorically presented as a viable path to solve the crises of finance and facilitate a green transition by their main advocates, in fact they are undergirded by distinct class logics—some of which will only deepen financial crises. Control reforms, which aim to subject flows of investment and credit to popular say, are hegemonic, as they most radically upend finance's three sources of leverage and offer an alternative democratic path to the private allocation of investment by subjecting the asset power of finance to the will of the demos.

Thesis 5. Weakening finance alone is insufficient for building durable emancipatory institutions. To be dynamically durable, these institutions must also be democratic. Democratic ruptures reverse the atomization and internal fracturing of working-class political life and draw ordinary people into meaningful dialogic participation and deliberation about economic decisions. Therefore, popular capacity to democratically direct flows of credit and investment is a critical additional step. There are three modes of democratization plausible for finance: *representative government*—that is, the governing status quo—*direct democracy* and *democratic mini-publics*. Minipublics, small deliberative governing bodies populated by random selection from the demos, are the most feasible and desirable way to draw working people into meaningful political deliberation and decision-making. I argue that democratic financial institutions that are governed by a combination of people's assemblies filled through lot and class- and issue-based standing commissions can produce the most democratically desirable and durable outcomes.

The argument that I lay out in this book is a stark alternative to the centralization versus decentralization debates that pervade the discussion of finance and our ownership society more broadly. Because contemporary culture is so highly individualized, a fetish is regularly made of both, especially with respect to the en vogue idea of DeFi (decentralized finance) in the world of blockchain, crypto, and Web3. I will argue that while this is a world of experimentation, on balance it is one built on deceptive mythologies about what it actually offers and what is possible. Hardly a break, it is, in many respects, the ideology of finance capitalism itself. Alternatively, with the use of minipublics, I argue that the financial allocation should be centralized, and control of that allocation should be decentralized following a principle of subsidiarity. But new democratized financial institutions, at every scale, should be built on dialogic processes of deliberation that not only identify socially and ecologically desirable ways to allocate investment and credit but also help to articulate a common working-class political culture and identity while at the same time giving a platform to the particular needs, grievances, and concerns of subsections of the demos. In doing so, I offer up a new framework for thinking about democratizing finance and democratic transformations more broadly. I develop each thesis at the conjunctural level of abstraction.

Thinking Conjuncturally

When we make sense of the world, we break down our experiences into different components and generalize from them. We think at different levels of abstraction. At first the concept of levels of abstraction may strike the reader as an obscure idea better left to the philosophy of science. But this is far from the case; abstraction is a crucial method for the development of new concepts and for critical analysis of any sort. It's not simply something used in social theory; it is something we use every day.

Levels of abstraction principally concern concepts—their formation and how to relate those concepts to others. Concepts are crucial because they are the basic data containers that we use to fill with our experiences and observations, both in scientific projects and in daily life. All concepts have a hierarchical structure organized along a level of generality or abstraction. For each, there is an overarching concept under which there are subconcepts nested within each other in a laddered logic.[4] Levels of abstraction are a way of *organizing* concepts and are therefore how we make sense of the things, experiences and meanings in our world.

They are illustrated nicely with an example from the natural sciences. In biological classification, we have taxonomic ranks such as domain, kingdom, phylum, class, order, family, genus and, finally, species. Each of these are different levels of abstraction for understanding the living things that populate the planet. As they move from the highly abstract, the domain, to the most concrete, the species, more and more information and determinations become relevant for why something is put into one classification or the other. The level of abstraction at which we think about anything in the world depends principally on what we are trying to explain. If we are trying to make sense of the characteristics of the organic life that gives birth to living young as opposed to laying eggs or dropping seeds, then *mammal* at the class level of abstraction is usually appropriate. But if we are trying to understand why some young are born and almost immediately strike out on their own whereas others spend decades in their parents' basements, then the level of abstraction of species is far more appropriate.

Table 1.1: Theorizing Capitalist Politics

Level of abstraction	Object of analysis	
	Structure of class politics	Form of the state
Mode of production	Polarized	Capitalist state
Social formation	Noncapitalist classes & cross-class alliances	Democratic, fascist, predatory
Conjuncture	Intraclass fractions & hegemonic formations	Neoliberal, corporatist, social democratic

Within social theory, we might distinguish between three levels of abstraction when thinking about social and political life within capitalism (though more can and have been added): mode of production, social formation, and conjuncture (see Table 1.1).[5] A mode of production constitutes the highest level of abstraction for thinking about capitalism but is also used to detail the basic social relations of feudal societies, slave-based societies, prehistoric communal societies, and even the fictional societies that might exist in the future. Here capitalism is treated as a system largely constituted by a polarized class structure consisting primarily of workers and capitalists who are engaged in a class struggle in which capital has the decided upper hand. It is an "abstract-formal object" or, more simply, an overarching concept in which many varieties can take form.[6] At this level of abstraction, all capitalisms share certain fundamental features; here, the key points of variability between, for instance, social democratic capitalisms, crony capitalisms, and liberal capitalisms largely fall from view. Instead, the continuities across capitalisms are emphasized.

At all levels of abstraction, we can identify a corresponding object of analysis. This book takes *capitalist politics* to be that object. By *politics*, I do not exclusively mean formal politics institutionalized in governments, courts, and political agencies. I consider politics more broadly to include all of the social practices that transform and reproduce power relations in society. In this more expansive view, relations of domination within the workplace between managers and employees are constituted through politics. The "means of production" for those power relations certainly include political parties and states, but they also involve other organizations as well, such as firms, business associations, interest groups, unions, schools, churches and the family. The kind of politics that I concern myself with is *capitalist* politics precisely because they relate to the transformation and reproduction of the power relations central to the production and distribution of goods, services, and—chiefly for this book—flows of credit and investment.

If we consider capitalist politics at the highest level of abstraction, that of the mode of production, we get a necessarily partial view of things. With respect to the structure of class politics and the form of the state itself at this level, capitalist politics appears to be a polarized class struggle in which the state takes a "pure" capitalist form, functioning with a singular purpose to reproduce business power and ensure that capitalist accumulation and legitimacy are secured. At this high level of abstraction, for analytical purposes, our snapshot of capitalist politics typically casts the working class in a state of disempowerment and the state as operating in a seamlessly smooth way to ensure the reproduction of capitalism and its relations of exploitation. Such a snapshot of politics is free of contradictions, variation, and points of plausible hope. In other words, at a very high level of abstraction we can only understand capitalist politics as a set of static constraints on workers' movements that protect private property and flows of capital for accumulation.

If you squint tightly and let all the complications that are built on this skeletal description fall from sight, what is left is the general structure of capitalist politics. But social structures are not law-like regularities; they are contested tendencies. The problem, therefore, lies in failing to move below this level of abstraction in making sense of capitalist politics to understand its permutations and varieties. We can, for instance, move down to the level of a social formation, where concepts are developed that are richer still in complexity and variability but are nested within a mode of production. These lower-level concepts are not developed apart from the more general ones; quite to the contrary, they presuppose them. This level of abstraction is best suited for studying the ways that societies combine different modes of production, even in cases in which one mode remains dominant over the others.[7]

With respect to class politics and the forms of the state at the level of a social formation, we find increased complexity in our object of analysis. In the structure of capitalist politics, non-capitalist classes (such as the peasantry, surplus labor, and so on) enter the picture, profoundly complicating the character of class struggle, which is no longer easily presented as a polarized battle between workers and capitalists abstractly conceived. This opens up critical analytical and strategic space for pursuing alliances between various class fractions that make up the social formation. The forms that the state itself takes also become more complex. Here the capitalist state is further differentiated into possible subtypes: liberal democracy, fascist, authoritarian, and so on. We need not get even further into the conceptual weeds. Here is the crucial point: To understand how institutional changes can go beyond solving economic problems to also upend the current configuration of social power, we can begin at an even lower level of abstraction, that of the conjuncture.

If the power formations and contradictions in the state are not static—something that can be articulated at the level of a mode of production and assumed true of *all* capitalist modes of production—but rather develop dynamically through capitalist development and crises, then the changing forms of power and possibilities for ruptural breakthrough must be deeply intertwined with this development itself. This makes an analysis of radical emancipatory transformations at the level of mode of production wrongheaded and simply inadequate at the level of a social formation. It is essential, in other words, to have a concrete understanding of power at the present as it has developed *historically* and, crucially, of how that power and its accompanying institutional transformations are defined by an accumulation of contradictions that generate emancipatory possibility.[8] Without a conjunctural perspective, such emancipatory possibilities would fall from view.

A conjunctural analysis of capitalist politics is therefore how we answer Lenin's oft quoted, "What is to be done?" for the present, at least with respect to how we produce, distribute, and finance things. This level of abstraction demands that the analyst identify the crucial features of accumulation, the key power blocs and fractions of capital where power is principally exercised, and the contradictions that it throws up for social and ecological life. Finally, the analyst must suggest precisely how, in design terms, it can be transformed. Intraclass dynamics, therefore, are a fundamental point of relevance. At the conjunctural level, the analyst is pushed to identify the hegemonic fraction of the ruling class, their sources of power, and the potential alternative sources of democratic power available to the many segments of the working class. Such a conjunctural analysis is the very basis of meaningful problem-solving, movement building, and strategy formulation. It also pushes the analyst to identify further differentiations in the form that the state takes. Capitalist democracies, for instance, can be further broken into subtypes such as neoliberal, corporatist, social democratic, and so on.

The theory of democratic ruptures laid out in these pages involves two key analytical moves, both of which break with abstractionist theorizations of capitalist politics.[9] The first is to make an inventory of the key causal phenomena in the terrain of capitalist politics broadly conceived and to compare and contrast them in order to create an accurate picture, or snapshot, of how the balance of power has taken hold in the present historical moment. This is why I spend several chapters showing both what exactly finance capitalism is and what its core sources of political power are. The second task involves an emancipatory twist. It is not enough to simply describe and categorize our historical period with respect to the operation of political power. We must take the additional step to identify the key problems that the conjuncture throws up for society in order to think through how those problems might be responded to. To put it still another way, the conjunctural analysis I develop here is an analysis of the key contradictions in a historical moment and how they might be resolved along lines that promote human flourishing.

As we will see in the coming chapters, finance capitalism, especially in its power centers in the US and the UK, rests on a core contradiction: it both is a key driver of the major dilemmas that beset the planet and provides the architecture of an institutional infrastructure that might address these dilemmas if they are democratized. Finance has become deeply intertwined with and empowered by strong state intervention. By moving beyond the too neatly presented divide between the private and the public, we can begin to empower the demos itself. The master's tools, the politics of finance, can and should be turned against him. A conjunctural analysis allows us not only to offer a diagnosis of finance capitalism but also to envision concrete institutional alternatives, which I do in this book with a democratic design for investment.

On Democracy

This leads us to another thorny problem: democracy. It's hard to imagine another concept that is more ubiquitous and contested. Everyone stakes a claim to it. The far right, the revolutionary left, all the varieties of pragmatists in between, hard constitutionalists, and even solarpunk technologists all rhetorically present their respective political tribes as the "real" defenders of democratic ideals. As I will show in this book, especially when applied to money and finance, the concept is often shrouded by mythologies and conceptual sleights of hand. Whatever the agenda, from doubling down on joke currencies like Dogecoin by taking out a second mortgage to replacing usurious check-cashing outlets with more reliable services from a Postal Bank, advocates claim the goal of democracy.

The idea of democratizing finance fueled the global debate about the retail traders that triggered a January 2021 short squeeze of the stock of GameStop, a dying brick and mortar video game store. Democracy has been the paramount value of celebrated financial economists like Yale's Robert Shiller, who argued for the need to make financial markets available to the middle and lower classes as a means of democratizing finance. And, most recently, the rhetoric of democracy has pervaded the marketing of cryptocurrency. Here, democratizing finance is framed as righting of the historical wrongs of financial exploitation, exclusion, and dispossession. The dollar, or "old money," is the currency of slavery, colonialism, and bigotry. Spike Lee's celebratory narration in a flashy commercial for Coin Cloud, a maker of digital currency ATMs, treats digital assets as the great equalizer for America's illiberal past: "But new money—new money is positive, inclusive, fluid, strong, culturally rich," Lee proclaims definitively on the screen. Reflecting on the commercial, the Coin Cloud marketing chief at the time said, "I had a vision of us creating more than a commercial and actually starting a real conversation as we are talking about a major flex in the financial market: the democratization of currency."[10] Just a year and a half after the commercial aired, Coin Cloud filed for bankruptcy with liabilities on its balance sheet somewhere between $100 and $500 million.

In this book, I show that these visions of financial democracy are built on mythologies, both about the desirability of such projects and about the concept of democracy itself. In practice, democracy understood narrowly as increased access to financial markets only leads to more unequal outcomes, macroeconomic instability, and a deepening atomization and fracturing of the demos. Just as fundamentally, the access view of democracy distorts what democracy has always been about, even dating back to its deformed origins in ancient Greece: the ability of the demos to debate, deliberate, and make binding decisions about the things that matter to their lives. I argue that it is only through such dialogic processes that atomization can be reversed and a shared political identity within the demos itself be articulated and established. We will turn later to the technologies of ancient Greek democracy to counter the insufficient access view of democracy.

Among the left, it has become standard to call for the need to extend democratic processes beyond the state into the economy—indeed, to extend the scope of the state itself. Yet when it comes to financial institutions, democracy is often treated like a residual category. Many would agree that our financial system should be more democratic, but, we are treated to precious few concrete descriptions of what a democratic financial system would actually look like.[11] Models for democratizing firms, ranging from unions and sectoral bargaining to co-ops to ownership transfers akin to the historic Meidner Plan in Sweden, are increasingly put under the microscope of scrutiny. And new work from political theorists increasingly bridges the gap between democratic theory and economic activism.[12] Within finance, thinkers and activists in the Debt Collective have built innovative ways to achieve debt abolition. But when the word democracy appears in relation to finance, it is almost always applied to the options-trading world of retail investors or haphazardly thrown into a list of demands. Democracy needs to be explained, and the basic features of a democratic financial institution need to be designed. This book takes up both intertwined tasks.

But first, some more conceptual ground clearing is necessary. Before delving into the specifics of finance I will turn to a more general theorization of democratic ruptures. This will be the conceptual scaffolding that the rest of the book will hang on. The next chapter explores some of the basic conditions under which capitalist democracies can be transformed and the working class, what I consider to be synonymous with the modern demos, empowered through democratic rupture. There, a general framework and scaffolding for this book is provided.

2

The Frankenstein Problem

> Yet you, my creator, detest and spurn me, thy creature, to whom
> thou art bound by ties only dissoluble by the annihilation of one
> of us. You purpose to kill me. How dare you sport thus with life?
> Do your duty toward me, and I will do mine towards you and
> the rest of mankind. If you will comply with my conditions, I
> will leave them and you at peace; but if you will refuse, I will
> glut the maw of death, until it be satiated with the blood of your
> remaining friends.
>
> The monster, in Mary Shelly, *Frankenstein*

Making Monsters

We are living in a time of deepening democratic deficits and
increasing concentrations of elite power, the likes of which have
not been seen since perhaps the Gilded Age well over a hundred
years ago. But this need not be the case. This chapter identifies the
core ways that capitalist states vary with respect to their autonomy
and distribution of class power and thereby provides a brief sketch
of a theory of democratic ruptures. Frankenstein's monster is an
analogy that lies at the heart of this theory. This chapter casts the
class functionalist view of capitalist democracies, that they invar-
iably govern for the reproduction of capitalist social relations, into
serious doubt. Something more contradictory lies at the center of
their operation, something stitched haphazardly together, in
response to crises, with a mind all its own.

While states do tend to govern for capitalism, they require a
degree of autonomy to do so, especially in periods of crises like

our own. I show that the very autonomy that is necessary to promote capitalist accumulation and to secure governing legitimation also allows for the various institutions and apparatuses of the state to be subject to subordination not only by capitalists but also, if rarer, by working-class movements, organizations, and parties for economic democracy. Perhaps ironically, to develop the capacity to govern in a way that promotes capitalist accumulation and growth, the state, like Frankenstein's monster, must also develop vulnerabilities that allow it to be subordinated and turned against its master. Capitalist states can also act in ways destructive to capitalist social relations. This chapter argues that democratic ruptures extend these political processes into the economy but do so in such a way that they are subject to the dialogic control of the demos itself.

Obeying Its Master

We will return to patchwork monsters momentarily. First we must revisit André Gorz's idea of "non-reformist reforms." Gorz noted that to fight for emancipatory improvements within capitalist systems, it is necessary to design and construct "counter-powers" that can undermine, disrupt, and weaken the private and public powers of capital owners. Gorz understood, quite sharply, that intermediate emancipatory transformations of the state were not reducible to expansions of the state and its social functions relative to the private sector. He therefore rejected the sharp public-private evaluative distinction that is so often taken for granted in debates about public policy. For Gorz, what is most important to consider is the *distribution of power*. As he wrote,

> whether it be at the level of companies, schools, municipalities, regions or of the national Plan, etc., structural reform always requires a *decentralization* of the decision-making power, a *restriction on the powers of State or Capital*, an *extension of popular power*, that is to say, a victory of democracy over the

dictatorship of profit. No nationalization is *in itself* a structural reform.[1]

Gorz's arguments pivot on a critical concern for emancipatory politics: What role do the legislative and policy apparatuses of the state play in the reproduction of basic capitalist social relations? To what degree, if any, are the institutions of the state functional and necessary for the reproduction of relations of exploitation and domination? The *class functionalism view* of the capitalist state sees it as serving a singular function: capitalist accumulation. States are central to the stability of capitalism, and it is hard to imagine basic relations of production, exchange, and investment working at all without legal rules in place to ensure order. This perspective treats the state role with iron-law-like invariability. It represents the left inversion of the bourgeois utopian view of the state, captured by Ronald Reagan's pithy inaugural address line, "Government is not the solution to our problem, government is the problem." For the utopian right, whom we will revisit in our exploration of crypto assets, capitalism works best when the state is as small as possible and is least involved. In this fantasyland, the state, especially in its role provisioning welfare, weakens capitalism's dynamism.[2] The left inversion treats the state as the source of that dynamism. Perhaps ironically, subsections of both the left and the right, at least rhetorically, therefore see the state as *the* problem to be overcome and done away with, whether as a the swamp to be drained or as capital's machine-like golem to be smashed.

The class functionalism view offers an unsatisfying account of capitalist politics, for reasons explored below, but it does contain partial truths. There is overwhelming evidence that capitalist democracies *tend* to govern for capitalism, and there are good reasons why. First, capitalists have greater ease of entry than do workers and the non-elite into the formal apparatuses of the state to do the work of interest group politicking. The lobbying tentacles of business dwarfs that of labor unions in its spending and personnel power. The policymaking apparatus, with its field of intersecting foundations, think tanks, and nongovernmental organizations is fueled by corporate funds and private donors. And the social worlds of many politicians, who are themselves overwhelmingly culled from the rich, overlap and intersect with those of capitalists as well. Second, because the economy is principally capitalist, politicians have an interest in making sure they pass laws that do not disrupt the growth of accumulation, jobs, and ultimately the tax revenue that finances many state initiatives. So, even if the state is not dominated by capitalists, by virtue of it being a capitalist state, its functions are informed by the capitalist context in which it is situated.

In functionalist causal accounts of what capitalist states do, the beneficial effects of a pattern of action are used to explain that pattern of action, but neither the intentions of the actors in generating those effects nor the feedback loops where the effects themselves sustain their original causes are shown.[3] The features of the state are explained in the class functionalist view by how those features allow the state to organize the power bloc—the ruling coalition of capital—and disorganize the working classes to promote stable capitalist accumulation.[4] Functionalism worked for Charles Darwin's evolutionary theory, as in the argument that birds have hollow bones so they can fly, because he identified the mechanisms: mutation and natural selection. But no such mechanisms for the state's *invariable* functionality can be pointed to. It is simply not the case that the state must solely function to the benefit of capitalist relations and capitalist growth. And yet, so much of radical emancipatory theory takes this as a presumption.

Both the influence of capitalists and the context of capitalism itself are subject to challenge and transformation. When labor unions and left parties have become socially strong enough, they have radically reshaped the labor-management relation, as was the case with the radical unionism during the New Deal in the US and sectoral bargaining won by social democratic labor organizations in the Nordic countries. And when the economy itself has been transformed by noncapitalist institutions—for example, when public enterprises and worker cooperatives have been created—they have offset capital's power in structural terms. In short, while the capitalist state does have strong internal biases to govern for capitalist reproduction, these are historically constituted and subject to contestation and change.

Instead, the capitalist state is a *contradictory* social relation. Its various apparatuses and governing bodies are not a thing or instrument acting at the sole behest of the capitalist class or capital broadly.[5] It is not a monolith. Nor is it a unitary bureaucratic subject with its own predefined organizational interests dominated by bureaucrats and experts.[6] Nor is it an alienated socio-political form that is superimposed upon humanity's democratic essence to be smashed wholesale in a great final battle once working-class power has been sufficiently built up outside of it.[7] Lastly, it is not a political form that can be thought of as derivative of the logic of capital itself.[8] The state is instead a strategic field composed of governing apparatuses, agencies, and a bureaucratic corps that are themselves expressions and results of class struggles. States are always a product of ongoing history. This means, importantly, that it is not simply a thing that can be taken by a left government in a single election or even progressively won through a series of elections.[9]

The capitalist state is a social relation in much the same sense that capital itself is a social relation. It is the political expression of active material forces—in particular, class struggles—whose power is both produced and reproduced through its formal institutions. This conception of the state in capitalist democracies, where the relations of class struggle are both constituted by the state and traverse its institutions to produce and resolve internal contradictions, is a useful starting point for developing the notion of a democratic rupture. The upshot of this view is that while, as we will see below, there are structural biases in the institutions of the capitalist state to govern in favor of the reproduction of capitalism—that is, to function for capitalism—those biases coexist with opportunities for democratic forces to create counter-powers on that same terrain precisely because the institutions themselves are changeable. It is contradiction, in this respect, all the way down. The rest of this chapter aims to demonstrate this first by showing how the class functionalist view of the state rests on an untenably abstract view of the state itself and then by turning to an alternative that emphasizes the state's contradictions.

Abstractionism's Cul-de-sac

State, Power, Socialism by the political sociologist Nicos Poulantzas is an ideal entry point because it illustrates the limits of abstractionist thinking about capitalist politics and the promises of moving beyond.[10] To date, nobody has done more to construct a complex model of capitalist democracy's internal contradictions in order to develop ruptural strategies fit to the political terrain. In *State, Power, Socialism*, Poulantzas remapped left politics, arguing that the antistate, mass-insurgent, and antidemocratic "revolutionary" road and the incremental, legalistic, and democratic "reformist" road were not the only two nor the most desirable routes available for emancipatory politics. Through his relational theory of the state, which argued that the state itself was the contradictory institutional expression of class struggles, he showed that emancipatory politics always had to fit the conjuncture. Because political theorists, in Poulantzas's view, are simply incapable of devising ahistorical formulas for emancipatory politics for going beyond capitalism, he concluded that there could be no general strategy.

The starting point must be states and their mutually constitutive intertwining with societies as they actually are. Writing on European democracy in the during the Cold War, Poulantzas demonstrated that the institutional terrain of politics is a key site for working-class ruptures that break with the structural imperatives of capital—imperatives that are iron-like in the class functionalist view. To create ruptural breaks with the pull on politics capital's power obtained, Poulantzas proposed to deepen democracy in both actually existing democratic institutions, the so-called state apparatus, and to extend democracy via direct forms of economic democracy and self-management in the spheres of production, distribution, and investment. In contrast to the strategic views he identified with Lenin and, more subtly, Antonio Gramsci, for Poulantzas the "democratic road to socialism" advanced a view of rupture that at once combined direct forms of democracy in capitalist institutions with expansions of worker rights and capacities in formal political institutions.[11] This book follows his navigational suggestion to think in terms of rupture, taking a path right into the Gordian contradictions of capitalist politics as they exist today.

But as crucial as they are, Poulantzas allows his conjunctural insights to be pulled back, almost as if by a gravitational force, to functionalist generalizations about politics pitched at the level of the mode of production. As he writes in the chapter "The Limits of the Moloch-State," "the capitalist State is constituted by a *negative general limit* to its intervention—that is to say, by *specific non-intervention* in the 'hard core' of capitalist relations of production."[12] This is the preferred level of abstraction in Poulantzas's early work, where instead of contradictions we find functional limits, which he never quite frees himself from. A study of abstract-formal objects, such as the capitalist state, that neglects how the state ensemble of institutions takes concrete historical form is a crucial barrier to developing an approach to democratic ruptures. Actual states, like actual capitalist economies, are far more heterogenous than it is possible to see from such a bird's eye view. Even if internal biases make the tendency to reproduce capitalism dominant, it need not follow—and doesn't—that states solely function to reproduce capitalism as the class functionalism view would have us believe.

In his first major book on the state, *Political Power and Social Classes*, Poulantzas develops a class functionalist theory that begins from the highest level of abstraction, the capitalist mode of production, and treats the capitalist state as a specific region within it. And to the extent that the concrete facts are engaged, they are used to illustrate that abstract theory. Yet such abstract theorizations render invisible the institutional variability, both internal and external, of capitalist democracies, which are observable only at lower levels. That variability is the raw institutional material of democratic ruptures. Political analysis limited to the abstract level like this therefore leads to a monolithic view of democratic institutions as seamless machines free of internal contradictions functioning to reproduce capitalist power. But capitalist states are not like biological organisms whose separate organs and systems function for a common goal, the life of the organism itself. The various institutions of capitalist democracy do not simply remake and reproduce capitalism. This is the cul-de-sac of abstractionism. While the class functionalist view is right to identify the ways that the capitalist state is constrained, it errs in presuming these constraints are static and timeless facts of capitalist politics.

Therefore, our analysis of capitalist politics needs to be articulated at a level of abstraction that can explain both variation across the forms of capitalist states (i.e., fascist, military, and liberal) and also variation *within* the state forms.[13] This book takes on financialized liberal democracies—such as those that obtain in a good part of the contemporary capitalist world—to argue that our evaluative concepts of politics need to be developed at a more *conjunctural* level of abstraction in order to explain their variability across time.

Poulantzas understands that this problem of abstractionism is a real one. He notes that it is "a theoretical conception that neglects the weight of class struggle in history."[14] But he leaves incomplete the task of freeing himself from it.[15] *State, Power, Socialism*'s final chapter is a sharp defense of a democratic socialism, which aims

> to transform the State in such a manner that the extension and deepening of political freedoms and the institutions of representative democracy (which were also the conquest of the popular masses) . . . [are] combined with the unfurling of forms of direct democracy and the mushrooming of self-management bodies.[16]

Yet the political theory that precedes it, contradictory as it is, snuffs out the contingent effects of transformations of democratic political institutions, leading us back into the impasse that, like clockwork, capitalist democracy must reproduce the capitalist mode of production at the eleventh hour. Poulantzas is always aware of class struggle as expressed in divisions in actual state institutions and parties, in the ruling power bloc of capitalists and their competing segments, and in contradictions within classes themselves. Yet despite his fidelity to a middling path between reform and revolution, he largely elides a discussion of how trans-formations in state structures through class struggles also transform state *functions* themselves. On this crucial point, his theory remains undynamic. This is the abstractionist trap of the class functionalist account of the state.

The notion of relative autonomy illustrates this. The concept emerged in the context of debates about the state and was intended to offer a counter-perspective to the reductive notion that capital-ists control democracies like puppet masters. Instead, relative autonomy suggests that the state in capitalist society needs, and therefore has in functionalist terms, a degree of autonomy from particular capitalist-class segments and individuals within the capitalist class "so that it may ensure the organization of the general interests of the bourgeoisie."[17] In much the same way that birds have hollow bones so that they can fly, in this view, the state has some autonomy so that it can organize the power bloc—the ruling coalition of capital—and disorganize the working classes. This is a hard pill to swallow when capitalist states have not simply broken strikes but have also protected and promoted the organization of the working class through legislation that enshrines labor organization as a liberal right.

Writing two years before the publication of *State, Power, Socialism* in response to a critic's provocative question "*How relative* is relative autonomy?" Poulantzas argued that

> the degree, the extent, the forms, etc. (*how* relative and *how* is it relative) of the relative autonomy of the State can only be examined . . . with reference to a given capitalist State, and to the precise conjuncture or the corresponding class struggle.[18]

Such an insight demands a conjunctural perspective that identifies the way class power varies. Yet his inability to specify the elements that account for the variability of relative autonomy itself forced his own account back into the impasse of abstractionism that he had hoped to move well beyond. When push comes to shove, the state's basic role is the reproduction of capitalism, which it happily fills at the end. While *State, Power, Socialism* argues that "the establishment of the State's policy must be seen as the result of the class contradictions inscribed on the very structure of the State," it does not show us why.[19]

If relative autonomy does tend to serve some function, then political autonomy is contingently realized rather than a static structural feature. This leads to a critical contradiction present in any capitalist democracy that might be termed "the Frankenstein problem." This contradiction is key to understanding the contingency at the heart of capitalist states and therefore the possibility for democratic ruptures within them.[20]

Contradictory Functionality

Thankfully there is an alternative that begins to help us understand states conjuncturally and therefore the conditions under which democratic ruptures arise concretely, the *contradictory functionality view*.[21] The capitalist class structure helps explain why democracies tend to govern in favor of capital. And the conjunctural class structure similarly gives ample evidence for the financial sector's leverage over politics—as the next section of the book shows. But if the capitalist state needs autonomy to help reproduce capitalist property relations and to prevent capitalism from destroying itself through crises, then like Frankenstein's monster it also has the capacity to wield its power against those capitalist relations—or at minimum to withhold its help in reproducing them. Even if capitalist democracy is typically governed by its capitalist masters, those political institutions hold a latent capacity to be turned against them as well. Much like capitalism itself may create its own gravediggers in the proliferation of the working class, the political apparatuses that afford it governing capacities can be used for other purposes. Autonomy can be subordinated by capitalists and workers alike.

The political sociologist Claus Offe identifies this problem in his pivotal essay on "the crisis of crisis management."[22] Solving crises in capitalism are key to his story. Offe shows that to overcome recurrent crises in capitalist development, the state develops "flanking subsystems," such as state agencies, committees, programs (such as welfare), and quasi-governmental entities such as central banks, that actively intervene in relations of production, exchange, and investment.[23] The interventions of these subsystems aim to legitimate the economic system with the population as a whole, but they also need to promote accumulation and profit making for firms. In some circumstances—for example, where there is rapid growth and markets tighten to increase wages—accumulation leads to legitimacy for the system; these need not be inversely related. However, the systemic need for both legitimation and accumulation might also contradict each other, by running counter.[24]

For capitalism to survive Offe reasoned that capitalist democracies pursue stabilizing interventions that overcome capitalism's own anarchic and self-destructive tendencies. This notion should be an intuitive one for readers who lived through the bailouts of the Great Recession, the passing of the CARES Act during the COVID pandemic, and the subsequent interest-rate hikes the Federal Reserve triggered to respond to inflation. While there were other options left unpursued on the table—for example, in the case of inflation, price controls—the debate was nonetheless about stabilizing the economy. Finance capitalism might, as will be suggested in the next section, require the near continuous presence of a bailout state.[25] There is a whole host of policy interventions that states use, but the key point is that they do not simply enforce property rights and allow the chaos of the market to ebb and flow, they actively and continuously manage it.

In short, capitalism runs into crises that require political coordination in order to be overcome. And states are the social institutions that play this role in the most decisive way. This inter-vention, as Poulantzas himself noted, would not be possible without a degree of autonomy from the direct influence of the business class and its various segments. Sometimes what capital-ists want is not what they need. And therefore, to effectively stabilize capitalist social relations, capitalist states need to govern on behalf of capitalism not necessarily at the behest of capitalists.

This stabilizer role gives capitalist democracy a contradictory double character. It must protect capitalist relations of exploita-tion and domination from the very conditions those relations produce while also ensuring that capitalist relations remain dom-inant in the political economy. As Offe writes, "This precarious double feature of the capitalist state continuously demands a com-bination of intervention and abstention from intervention, of 'planning' and 'freedom,' in short it demands an 'opportunism.'"[26] But here is the rub. In asserting itself over economic relations in the effort to protect those relations, it necessarily reveals those relations to be profoundly political in their basic constitution and reproduction and therefore calls into question for the demos the private and by extension the capitalist character of production, exchange, and investment it seeks to protect.

When states develop the bureaucratic autonomy and capacity needed to save capitalism from itself, that very autonomy becomes vulnerable to being subordinated to interests and, counter-intuitively, to being used against capitalism itself. If capitalism survives by creating monsters that it cannot itself fully control, then those monsters must also have the capacity to harm the thing that brought them into existence—that is, capitalism itself. Like Frankenstein's monster, they might destroy their own master. Therefore, when capitalist economies become more firmly prop-ped up by flanking state subsystems designed to keep accumulation afloat, which is an endemic feature of finance capitalism, they begin to face a political threat to the autonomy of those systems. This is the recurrent Frankenstein problem for capitalist states. That contemporary states prop up our dominant financial insti-tutions makes clear their political character.

The Frankenstein problem of capitalist democracies leads to three contradictions. First, once this capacity is created, interest groups—most often capitalists themselves—will try to command it. Such state capacity underscores the pivotal centrality of the state and its agencies in class struggles for power.

Second, there is no stable equilibrium between regulation and marketization, bail outs by flanking subsystems and letting the market decide. As capitalist societies develop, the state follows a dialectical dance of capacity construction, dismantling, and redesigning in ways that never look the same twice. Our most recent dismantling period, the neoliberal revolution lead by Reagan, Thatcher, and Xiaoping might in part be treated as a reaction to this enlarged state capacity with its flanking subsystems, which notably took the form of public entitlements such as housing in the UK and welfare provisioning in the US. In our monster analogy, who were the neoliberals other than Shelley's late-act villagers wielding lanterns and pitchforks? But in our downturn era of finance capitalism, industrial strategy, and sovereign money, central bank capacities are enlarged, redesigned, and monstrous; the bailout state is firing on all cylinders.

And third, as the state intervenes, it also transforms people's expectations for what can be achieved via the state itself. These interventions have *cultural* effects. This adds a critical normative wrinkle to the Frankenstein problem. As states intervene to support private accumulation, typically with bailouts for private firms, they transform workers' perceptions and expectations about what is politically desirable and feasible, making it harder to justify not also allocating intervention power to working class people also ensnared by the given crisis. This is why, in the age of the bailout state, it has become easier to imagine the end of capitalism than it has to reverse climate change. The Obama-era Recovery Act bailed out firms but did not offer similar assistance to families that were losing their homes. By the Trump-era Coronavirus Aid, Relief, and Economic Security Act, such a one-sided intervention had been made normatively impossible. CARES injected cash into the pockets of both firms and workers, playing an accumulation role that needed cash transfers to workers to be legitimated.

This process of the enlargement of state capacity can lead to contradictions that create dysfunctions in the state. When spending and state interventions become detached from accumulation, state budgets can become squeezed, leading to fiscal crises. As the state becomes larger and more differentiated, it then increasingly loses its capacity for rationally intervening to support accumulation. The internal differentiation of the state leads to these various parts being subordinated to competing interest groups, typically sectors of business but also other special interests or labor interests as well. Ironically, the very expansion of the administrative capacity of the state undermines the capitalist state's ability to engage in rational planning and long-term forecasting. Finally, as the state becomes increasingly dysfunctional, it risks losing the "mass loyalty" of the population and undermining its own electoral sources of governing legitimacy.[27]

While liberal capitalist democracies *do* tend to govern for capital because of a combination of structural constraints and historical contingencies that I will turn to below, like Frankenstein's monster, they can—and indeed have—become a force against capital itself. A long history of movements of the demos show how working-class politics have subordinated the interventionist arms of the state and in turn changed their very structure. In the US, in the context of the Great Depression, a disruptive workers movement helped to pass the National Labor Relations Act, which instituted the National Labor Relations Board. The board imposed stricter constraints on capitalists and extended wider organizing freedoms to workers. A few decades later the civil rights movement won massive legislation that was enforced through an empowered division of the Department of Justice, significantly transforming the basic freedoms of Black workers.

These transformations lay at the center of the emancipatory potential of politics. But to be durable and resistant to elite capture and degradation, subordinating the interventionist apparatuses of the state to the demos also requires the institutionalization of deliberative and participatory democratic processes. Democratic ruptures do not simply require making something public—as I have shown, the public/private distinction is an illusion. They require making processes democratic such that the working-class demos itself has a say.

Class Subordination of Democracy

The apparatuses and institutional bodies of liberal democracy and its flanking subsystems are not just created by class struggles but are sites for them. But capacities for struggle between classes on this terrain are widely different. Capitalists do not sit idly by waiting for direction from state personnel but instead use their resources to directly shape and imprint their interests on internal processes and the policy outcomes of formal politics. Working classes, though profoundly out resourced and beset by collective action problems, do so as well. To explore the variation in class capacity to subordinate the otherwise relatively autonomous institutions of the state, it is again necessary to come down to the more conjunctural level. Not only do class struggles *outside* of capitalist democracies shape its institutions, but the ones *inside* the state's formal institutions do as well. Those institutions are subject to possible capture. Capitalists and the organized working classes know this and expend huge amounts of resources to achieve greater leverage in them. And yet, capitalists and workers follow very different logics for collective political action.[28]

Political organization of capitalists

For their part, capitalists have control of key resources in society—namely, income-producing wealth. In capitalist societies, as Marx laid out with the general law of capitalist accumulation in *Capital*, this control tends to become concentrated. Rising levels of inequality in income and, in particular, wealth, unless mitigated by countervailing forces of wartime devastation or growing labor power, has been borne out in capitalism's historical record. In short, resource inequality gives capitalists greater capacity to influence the policymaking process. In a context of inequality, they are better able to use concentrated resources to both control and influence politics by hiring legal talent, contributing to campaigns, developing coordinated lobbying efforts, hiring technical consultants, enhancing social prestige, and reshaping information available to the electorate.

These resources also afford the segments and sectors of the capitalist class a networked status that other classes simply do not have access to. In most capitalist democracies they are a fixture of the policymaking process, using their involvement in think tanks and research institutes to write the policy papers that become law. They also share a similar cultural background with most politicians. That their children go to the same elite schools and that they have vacation homes in the same places affords them additional political capacities. This combination of material and social resources simply makes the capitalist democratic state more easily traversable for capitalists than ordinary workers (power-elite theorists have most thoroughly explored these linkages).[29] Taking a conjunctural view, as I will show more thoroughly in the next chapter, the financial sector occupies a hegemonic role in the advanced capitalist world, sitting in the driver's seat of the global accumulation model.

Political organization of workers

How do the working classes fare in their struggles within and via the state? Prior to even beginning to wage their battle inside or outside of formal political institutions, workers first must discover their own political aims and then their shared political commitments. The organizational interests of capitalists are more transparent: profits. This objective is defined in competitive capitalist markets by the very structure of the firm itself, which compels them to seek profit and innovate or go out of business. On the other hand, workers have a heterogenous set of interests as workers, which are made complex by their skill level, their geography, their race, their gender, their citizenship, their sexuality, and so on—all of which account for why one person's views of what is desirable might diverge from another's.[30] This poses a serious challenge to building a working-class politics.

Working-class—and therefore emancipatory—politics are not a simple class structural mold to be filled with action. Thus, while it might be possible to theorize capital abstractly, it is a mistake to think that politics and emancipatory strategy can be as well. In one view, to the extent that the class struggle is weak, this is because workers opt out and pursue more individualized and atomized strategies for survival. In this take, the challenge is simply to achieve class-based collective action. But this binary view of class politics suffers from a vertical conflation of class structure abstractly understood with all class structures and a horizontal conflation of class structure with other social structures that define people's interests and political identities and formations.[31]

The horizontal conflation entails conflating class structure with social structure as such. But class experiences are not the sole set of life conditions shaping and producing political action. Workers—indeed all people—are embedded in multiple structural locations (relating to gender, race, citizenship, geographic location, and so on) that bear on the possible political formations that they are in or might form. Political sociologist Göran Therborn referred to this more broadly as the "material matrix," in which affirmations and sanctions related to the multiple structural locations and roles that people fill bear on their ideologies—what they think exists, is good, and is possible.[32] Working-class formation, unlike capitalist-class action, is not therefore structurally given by something akin to a firm's profit motive but instead must be forged alongside overlapping and sometimes competing pressures of political identification along nonclass lines. Working-class politics requires that workers be organized as a demos.

This runs counter to the economistic tendency in some sectors of contemporary critical social theory, which assumes that so much takes place solely within the economic sphere of work but pays little attention to how class conflicts at work or at the level of the community are translated to the level of emancipatory politics broadly. The common economistic view is that because workers are the majority and understand their interests straight-forwardly, emancipatory politics is a matter of articulating party politics and platforms in a way that appeals to majoritarian working-class interests, abstractly understood.[33] Class formation, again, is a simple structural mold to be filled with action—and class struggle a binary outcome of a collective action problem with workers either acting individually for their own good or acting collectively for their shared interest. But this presumes that people's class interests, abstractly conceived, are the *sole* driver of their political behavior and collective political identifications—which, of course, they aren't, never have been, and never will be.

The problem with the binary view extends to how it conceives of class structure itself—a problem that can be termed vertical conflation. This analytical conflation treats class structure in its simplest and most abstract articulation—at the level of the mode of production as that between workers and capitalists—as the only structure relevant to emancipatory politics. The problem is not only that this turns a blind eye to the bulk of the Western Marxist tradition, which was principally aimed at understanding how various intermediate class and social strata bear on socialist politics in given historical conditions, it also makes the analytical error of glossing over the salience of class structure itself at a more conjunctural level of abstraction. The material matrix in which a worker is embedded is not limited to their position as a wage-earner (abstractly conceived) but is also determined by a host of other class-structural locations, such as their industry, firm, occupation, skill level, degree of autonomy and authority at work, and so on.

This is of course crucial for building a class politics rooted in the demos, because as capitalism has developed it has not led to class homogenization, as Karl Kautsky incorrectly predicted it would, but instead to incredible class and social differentiation. The emergence of the "middle classes," what in debates about advanced capitalism is often referred to as the professional-managerial class, is not a bourgeois illusion but is instead indicative of the ways in which the contemporary class structure has become differentiated over time.[34] Given the complexity of class itself, as Erik Olin Wright argued in his pathbreaking *Classes*, "It is hard to see how a definition of the working class as all wage-earners could provide a satisfactory structural basis for explaining class formation, class consciousness, and class struggle."[35] To put it another way, none of the key dimensions of class politics can be explained by such an abstract structural category.

Alternatively, workers, differentiated along both class and nonclass lines, must therefore engage in a dialogic process of communication with each other to discover their common interests—and hence common purpose—in order to act collectively *as* workers instead of acting according to other political formations based on occupation or ethno-nationalistic identity. This is doubly necessary for workers because their power is associational and dependent on forming collective organizations, such as movements, unions, or parties. The most fundamental power of capitalists is structural and not dependent solely on collective organization or conscious political action at all—even though they certainly do a lot of both.[36] They must act, therefore, deliberatively as a demos.

But class struggle does not simply follow once workers come to recognize their shared situation qua workers. They must then forge strong solidarities to overcome both free rider problems and the internal divisions within the demos itself and its pockets of political atomization. Crucially, when capitalists do act politically, they are better able to get what they want in politics because of their willingness to pay via lobbying, campaign financing, and associational interaction. Workers, on the other hand, derive their political power from their willingness to act collectively through strikes, protests, voting, and building organizations together. The power of the demos is an associational power. Yet these forms of political action are much more prone to collective action problems, especially if they come with significant personal costs. In the absence of solidarity, there is a strong risk of ordinary people opting out of the struggle itself by free riding, ultimately under-mining it entirely. These contradictions in capacities for struggle between capitalists and workers are the raw material of the strug-gles that unfold on the terrain of the state. Democratic ruptures in state structures will weaken capitalists' advantage in subordi-nating the state and instead institute processes that help to overcome the collective action problems that undermine the polit-ical capacities of ordinary people.

Though popular sentiment around the world has decidedly shifted against finance capital in the last two decades, it is also hard to imagine a moment when the working classes, especially in the advanced capitalist countries, were more differentiated and in pursuit of distinct emancipatory projects, compounding the problems of collective class-wide organization.[37] Today, spider-webbed supply chains, a shift toward a gig economy, and remote work spurred on by the pandemic have all resulted in a working class that is increasingly disconnected both spatially and communicationally.[38] And the global working class is increasingly fragmented and differentiated by skill, authority, and other basic conditions of life both at work and outside.[39] This renders salient in politics myriad other structural positions, such as citizenship, gender, sexuality, race, and place—further raising challenges to workers engaging in collective action against capital as such. The crucial factor for generating working-class power today is a simple one: economic democracy—that is, deliberation over and the power of the demos to make decisions that are binding about how we produce, distribute, and allocate investment and credit.

Democratic Ruptures

Let me recap the broad conclusions drawn from the previous sections of this chapter, as they are the theoretical scaffolding for what is to follow. First, only by understanding capitalist politics conjuncturally can we begin to understand how ruptures might be achieved. These ruptures involve extending democracy to the spheres of the economy and thereby deepening democracy within the formal institutions of the state. But no general formula is available for such ruptures; conjunctural analysis is the necessary precondition. Second, the state responds to crisis by installing flanking subsystems to support capitalist accumulation, whose autonomy is subject to class subordination at the outset. These subsystems very often become the master's tools.

Crucial loci of rupture lie precisely in the establishment of and democratic control over these subsystems, which traverse the institutional boundary between the public and private by extending the scope of the state. An aim today should be in the installation of democratic subsystems to respond to our most pressing social and ecological crises that are governed by the demos. Finally, the working class—or demos—is structurally and therefore also politically differentiated along both a vertical and horizontal axis. As such, its subsections have already forged solidarities that are culturally and politically articulated in nonclass terms. Democratic ruptures build a class politics out of the conjunctural character of class politics as it *already* exists, not as it might be in theory. The fundamental character of such a building is that it be done dialogically, through participation of and deliberation within the demos itself.

In this final section, I further specify this argument and argue that democratic ruptures are the principal means to transform the state against capital. I draw the concept of rupture directly from Poulantzas himself, who argued that they need not be singular and decisive or emerge between the state en bloc and an externally mobilized working class. Instead, in his later writings and interviews, ruptures occur within and outside the state apparatuses themselves simultaneously. As he commented in an interview with the French militant Henri Weber,

There will be a rupture, there will be a moment of decisive confrontation, but it will pass through the state. The organs of popular power at the base, the structures of direct democracy, will be the elements which bring about a differentiation inside the state apparatuses, a polarization of the popular movement of a large fraction of these apparatuses. This fraction, in alliance with the movement, will confront the reactionary, counter-revolutionary sectors of the state apparatus backed up by the ruling classes.[40]

There can be no general strategy for economic democracy against capitalism. In contemporary capitalist societies, which rest on liberal democratic rights, it is both feasibly unlikely and flat-out undesirable to "smash" the state precisely because of the extent to which its flanking subsystems have become integrated into people's lives. Moreover, the demos have imprinted upon these very institutions working-class gains that would be disastrous to do away with (such as, for instance, universal suffrage). And even were the state thoroughly captured by and bound up with the interests of capitalists, sweeping the state away would lead to chaos in even the most basic forms of social, economic, and political coordination that people depend on at least in the medium term. Erik Olin Wright has called the ensuing chaos of a dismantled state a "transition trough"; he argues that the immediate costs of such smashing might not only destabilize economic democracy projects themselves but make the goal of destroying the state in the service of social and ecological flourishing highly unlikely in the first place.[41] Under what conditions, then, might democratic ruptures occur?[42]

Democratic ruptures principally entail the *transformation of democratic institutions* and the *reconfiguration of state-mediated power relations in the economy*. As I showed in the prior section, the form that liberal democracies take are constituted and vary in a multitude of ways. On this institutional terrain, democratic ruptures involve four distinct breaks that expand the power of the demos, thereby diminishing the power of both capital as well as the elected members and hired bureaucratic corps of formal democratic institutions:

Extending formal decision-making rights into the economy: Empowering the formal participation of the demos in economic

46

decision-making processes in capitalist politics—that is, the fateful decisions about production, distribution, and flows of investment and credit typically left to private actors—is the first feature of a democratic rupture. Historically, a vital way in which working classes have influenced these decisions is through extra-institutional and contentious politics such as strikes, protests, and riots. Yet the formal extension of democratic rights and capacities to make deliberative collective decisions to the working classes is essential for establishing and securing durable political power. Formal rights here are not limited to political representation in politics but more critically are economic rights within the workplace, such as cooperative ownership models and union codetermination, and economic rights with respect to how investment is allocated.

Expanding the democratic composition of the economy: Enlarging in the democratic sector of the economy relative to the private profit-maximizing sector and the state capitalist sector is the next feature of a democratic rupture. Because most capitalist democracies have very small and weak democratic sectors, they remain politically vulnerable to private investment moves, slowdowns, and capital strikes. Contrary to standard progressive presumptions, merely enlarging the public sector is insufficient for countering the power of capital. In this respect, we must push beyond the public-private dichotomy in policy debates. A public sector entangled with the financial sector, state capitalism, will prioritize financial returns on investments over the allocation of investable assets into social and ecological goods.[43] Instead, only economic democracy has the potential to deliberate beyond the short-term profit interests of business. As the democratic sector, situated in both formally private and public institutions, crowds out the capitalist private and public sectors as generator of economic activity, the relative autonomy of the demos to govern will be strengthened. As the democratic sector responsible for production, distribution, and flows of investment and credit are expanded, the relative autonomy of the realm of politics will be as well—and like Frankenstein's monster, it can better wield its powers against its master.

Class consolidation of the body politic: Reorganizing the experiential level of capitalist politics for the demos as a terrain of class struggle is a crucial cultural factor. Liberal capitalist democracy atomizes the working class into legally equivalent monads—individuals—and fosters a political culture that obscures the class relations of exploitation, domination, and extraction.[44] And capitalist class development differentiates the working class along both the vertical and horizontal dimensions identified above. The extent to which formal state structures consolidate working-class political actors *as* classes, rather than as individuals or as groups bound in solidarity over reactive or exclusionary forms of claims making, shifts power to the demos in democratic politics. Such consolidation cannot be imposed by the theorist's will. Instead, they must be articulated in the terms of the existing class politics. Because dynamic capitalist development is uneven, it generates profound heterogeneity within the working class; working-class politics are always already expressed by myriad class subjectivities and political identities anchored in their distinct social contexts. A dialogical political process between workers as they are is the means to consolidate the body politic along the lines of class.

Decommodification of labor: Minimizing the degree to which states subject their residents to capitalist market imperatives for survival and formalizing survival means into rights (e.g., universal basic income, universal health care) is the final feature of a democratic rupture. Decommodifying labor disentangles the demos from the capitalist sector, thereby reducing their dependence on the private activity of firms and reducing the power of those firms in their lives, and thereby in formal politics. Conjuncturally, as will be shown, this is particularly critical in the realm of finance, where so many workers' savings and assets are tied to returns in extractive financial markets.

Democratic ruptures transfer power from the elite to the demos, the working classes, leaving an imprint on the formal institutional terrain of politics, the economic institutions such as the workplace, and even civil society institutions such as the household. As we have demonstrated, the state is already intertwined with the economy, and capital in turn intertwined with the state. The imbricated institutional character of politics and the economy should at the least cast serious doubt on too clean a differentiation of the public and the private. To the extent that capitalism entails a separation of the political and the economic, where market imperatives are allowed to operate independently of political control or obligations, that separation is again constituted by the state itself.[45] The rule of law, property rights, and both the physical and market infrastructure necessary for economic transactions are both produced and maintained by formal politics. As I will demonstrate in the next section, in finance capitalism financiers bit the hand that feeds by eroding and plundering the very politics that constituted their power in the first place. They engage in what the political philosopher Nancy Fraser refers to as "cannibal capitalism," by consuming their own existential prerequisites, including the sphere of democratic politics.[46]

Democratic ruptures do not seek to restore a golden age of capitalism, by recalibrating the state and economy into a more stable symbiosis. Instead, they break with the ontological presumption that the public and private are indeed at odds and with the view that the state and economy are in practice separate. Their aim is a third path, the empowerment of the demos at the expense of the power of business and the state. By extending democracy to the economy, democratic ruptures deepen democracy in the formal institutions of the state itself. In the remainder of this book, I argue that the sector most in need of such democratization is finance itself and argue for how such a transformation might be democratically designed and installed.

PART II

CONJUNCTURE

The Political Contradictions of Finance

3

A Primer

The terrain is defined, not by forces we can predict with the certainty of natural science, but by the existing balance of social forces, the specific nature of the concrete conjuncture.

Stuart Hall, "Marxism Without Guarantees"

Finance Capitalism

The global world economy has become increasingly hitched to the volatile rhythms of financial markets. At the core of finance capitalism is the growth of the sphere of circulation, in which claims on the creation of value in the future are priced and traded relative to the sphere of production as a center of revenue and income generation. On this point, it is crucial to note, finance capitalism does not only pertain to the income of corporations and the elite but also to that of the demos, the working class both in blue collar and more credentialled positions. Even if situated in a global economic ecology that depends on labor-intensive manufacturing in the Global South and nonurban centers of the global core, the circulation and the management of money and other financial assets has become a key mode of value extraction and income production in every advanced capitalist country.

Even so, there are many confusions that persist about what finance capitalism is and where it came from. Depending on how one defines it, financialization denotes widely different processes. This chapter will show that it is not a speculative casino adjunct to and wholly detached from the so-called real economy as is the popular conception. The revenues and income from financial assets themselves are directly tied to the so-called productive sector, so it is impossible to separate these out as distinct and unconnected realms of economic activity. In simple terms, financialization is the process through which money capital—that is, money advanced with the purpose of being returned with interest—becomes more salient in economic activity, politics, and the everyday lives of the demos. And this process is deeply intertwined with and dependent upon the production and distribution of real things. As I will show in the final section of this chapter, it is not that financialization has led to an underinvestment in the productive economy but instead to an underinvestment in the specific productive projects that society desperately needs, socio-environmental ones to rebuild our broken social worlds and cool the planet. We have plenty of goods but not enough clean green energy and infrastructure, affordable housing, empowering workplaces, and mutually supporting forms of social solidarity. It's not that finance simply diverts investment from production but rather that it diverts it towards investments, both real and financial, that solely maximize financial returns. This has come at the expense of so much else.

The genesis of its contemporary form can be traced to the crises of the 1970s precipitated by the seismic interest rate shocks administered like medicine for capital by the Federal Reserve. With its uneven development, modern finance capitalism has profoundly altered the structuring of contemporary capitalist society, the allocation of income and its sources, and the mechanisms of upward redistribution to the elite. This has occurred through three distinct but intertwining transformations: the transformation of the accumulation model that allocates increased investment into financial asset transactions; the rise of shareholder value as a principle of corporate governance; and finally, the transformation of elite assets and the financialization of people's daily lives through their incorporation into financial schemes for survival. These features are largely intertwined in terms of their causality; each adds to the other, making finance capitalism a large and complex mutually reinforcing system that does not merely leave working class people on the outside but ensnares them in its maw. Changes in the accumulation regime (the growth of the financial sector relative to others in advanced capitalist economies) leads to changes in corporate governance and vice versa, which leads to changes in the character of income-producing assets that the demos itself depends on. This is no simple one-dimensional system.

The task of this chapter is one of descriptive simplification, historicization, and evaluation. In addition to exploring the transformations in the accumulation regime and regimes of corporate governance in the global centers of finance—namely, the US and UK—the chapter explores how this conjunctural configuration of capitalism came about. It then evaluates the faultiness of this model of accumulation by turning to four intertwining crises that finance hoists upon humanity and the planet.

Accumulation

Viewed through the lens of accumulation broadly, capitalism is intrinsically financialized. However, following a protracted period of stagnation and high and unstable interest rates, financial firms, actors, and assets have assumed a more pivotal role in the allocation of investments, the prioritization of investment avenues, and the distribution of income.[1] There are many features of this story, including the more familiar rise of a rentier class, the proliferation of new financial instruments that are coded into law in ways that protect creditors, and the rise of titanic asset managers who control massive stores of both financial and physical assets, often on behalf of other people.[2] This chapter argues that a critical dimension of finance capitalism for the current conjuncture is that the appreciation of the value of financial assets accounts for not only a significant source of income for capitalists and the rich but also wealth for working people. Today financial organizations like banks and nonfinancial firms in sectors such as manufacturing accrue more income though speculative financial assets than they did prior to the 1970s.[3] But, increasingly, the wealth and lives of workers are also tied to ups and downs in financial markets.

Figure 3.1. Gross Value Added as a Ratio of Total Value Added, US, in 2005 Prices

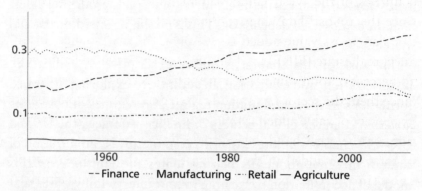

Source: Groningen Growth and Development Centre 10-Sector Database (author's calculations)

Figure 3.2. Gross Value Added as a Ratio of Total Value Added, UK, in 2005 Prices

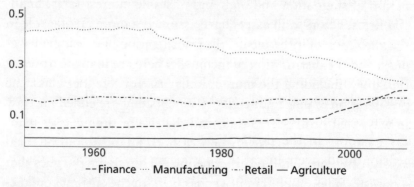

Source: Groningen Growth and Development Centre 10-Sector Database (author's calculations)

In the period following the monetary shocks engineered by Federal Reserve chair Paul Volcker in the early 1980s and the high interest rates produced by monetary policy through the

1990s, the global financial sector has ballooned. As a share of value-added, with a few exceptions, the mass of the financial sector has grown dramatically across most of the countries within the Organisation for Economic Co-operation and Development (OECD). And this is hardly a feature solely of the rich capitalist countries of the West. China's financial sector has quadrupled since the 1980s.[4] Drawing from national accounts data used to calculate gross value added by sector in the US, finance, insurance, real estate (FIRE), and business services contributed about 17 percent of total value added in 1949, as is shown in Figure 3.1. Since then, the sector has steadily risen and by 2009 contributed 35 percent of value added. Manufacturing, mining, and construction, on the other hand, began to decline from about 30 percent of total value added in the early 1960s to about 16 percent by 2009. In the UK, as is shown in Figure 3.2, manufacturing, mining, and construction accounted for nearly 45 percent of total value added in 1950 and by 2009 was down to just 24 percent. Finance, insurance, real estate, and business services, on the other hand, rose from about 5 percent of total value added in 1950 to over 20 percent in 2009.

There are, of course, many institutional subcurrents in this broader story. For one, banks have increased in power and size. In 1960, UK banking sector assets amounted to 32 percent of GDP; by 2010 they had increased to 450 percent of GDP.[5] And nonbank financial groups—that is, asset managers such as pension funds, mutual funds, and other investment funds—have grown to even greater comparative heights. Financialization has its roots in the postwar period, when massive workers' pension funds were installed and became key drivers of financial asset price appreciation. Today, the so-called Big Three, BlackRock, Vanguard, and State Street, have become the new masters of universal ownership, owning significant shares in 98 percent of all the firms in the S&P 500 index. Combined, the Big Three manage more than $20 trillion in assets. Other asset managers have come to convert real physical assets into their own speculative assets.

The speed of the transformation of the ownership structure has been jaw dropping. Blackstone, an American asset manager, is currently the world's largest real estate owner. Astoundingly, all the housing assets in its current portfolio were acquired since the housing collapse in 2008. All of them. This shift toward asset manager–owned housing has been at the heart of staggering housing price hikes and rent increases.[6] And by buying Global Infrastructure Partners for a cool $12.5 billion in 2024, Blackstone became the second-largest manager of private infrastructure on Earth. Financial firms don't simply manage most of the financial assets, they manage an increasingly large portion of the physical assets we rely on as well. Crucially, they often do so on behalf of others, including workers themselves.

Stepping back from this complexity, financial operations are part and parcel of the circuit of productive capital in the so-called real economy where physical goods and services are bought and sold. As the political economist Costas Lapavitsas has shown,

> Such operations include committing money capital to the initial investment, receiving commercial credit to buy inputs, advancing commercial capital to sell output, borrowing loanable capital to expand or maintain circuit flows, handling receipts, payments and hoards of money, lending temporarily idle money to others, and, far from least, receiving the money value of output with sufficient regularity to prevent the circuit from stopping.[7]

As a result, nonfinancial firms are deeply and intrinsically involved in financial operations. Finance is not new; the scale of its significance and relative weight in the economy is. Focusing on the US, we can see in Figure 3.3 that the finance sector's share of total profits rose from under 10 percent after World War II to nearly 40 percent in the early 2000s. It has held steady since the 2008 downturn at approximately 26 percent of all profits. That's not small potatoes.

Figure 3.3. Share of Domestic Corporate Profits, Financial Sector versus All Others, US, 1948–2019

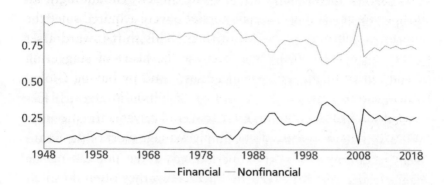

Source: Bureau of Economic Analysis, Table 6.16 (author's calculations)

What about the place of financial profits for nonfinancial firms? This is an area highly debated. On the one hand, it is clear that leading nonfinancial corporations have become less dependent on bank credit to finance their operations. Instead, with monopolistic forms of concentration, the largest nonfinancial firms have become increasingly self-financed by supporting their circuits of capital with sales revenue.[8]

Yet nonfinancial firms have also increasingly engaged in financial transactions for revenues. There now exist piles of research showing that nonfinancial firms in the US and the UK have become more deeply intertwined with the financial sector for their returns as well. In addition to increasingly tying managerial remuneration to financial asset performance, nonfinancial corporations have become increasingly involved in financial speculation and lending. Researchers have found that an increasing share of their profits are derived from interest, dividends, and capital gains. Throughout the 1950s and 1970s the ratio of portfolio income (earnings on interest, dividends, and capital gains) to corporate cash flow (profits plus depreciation allowances) was low and stable. It began rising in the 1970s, and by the early 2000s, nonfinancial firms derived nearly half of their profit from portfolio income, the bulk of which came from interest payments.[9] As a result, though large nonfinancial firms increasingly finance themselves internally through profits, they have also become increasingly skilled at obtaining external financing through open markets. This process has been confirmed at both the industry and firm level—and is evident in both the US and the UK.[10]

As nonfinancial firms have become less dependent on traditional banks for financing, banks have also gone through deep transformations in corporate strategy themselves. They too have turned toward open markets as both a source of trading profit and a source of profit on fees and commissions on their investment accounts. In the postwar period, investment and commercial banks traded very little securities in their own accounts. Since the 1980s, proprietary trading became a critical source of earnings for investment banks and a growing number of commercial banks who bet their own capital on future market moves. Although this practice has been significantly reduced since the crisis, especially in the US where the Volcker rule restricts it to only a few exceptions, postcrisis capital rules in Europe make proprietary trading possible, if more expensive.

The shift in banking strategies is a part of the broader accumulation model of finance capitalism, which is profoundly political in character. To understand it, it is essential to understand the political institutions that prop it up. As explored in the previous chapter, "flanking subsystems" play a key stabilizing role in reproducing the conditions under which financial assets are key sources of returns. Central banks and public debt, in particular, help to keep finance capitalism afloat. The core task of monetary authorities in advanced capitalist economies is to manage the money supply, interest rates, and the system of payments. In doing so, central banks have been part and parcel of financialization. In the US, the Federal Reserve embraced market solutions to money creation, expanding shadow banking through asset-backed securities as a substitute for money issued against government debt. Similarly, the European Central Bank turned aggressively to shadow euros, lending to banks through repo transactions instead of buying and selling government bonds.[11] Central banks also encouraged capitalist growth by converting private liabilities into public ones. They have done this since the crisis by maintaining extremely low interest rates and engaging in large-scale government-debt purchases with money they create, a practice called quantitative easing. In the postcrisis era, this program, most aggressively adopted in Europe, Japan, and the US, has generated an asset price bubble of stock values and has indirectly contributed to a new asset-price bubble in housing. And it reached its greatest heights yet in response to the COVID-19 pandemic.[12] We will turn most directly to the political dimensions of finance in the next chapter on political plunder; first I want to travel into the corporation itself, to show how finance capitalism has transformed the way businesses are governed.

Corporate Governance

The financialization of the nonfinancial firm has led to deep transformations in their income distribution strategies. Central to the story of corporate governance is the ascendence of shareholder primacy, a legal governance framework that is predicated on the idea that the sole purpose of a corporation is to maximize value for its shareholders. The basic implication of this is the prioritization of a firm's stock price in its corporate strategy. Therefore, in the boardroom, concern for this financial metric as the paramount signal of value creation for shareholders within the firm has come to crowd out other possible governing concerns. This transformation does not merely apply to the US and UK; it has significantly reshaped firms across the rich capitalist countries of the North in both liberal and social-democratic market economies.

It is no surprise then that shareholder primacy has led to major shifts in how firms conduct their business. The economist Lenore Palladino demonstrates that shareholder gains have come at the direct expense of the wages of the employees in those publicly traded firms.[13] Since the 1970s, wages for workers have not grown with productivity, leading to a significant decline in labor's portion of total profits, the labor share. Where is all the money going? A large portion of income from publicly traded firms has been siphoned off into financial markets through stock buybacks. Were publicly traded firms simply to refuse and embrace high-road strategies that undermined stock value, they would face hostile takeovers by activist investors demanding their value. Executive heads would roll. Economists William Lazonick and Mary O'Sullivan have described this as a shift away from "retain and reinvest" with respect to workers and profits to "downsize and distribute" so as to prioritize raising the company's stock price.[14] This transformation has significantly benefitted the C-suite, where the executives and managers are compensated with exorbitant stock options and bonuses.

Household Assets

The impact of financialization extends beyond corporate governance, reaching into the very character of the wealth held by both the elite and the demos. We can illustrate this with historical data on household assets. Data from the Federal Reserve's Distributional Financial Accounts reveals that in 1989, the top 1 percent of wealth holders held most of their assets in private businesses with a smaller portion in financial assets, such as corporate equities and mutual funds (see Figure 3.4). Middle- and lower-wealth workers, by contrast, held most of their assets in real estate and pension entitlements. Much has changed in just thirty years. By 2019 the top 1 percent of wealth holders had most of their wealth not in private businesses but in corporate equities and mutual funds—liquid financial assets. Similarly, an increasing share of the wealth of the demos is held in pension entitlements and other financial assets (see Figure 3.5). Comparing these different time periods, the top 1 percent of households by income saw financial assets as a share of their total wealth increase by 59 percent, the next top 9 percent of households had 57 percent increase, the next 40 percent of households 49 percent increase, and finally even the bottom half of households by income saw a 30 percent increase in the share of their total wealth made up by financial assets. The financial assets technically owned by workers are typically controlled by fiduciaries and asset managers that invest them in ways that prioritize returns over all other considerations.

Figure 3.4. Assets of US Households, % of Total, 1989

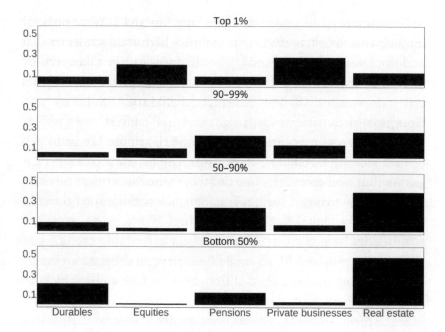

Source: Federal Reserve, Flow of Funds Accounts (author's calculations)

Figure 3.5. Assets of US Households, % of Total, 2022

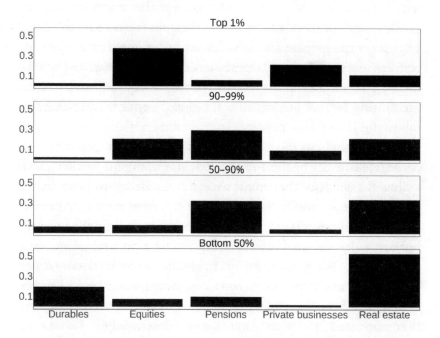

Source: Federal Reserve, Flow of Funds Accounts (author's calculations)

Nowhere is this more evident than in the large pools of finance that workers and their families already own in the US and the UK in pension funds.[15] Large pools of labor's capital sit in retirement funds, a fact that some analysts see as "labor's last best weapon."[16] The American Federation of Labor and Congress of Industrial Organizations (AFL-CIO) and the Service Employees International Union (SEIU) in the US and UK's largest union, UNISON, have large capital stewardship programs that aim to exert some control over this worker finance. Controlling workers' capital is hardly a postcrisis idea though. In 1923 the Amalgamated Clothing Workers of America founded its own bank to offer workers affordable credit. And two years later the AFL's Samuel Gompers established an insurance company (today called Ullico) to offer financial services to union members.

Since then, however, unions have focused most of their attention on pension funds because of their massive size. As of 2024, the US pension market is the largest in the world, holding assets across different types of retirement accounts, including individual retirement accounts (IRAs), defined-contribution plans such as 401(k)s, and defined-benefit plans, totaling nearly $40 trillion.[17] That staggering figure accounts for over 60 percent of total global pension assets. The next largest pension system is that of the UK, whose assets under management reached $4.25 trillion by 2024, accounting for 5.8 percent of total global pension assets, closely following Japan's 6.1 percent.[18]

Pension funds in the US came to own nearly 25 percent of all corporate equities by the 1970s. Their size in capital markets, providing the jet fuel that made American capitalism soar in the postwar period, might imply a relative empowerment of the union workers who negotiated and won them. But their actual history reveals a deeper story of corporate subversion and democratic backsliding. With support of the state, corporate-controlled boards and asset managers took control of the assets from the actual beneficiaries, the workers. As a result, these funds have been invested in ways that drove down labor standards, contributed to deindustrialization and the modern wreckage of American cities like Detroit and Pittsburgh, financed leveraged buyouts during the merger wave in the 1980s that led to firings and asset stripping, heightened financial risk and global turbulence, and weakened the unions that had fought to win them in the first place.[19] Somewhat ironically, workers' financial assets are largely managed by others and move with the same market signals as those assets held by the rich. The use of worker finance to dismantle what little was left of the postwar system of labor management relations paved the way for the most common destructive investment strategies of private equity funds, which buy, strip, and sell off people's former workplaces. Quite simply, huge pools of worker assets in finance capitalism are managed by others, in ways that run counter to the collective interest of the demos. Ownership, in the case of labor's capital, has no relationship to control.

Finance as a Political Project

The current configuration of finance capitalism did not arise behind our backs; it was the direct result of a devastating struggle from the top of the American hierarchy, largely engineered through representative democracy. American policymakers helped turn the global economy toward finance as a way to overcome a series of social and economic dilemmas that they faced. To put it simply, this shift toward finance principally involved a fight from above, in which the political establishment acted on behalf of capitalism in general to break the power of unions and workers in the US and the UK. Theirs was the craft of midwifery for the birth of the mode of accumulation I described above as finance capitalism.

The class struggle shift to finance capitalism has its origins in the postwar period, when Congress of Industrial Organizations unions such as the United Mine Workers of America, the United Auto Workers, and the United Steel Workers won collectively bargained packages that included funded pensions. Nearly as soon as they were established, the finance in these funds became a focal point of fiery contestation. Employers and the American political class, with support across the aisle, clamped down on labor's attempt to control these funds. What was at stake was the control of finance, massive pools of liquid capital. Politicians plainly understood this in class-struggle terms. In congressional testimony in 1946, Senator Harry F. Byrd, a Democrat from Virginia, said,

> I am endeavoring to strike against the attempt of representatives of labor to use such payments in establishing funds over which no one but the labor representative would have any control. I assert that if such a condition were allowed to take place, labor unions would become so powerful that no organized government would be able to deal with them.

Byrd and others viewed the possible control of these pools of assets as an existential threat to capitalism itself, suggesting that it might lead to "the complete destruction of the private enterprise system in the U.S."[20] With the passage of Taft-Hartley in 1947 and the Employer Retirement Security Act in 1974, the American political establishment effectively killed labor's drive for control over their own finance, diverting the funds to institutional investors who followed Wall Street trends. Indeed, these asset managers weren't just following Wall Street, they were Wall Street.

This corporate control of worker finance presaged a more fundamental shift in the 1970s, which reorganized American capitalism—and with it global capitalism—around a model of accumulation that was even more deeply intertwined with finance and dependent on asset price appreciation. Now the lives of the demos in retirement depended on the health of financial markets and their portfolio's performances in them.

There were of course many factors that led to the rise of finance capitalism and its turgid recent history; several tomes have already been written chronicling them and a thorough causal analysis of the various historical factors is beyond the scope of this book.[21] I will highlight here what I see as a crucial political component of that much bigger story—one that illustrates how undemocratic our governmental system of financial engineering actually is: the Federal Reserve's hawkish war against organized labor and its agenda of disorganizing the organized capacity of the American (and by extension, global) working class in order to break its wage-setting power. The result, perhaps intentional perhaps inadvertent, was also the deepening political atomization of working-class political life and the opening up of political terrain for the mobilization of people into politics on more proximate, subjective bases than class—be that basis citizenship, race, or place. Financialization has been part and parcel of class differentiation, and finance's intertwining into the lives of the demos has led to a historic deepening of the challenge social inequality poses to the viability of class politics itself.

At the center of the story is inflation, the silent thief that eats away at savings and investments. It is the bugbear of the financial sector. The inflation of the 1970s was a new beast, rising to a 13.7 percent high in March 1980. Inflation spurred politicians and the financial sector into action. By weakening American firms, breaking apart the Bretton Woods approach to exchange rates, and discouraging foreign direct investment, inflation threatened American planetary dominance. Yet, in addition to hitting people's pocketbooks and savings accounts, it also undermined government securities and eroded capital stock. It created political havoc and an urge to finds solutions that proved politically efficacious for the class politics of the financial sector. Their solution, the one that won out among a host of political competitors, hinged upon breaking labor.

In August 1975, amid Arthur F. Burns's reign at the Fed and his fruitless attempts to hobble inflation with moderate interest rate increases, Paul Volcker, a tall, grumbling, ten-cent-stogie-smoking economist, was named president of the Federal Reserve Bank of New York. The role gave him a permanent seat at the Federal Open Market Committee (FOMC), a key committee that sets the Federal Reserve's main policies and is protected by secrecy and outside the scrutiny of public feedback or direction. In some of his first contributions to the committee, he played the role of

Cassandra warning against the optimism of Burns and many others; but his prophecies fell on deaf ears.

The econometric models predicting continuing interest declines with marginal Fed rates hikes had one critical flaw for Volcker: they failed to take into account the rising expectations of American workers. American lore had become a truism: the next generation will do better than the last. If there was one thing that Volcker had to extinguish, it was the sense that if one simply kept working hard that they would do better and better in life—a feat that, despite its limitations and reproduction of longstanding racial inequalities in access to the good life, the so-called postwar labor accord had accomplished.

His pessimism was correct. In the beginning of 1977, inflation began to bubble back up again across the American economy. By 1978, the confidence barometer of Wall Street signaled major worries about the dollar—the price of gold had skyrocketed. Wall Street certainly had something to brood over; America's currency was losing against its competitors, especially the German mark. Financial investors understood that a weakened dollar was a source of volatility in the international money markets. According to Volcker, embodying the contradictory position of being at once a custodian of the state and a representative of finance, "Our moral obligation to prevent debasement of our currency coincided with our self-interest."[22]

The political class across the rich democracies of the West had a long history of targeting organized labor as the problem during periods of inflationary upticks. They termed their view the cost-push theory of inflation. It had become governing dogma for Volcker and the other members of the Federal Open Market Committee (FOMC). But it wasn't a new perspective on the cause of inflation. Though it became common to talk about the quantity of dollars in circulation, central bankers and policy makers have long understood inflation in terms of the balance of class forces in society. Theirs is a straightforward, crude Marxism. When wage and price controls were lifted following World War II, the spike in inflation from 8.5 percent in 1946 to 14 percent the next year was explained by many members of Congress to be the result not of printing too much money but of the spread of union-negotiated industry-wide contracts that included wage increases.

In 1970, The OECD released a new report on inflation's return, *Inflation: The Present Problem*. Labor victories and working-class power were identified, albeit in different terms, as the cause of the uptick. This reintroduced the cost-push theory to a new cohort of sharp-suited policy men. The recommendations of the report were put plainly: give up the hope of achieving full employment and instead use a combination of monetary and fiscal policy to increase unemployment. The aim, perhaps counter-intuitive at first, would have the net effect of weakening the ability of organized labor to make wage gains through contract negotiations.

A similar view was developed at the Fed. In 1977, central bankers worried that "business did not appear to be pressing as actively as they might to hold labor costs down, fearing the impact of strikes and assuming that inflation would continue."[23] In 1978, the sense of urgency within the central bank about labor power intensified, and many of the central bankers worried that wage settlements would in turn lead to further inflation increases. In April, members of the FOMC honed in on contracts being nego-tiated in the coal industry by the United Mine Workers. The committee agreed that if these contract negotiations set a pattern and others negotiated similar contracts that included wage increases, it would drive up inflation further.

Volker told Jimmy Carter in a short meeting in 1979 that he thought the only solution to inflation was a Fed-induced reces-sion. The Fed cut reserve supplies to banks through open-market operations and held non-borrowed Fed reserves at hard fixed levels. His predecessors would set a target rate and then reach it by selling or buying Treasury bills. The new strategy abandoned this, instead forcing banks who were running lower and lower on funds to compete for funds, driving up interest rates in the pro-cess. The process was one engineered to cause a recession. But by letting the markets decide, Carter erroneously believed it would buy himself significant cover in his reelection campaign. Milton

Friedman had said that "inflation is always and everywhere a monetary phenomenon."[24] But monetary policy was just a cudgel for Volcker in a class war, as it often is.[25] The real goal wasn't simply to reduce the amount of money in circulation, it was to alter the balance of class forces in favor of capitalists, in spite of the latter's own preferences (many actively opposed the Fed's hawkish turn).

The Fed's strategy to control interest rates indirectly manipulated the firms' behavior, making borrowing more expensive to push firms to be austere. This shift in monetary policy was central to disciplining and weakening unions as wage-setting institutions by changing the conditions under which firms made a profit.

There is no gainsaying the fact that the Fed chair had concluded that inflation was the result of wage gains. In a congressional statement in 1981, Volcker said, "So far, only small and inconclusive signs of moderation in wage pressures have appeared."[26] Just a year later, Volcker spoke in atypically simple language—he was notoriously vague in hearings—about the issue. He told Congress that "progress will need to be reflected in moderation in the growth in nominal wages. The general indexes in worker compensation still show relatively little improvement."[27] By improvement, of course, he meant the *lowering* of wages. By his own measures, the hawkish approach was a success.

Inflation declined by 1982 and fell further in 1983—recession had nasty consequences for working people and their organizations, but it also broke price increases. But much to the political establishment's frustration, interest failed to decline along with it. Mortgage rates had climbed well over 18 percent by the end of 1981 (they only fell under 10 percent again in 1986). The shock had severely depressed credit-sensitive industries like real estate, housing construction, and auto. Despite rising unemployment coupled with high interest rates, Reagan continued to point to inflation as the primary problem for American capitalism. At a press conference in February of 1982, in the midst of the

Volcker shock, when the unemployment rate was at 9 percent and climbing and Volcker himself was vilified throughout the country, Reagan called inflation "our number one enemy" and repeated his "confidence in the announced policies of the Federal Reserve."[28]

Volcker wasn't just loathed by American workers and those around the globe who felt the reverberation (as we will see in France under Mitterrand in the next chapter); large sections of capital were also hostile to the Fed's monetary policy. Home-builders and automobile dealers mailed two-by-fours and car keys to the Federal Reserve in protest. After the agricultural sector was hit, indebted farmers blocked the entrance to the Board of Governors with their tractors. The policies dealt an especially damaging blow to manufacturing—about $6 billion in manufacturing assets were decimated between 1980 and 1983 alone. The reconfiguration of the capital order ending with finance on top was a result of brutal battles within capital itself.

In Washington, both Democrats and Republicans looking out for the interest of these nonfinancial sectors of capital called for Volcker's head. But throughout the recession, Volcker remained beloved by finance for very good reasons. He was more sensitive to signals of confidence coming from Wall Street, for whom he'd advocated steadfastly at the Federal Reserve, than he was even to those from the presidency.

But perhaps the biggest victim of all was the demos itself— the ordinary people who over decades of labor and civil rights organizing had begun to scrape out a middle-class life. Defeating labor, whose stronghold was in the industrial sectors of American manufacturing, was a critical first step in setting the stage for the new finance capitalism. Between 1979 and 1983, 2.4 million American manufacturing jobs were lost—many of which were in apparel, metals, and textiles. But the policies of the Fed had an impact on working-class lives and struggles that lasted long beyond the official recovery from the recession. In what would soon be called the "Rust Belt," many plants shuttered their doors for good. By the end of the 1980s, more than a quarter of a million steel jobs were lost with plants being closed or downsized. In the next decade, many auto-parts-production operations moved to *maquiladora* plants in northern Mexico. But manufacturing moved to the Southern states as well, while workplaces were reorganized along the basis of lean production schemes. By 1990, 39 percent of American auto employees, over 318,400 people, were in the South.

But in the North whole cities, places like Detroit and Cleveland, which were once centers of industry, emerged as shells of their former selves and cauldrons of plight and so-called urban decay. Pittsburgh transformed from a "Steel City" built by a powerful United Steel Workers into a zone of precarious work in the health care industry.[29] A similar hollowing occurred in the UK. Manchester, once a textile powerhouse, and Birmingham, a center of metalworking and manufacturing, saw factory after factory closed. If capitalist development had born fruit for the English working class in the North, its rapid decline there engendered a new "structure of feeling."[30] The wine went sour. Despite efforts at reinvention, the recession for the working classes never truly ended in these places but instead became a permanent feature of everyday life. There has been a simultaneous proliferation of pawn shops and check-cashing outlets as factories have withered away or sprouted up with substantially poorer pay and benefits.

Job losses in manufacturing were large in the period, but unions and their members were the main ones on the chopping block. In the US, union density declined from 20.6 percent in 1980 to 9.1 percent in 2000, and by 2020 it was at about 10 percent. In absolute terms, union membership actually reached its peak in 1980 with over twenty million workers organized—a number that would decline by nearly five million over two decades. Between 1976 and 1983, the United Steel Workers lost 593,000 members, the Teamsters lost 422,600, the United Auto Workers lost 348,000, the International Association of Machinists lost 321,000, and the Amalgamated Clothing Workers of America, 249,000. Pressuring firms to discipline their workers did, however, contribute to reviving the profit rate for American capital.[31] In the UK, the destruction of working-class economic and political life also corresponded with a wild flowering of finance. In the Midlands and the North of England, there was a similar decline in union jobs; union density fell by over half of the working population in 1979 to less than a quarter by 2020.

Wall Street and the City had forced the other sectors of capital to take their bitter medicine. With labor weakened and shop-floor resistance at a multi-generational low, firms intensified work through speedup and reorganization and turned to financial speculation instead of capital investment as a means to generate additional profits. Finance capital gained the most from the Federal Reserve's policies, an effect echoed in the policy of quantitative easing from the 2008 crisis, which continued and intensified through the pandemic crisis. Investment in software and equipment grew much more slowly in the 1980s than it had in the 1960s, 1970s, and 1990s. The profit rate had been on a systematic decline since the mid-1960s and bottomed out in 1982 at the height of the Volcker recession.

A critical goal of the Volcker shock was generating higher labor productivity, producing more for less, which of course is just a euphemism for increasing the rate of exploitation. And study after study shows that after 1982, profit rates in America significantly began to recover. As wages stagnated while labor productivity continued to rise, profit rates themselves took off—increasing until 1997. Tight monetary policy that disciplined market actors contributed to a period of renewed capitalist expansion in the Reagan/Clinton and Thatcher/Major/Blair years.

The most direct solution to inflation would have been wage and price controls, which Carter had proposed with the support of the AFL-CIO prior to the first Volcker shock. Price controls had become a normal part of the American political economy over the entire length of the postwar period, so the proposal was hardly unprecedented.[32] And Carter's unrealized "reindustrialization plan" would have diverted American pension savings into good union jobs and redevelopment projects in areas facing severe job loss and capital flight. Because Reagan won instead, such areas were declared "free enterprise zones."

Instead, the high interest rates the Fed triggered kicked people out of the workforce and into the labor reserve. It increased the poverty rate from about 11 percent to 15 percent, with Black and Latinos disproportionally feeling the brunt of the firings. Union jobs in industry had become a key way for some Black Americans in Northern manufacturing cities to gain something that resembled a middle-class lifestyle. The shock broke the dream of union uplift and replaced it with the war on crime, leading to an over-policing of urban neighborhoods that defined the criminal justice regimes of the 1980s and 1990s. These were regimes based principally on the moral panics associated with broken windows, drug use, and moral decay. In the UK, the cultural analyst Stuart Hall and coauthors identified a similar breakdown and moral panic associated with muggings. Hall described the parallel process of increased precarity and social anxiety and an uptick in racialized state control in response as "policing the crisis."[33]

More than any other government agency, the Federal Reserve of the United States has been the primary architect of global finance capitalism. The marquee neoliberal governments under Reagan and Thatcher merely accelerated a process already underway. The sharp increase in inflation and the expansion of credit, in part needed to supplement worker's depressed and stagnant wages in the decades that followed, created the conditions for the extraordinary rise of finance in the 1980s and 1990s. Finance unleashed vast amounts of cash to circulate and feast upon. Though interest rates were the means to crush labor, since the 1980s they slowly declined to a point of rock bottom during the pandemic. Then they began rising again as another response to inflationary pressures. The turn to finance has been fueled by dirt cheap credit—the hope being that cheap money will drive growth both in and out of the financial markets. And after their pivotal role, the central banks have continued to guide our growth models, intertwining the power of the state with the power of financial institutions. This is not merely a story about the Federal Reserve but about central banking around the world.[34]

The New Deal regulatory agenda for finance crumbled in the 1990s and 2000s for two reasons, which were mutually constituting. One relates to tectonic shifts in finance itself and the other to the dismantling of the rules by Congress. Structurally, a wide host of new financial institutions began to sprout up that were quite simply outside of the scope of the New Deal's regulatory framework—the shadow banking sector and its activities. These include but are not limited to: 1) nonbank financial institutions like hedge funds, special-purpose vehicles, private equity firms, and check-cashing outlets; 2) the expansion of derivative transactions like the now-famous credit default swaps and collateralized debt obligations that sunk the global economy in 2008; 3) the regulated banking sector turn to shadow banking activities as an alternative to traditional bank lending by, for example, packaging and securitizing mortgages in order to be able to issue tradeable securities, holding securities assets on balance sheets, and borrowing against those balance sheets in what are known as repo markets.

As for what was left of New Deal reforms that had become ineffective because of changes in the market, the state made aggressive moves to dismantle it all. Rules governing banking were liberalized with the repeal of the Banking Act of 1933 and the passage of the Financial Securities Modernization Act in 1999. In short, this legislation allowed multipurpose bank-holding companies to fully integrate all financial activities into a single bank, hence bridging of commercial and investment banking, which the New Deal reforms had barred. This hardly marked a key moment in the turn toward finance capitalism, as some have suggested. Instead, the legislation was a clear message that the turn had already been made.

Like Reagan's and Clinton's, Thatcher's free market dream turned out to also be a utopia for financiers; the money flowed upward. The 1979 abolition of foreign exchange controls as well as the so-called "Big Bang" reforms of the London Stock Exchange opened the way for a hegemony of the City. The state made it much easier for financial companies to join the London Stock exchange, abolished fixed commission charges, ended the separation between stockjobbers and stockbrokers, and introduced electronic trading. The changes marked the City as a zone of financial freedom, resulting in a massive influx of financial companies that were more restricted by the rules in the countries they moved their money and operations from.

A new order emerged from this reorganization of Western capitalism, which former banker Tony Norfield describes astronomically as a double-planet system. As he writes, "rather than the UK simply orbiting the US, each country's financial market exerts a significant 'gravitational' pull on the other, even though the pull of the US is obviously larger."[35] Though their positions are hardly fixed and subject to changes in the global financial system itself, where new financial powerhouses like China have rapidly risen, this book will limit its focus to the economic and political implications of the rise of finance in the two countries in this two-planet system.

Finance Capitalism as Social Crises

The upshot of this transitional history and the organizational changes that have come about from it are four interwoven global crises that wrap people's everyday lives into the circuits of finance: debt and financial insecurity, stagnation, macroeconomic instability, and climate catastrophe. All are caused by finance capitalism's systemic underinvestment in socio-environmental goods.

The growth model of finance capitalism, which diverts gains away from workers to shareholders, depends on debt-driven consumption. Along these lines, middle-income and poor workers, together what I have called the demos, have been channeled into new financialized schemes for survival.[36] In the US, the proportion of debt to income lurched from 14 percent in 1983 to 61 percent in 2008.[37] Even more drastically, in the UK as a proportion of income it rose from 87 percent in 1997 to 148 percent in 2008.[38] Workers have been ushered into this debt down two unique paths.

For the racialized poor at the bottom of the labor market, welfare state retrenchment undermined and eroded the public sources of stability and security established in the postwar period. Financial intermediaries and financial companies in the private market have been the primary beneficiaries as poor people have desperately sought out new sources of income elsewhere.[39] Extraction is good business. It isn't a coincidence that as the state found new ways to undermine and retrench public support in the US, culminating in Bill Clinton's signing of the Personal Responsibility and Work Opportunity Act of 1996 just three years before he did away with Glass-Steagall, payday loan and check-cashing outlets offering credit at usurious rates began to flourish in poor neighborhoods. With little in the way of alternatives, their extraordinarily high interest deepens both the debt and the poverty of those that rely on them. Therefore, finance capitalism has intertwined itself into the dynamics of racial capitalism, not only extracting wealth from poor workers but also siphoning support away from those workers by municipal, state, and federal governments.[40]

In the US, the story of finance's ensnarement of the poor is part and parcel of the longer history of racial segregation. This is a story not of exclusion from the financial system but rather of extraction that leads to African Americans being locked into deteriorating urban neighborhoods. The historian Keeanga-Yamahtta Taylor has described this financial relation as one of "predatory inclusion," in which Black homebuyers in the postwar period were only able to get mortgage financing through banks at far more expensive rates than their white counterparts. As Taylor writes, "Where white housing was seen as an asset developed through inclusion and the accruable possibilities of its surrounding property, Black housing was marked by its distress and isolation, where value was extracted, not imbued."[41] It was banks simply going about their business, adjusting for so-called risk, that helped to produce the racially tiered system of housing that persists today and, in part, explains segregation, not just along racial lines, but in terms of wealth as well.

For middle-income workers, we see the flip of this story. Since the 1980s, wage stagnation has failed to keep standards of living affordable with rising costs. This has transformed them into what Lisa Adkins, Melinda Cooper, and Martijn Konings refer to as "Minskyan households," balance sheet entities tied to the speculative and future-oriented logics of financial markets and assets.[42] Much like the poorest workers, middle-income workers turned toward larger amounts of credit card debt and borrowing on home equity to finance household consumption. Household debt for the middle class has dramatically risen as a result. In the US, debt increased from nearly 43 percent of GDP in 1983 to nearly 100 percent in 2008.[43] Debt clogs many advanced capitalist political economies and makes their precarious accumulation model highly dependent on creditors offering it up. Prior to 2020, auto loan debt, consumer credit, and student loan debt all rose. Even mortgage debt, which rapidly declined with foreclosures, today surpasses the pre-2008 crisis peak. Household debt has become a source of deep new financial angst and anxiety for the working-class people in all income brackets because of the interest payments that come along with it. Fundamentally, this extraction of financial income out of workers at all points in the labor market has become a new source of profit, not simply from interest on debts but also through fees, commissions, and proprietary trading. Economist Costas Lapavitsas describes the appropriation of workers' incomes through such financial schemes in the realm of circulation as a "profit upon alienation."[44] For both poor and middle-income workers, if this debt source seized up, their ability to consume would be severely hampered and could trigger a demand-led recession.

It is fundamental to note, however, that despite the shift to what was termed the "ownership society" by George W. Bush, there remains a yawning gap in financial asset ownership. First, stocks and bonds constitute a far smaller share of worker wealth portfolios; the large bulk of working-class wealth is not held in financial markets but rather in real estate. Most middle-class workers hold the bulk of their wealth savings in their home rather than a brokerage account.[45] Second, the wealthiest families hold the large bulk of stock ownership. The top 1 percent of US households hold an astounding 40 percent of all stocks; the next 9 percent of US households take up another 40 percent of all stocks. The bottom 90 percent of all households own just 20 percent of all stocks.[46] But, as I illustrated above, even if it is a smaller share, more and more members of the demos are themselves owners of financial assets. And in most cases, these financial assets are managed by others, asset managers.

Debt also ensnares workers through the organizations that they work with, firms. As distinct from the monopolies, which are able to self-finance, many small and medium-sized firms have become more dependent on finance through debt. Since the global financial crisis in 2007–8, taking on cheap corporate debt has served as a magical way to increase profits for small and medium firms that have had shrinking profit margins. Nonfinancial-firm global indebtedness rose 13 percent between September 2008 and December 2019. Even prior to COVID-19, these firms were already holding down the wages of their employees and shifting from reinvestments to upward redistribution to executives and shareholders. Research by political scientists Joseph Baines and Sandy Brian Hager finds that small and medium-sized firms have had profit margins in the negative off and on since the dot-com bubble burst in the early 2000s.[47] To keep their shareholders appeased, these "zombie firms," which account for about half of total employment in the US, were already "feasting on debt" as Baines and Hager put it. While debt-to-revenue ratios have increased dramatically across the board, the rise has been greatest for the small and medium-sized firms. These are the firms that have had the most drastic layoffs during the crisis. The pandemic-fueled crises in 2020 drastically widened the debt divergence between these firms and those with monopoly power.[48]

Though nonfinancial firms turned away from traditional banking loans to finance themselves internally through retained earnings, many small and medium-sized firms are now saddled with shadow banking debt that they procure through open markets. And since 2008, nonfinancial companies have dramatically increased borrowing through corporate bond markets. In the OECD, between 2008 and 2018, nonfinancial companies increased their borrowing to $1.7 trillion a year—the average between 2000 and 2007 was $864 billion. There is a steady increase in the share of BBB rated bonds in this debt, just one level above non-investment grade.[49]

According to the Federal Reserve, in addition to volatility in the stock market, this corporate debt threatens to worsen the current economic slump. They suggest that

> the strains on household and business balance sheets from the economic and financial shocks since March will probably create fragilities that last for some time . . . Financial institutions— including the banking sector, which had large capital and liquidity buffers before the shock—may experience strains as a result.[50]

This is the basic risk that threatens the global capitalist political economy in the event of a credit freeze: firms become more and more indebted and default rates increase as they can't find revenue to pay back their loans. In such an event, more and more firms will go into bankruptcy at the same time that credit markets seize up because of the risk associated with lending.

Debt is not the only source of financial worry for the working class. Nearly as relevant is their financial uncertainty and insecurity. Financial insecurity for workers is not only manifested in the precarity of work though. Increasingly, social programs that afford a modicum of financial well-being are hitched to turbulent financial markets. This is true across a host of institutions but is particularly striking with respect to retirement income. In the US and the UK, assets held by both traditionally defined benefit pensions, 401(k)s, and individual retirement accounts (IRAs) are heavily invested in equities markets. As a result, workers' livelihoods depend directly

on how those markets perform. It is simply false, as some are wont
to say, that the stock market only matters for capitalists. In the
context of the 2008 downturn, workers in the OECD lost $5.4
trillion in savings. With US stocks plummeting 37.5 percent, American workers lost $2.4 trillion. By 2014, the Obama administration
publicly celebrated the recovery of these lost assets. But this was a
misleading assessment. All things being equal, retirement accounts
are over half a decade behind where they should be in terms of
investment returns. And, even more importantly, 45 percent of
workers with a pension saw further losses in their retirement funds
in the same period of stock market recovery between 2009 and
2011 when the S&P 500 was itself up by 54 percent.[51]

The macroeconomic result of these transformations has been
significantly more market instability. Volatility in asset prices and
the accumulation of debt has generated recurring financial crises
and heightened systemic risk. As political economies have become
more financialized, stock prices have become increasingly
detached from the underlying real economy. The largest asset-
price bubble in US history, which emerged in the 1990s and burst
with the dot-com failures, set the precedent. The 2008 downturn
was directly precipitated by losses on securitized loans held as
financial assets. Since 2008, new bubbles in home loans, housing
prices, auto loans, student loans, stock and bond markets, and
Chinese credit all threaten turbulence in the financial system.

Far away from Wall Street on Main Street, the financialization
of everyday life for the poor has had far-reaching effects beyond
poor neighborhoods. Considering the longer-term historical
causes of the 2007 housing crisis, the rollback of public housing
contributed to the housing debts among the poorest workers,
which directly precipitated the downturn, sinking capitalism
itself into a global slump. This volatility isn't solely the result of
housing practices, though. The financialization of workers'
health, education, insurance, and pensions all contribute to
market volatility. Short-term investment trends in vehicles like
401(k)s, for instance, greatly increase macroeconomic instability in financialized economies more broadly.[52] Financial

markets operate in ways quite different from markets for goods and services. All things equal, rising prices in markets for goods and services tends to lower demand while falling prices increase it. Because of the peculiarly speculative logic of financial markets, when prices go up, demand tends to go up. That demand falls with price makes the burst of an asset bubble all the more sudden.[53] Surely the extraction of circulatory profits is a major financial boon to those in the business, but when considered the cornerstone of a development model, financialization turns out to be fool's gold.

But far and away the most severe crisis that finance capitalism has hastened is the ecological one bound up with climate change. It has done this through two distinct mechanisms: allocation and greenwashing. First, as investments have prioritized returns over sustainability, there has been an underfunding of the kinds of investments that can decarbonize the economy. Retrofitting buildings, expanding public transit, building national energy grids connected to a global network of clean energy distribution, and offering cheaper credit to green projects and businesses are all areas that put the social good before maximal profit and have therefore largely been left underfunded.[54] There is no lack of eager investors for carbon-intensive goods. When Saudi Arabia's former state oil company Aramco went public at the end of 2019, they raised over $25 billion from large institutional investors like Godman Sachs. Unlike renewables, there is certainty in the money to be made in climate destruction. The oil majors continue to expand fossil fuel extraction and distribution and year after year report record profits and payouts to their shareholders.[55]

In short, finance capitalism does not allocate investment support into renewables anywhere close to the scale needed to deliver carbon neutrality. Currently, global finance capitalism barely puts a dent in the $9 trillion annual challenge needed to achieve a green transition (we currently have just over $1 trillion globally in climate finance).[56] Crucially, this is not because of a lack of assets. In the US alone, total assets under management today of public and private occupational pensions are nearly $40 trillion, of BlackRock $10 trillion, of Vanguard $7.7 trillion, and of State Street $4 trillion. Asset managers control massive pools of investment power that they choose to invest elsewhere.

The second mechanism is greenwashing, which despite this profound inaction allows asset managers to create the illusion that they are in fact financing a transition. Many of those very same institutional investors investing in a gas future with Aramco have also signed onto Environment, Social and Governance (ESG) investing pledges like the United Nations' Principles for Responsible Investment. The ESG funds attached to the trend, disproportionately based in Europe, became the fastest growing segment of the asset management sector, reaching $2.7 trillion in 2021. Yet with so little agreement on what these standards even are or how they are regulated, there is a widespread concern in the financial industry that the funds are hiding investment practices that are far from green.[57] The evidence for their effectiveness at financing a green transition is simply not there.

Were that not enough, there has been a profound investor backlash against them. In the US and UK, huge sums of investor money flowed out of (not into) ESG funds.[58] In many respects, this was a direct response to moves by anti-environment Republican lawmakers in the US to disincentivize these funds and attack the sectors of finance capitalism supportive of their Democratic rivals. Many red-state treasurers on an "anti-woke" mission have tried to blacklist some of the largest pro-ESG asset managers such as BlackRock, Goldman Sachs, State Street, and Wells Fargo. And red-state governments in Florida, Idaho, and Kansas have passed legislation banning ESG. If your working assumption is that asset managers are driven by the imperative to gain profit above all other considerations, which is the correct one, their response to the political backlash has been predictable. JP Morgan Asset Management, State Street Global Advisors, and BlackRock have all pulled out of Climate Action 100+ since. This was an effort by sectors of finance to use their power to prod airline companies, the oil majors, and other known corporate polluters to reduce their carbon footprint and embark on a green energy transition.[59] Perhaps toothless from the beginning, even expressing a symbolic concern for climate change was too costly for finance capitalism.

Finance capitalism therefore poses a problem for a ruptural change defining our core social dilemma: Who controls investment? The twenty-first century has thus far been a century of mesmerizing surplus extraction, worker precariousness, macroeconomic instability, and climate catastrophe. Ours is a time of profound overlapping and intertwining crises. Each level of crisis is deepened by financial activities related to the allocation of debt and credit. How have the financial institutions and actors that benefit from them—the asset managers, the banks, the nonfinancial corporations, and the elites that run them—pulled off this self-defeating heist? How do they continue to do so, despite having hardly any popular legitimacy at all? The answer is their power in politics and the near-complete absence of the power of the demos in modern democracies. The leverage of financial actors and institutions over formal decision-making in democratic governments has stitched this precarious financial order together and kept it from coming apart at the seams. The crucial levers of power that financial actors and organizations wield through politics and thus use, both intentionally and not, to disorganize and disempower ordinary people and workers is where we now turn.

4

Financial Plunder

The rich man consumes the poor man's losses, creating for him
a category of degradation and abjection that leads to slavery.
                    Georges Bataille, "The Notion of Expenditure"

Political Domination

Finance capitalism thrives off immiseration. Its massive balance
sheet apparatus is enriched through the degradation of nature,
the heating up of the planet, and the extractive rents it collects.
We live in an age of profound financial plunder by the very people
who manage the money of workers themselves. But how does
finance accomplish this upward extraction in democratic societies
where people would seem to have a say? Here is the upshot: the
vote is no match for the political power of finance capital.

There is a huge body of research on capitalist politics that sharpens our understanding of the various resources corporate interests
mobilize to secure their systemic advantage in the policymaking
process. From archive to statistical analysis to ethnographic obser-
vation, the critical research available is mainly concerned with the
processes by which money and interpersonal influence are mobilized within formal state institutions. Yet it has also become clear
in the debate on corporate power that in addition to the ability of
the wealthiest to directly influence politics through their interpersonal networks and political spending, their capacity to withhold
and redirect economic investments also profoundly constrains
what is possible in politics and shapes political outcomes.

This chapter develops an analysis of the social causes of the
disproportionate political power of finance and its wreckage of

democratic institutions. It makes four interlocking arguments. First, it argues that the heart of the power of capitalists in democratic politics in general are the productive assets at the core of a political economy's accumulation model that they direct. The character of those assets, which I will elaborate below, determines how they can be deployed in politics as means of controlling democratic processes. I term this *asset power*.

This extends conventional accounts of business power, which instead point to characteristics of businesses themselves and the interpersonal connections and formal involvement of their elites in the policymaking process. When we turn our attention to the kinds of assets mobilized in accumulation, what we find that is perhaps most insidious about the power of finance capital is that it works not solely through the leverage of capitalists but also through the leverage of ordinary workers. In this vein, the accumulation assets in finance capitalism are not the ones simply held by corporations or even wealthy households, though they hold the majority of them, but also those held by the demos through entities like pension funds and personal accounts. Somewhat ironically, in this view, the political power of finance capital is not *solely* exercised by particular businesses or the wealthy. It is in large part an effect of large numbers of people relying on financial assets to generate their own income and savings. Counterintuitive as it is, a worker's own personal wealth enhances the power of finance capitalism and the asset managers at its helm.

Second, the character of capital assets determines the way those assets are exercised, intentionally or not, as sources of capitalist power. When assets are primarily fixed in a territory during a democratic rupture, as occurred in the mining-intensive Chilean case under Salvador Allende, capitalist power exercised in the form of investment slowdowns can turn violent if they are not successful. Yet when income-producing assets are more mobile in similar emancipatory experiments, as in the French case under François Mitterrand, capitalist power is more easily exercised in the form of exit, or capital flight; there, democratic socialism experienced a more "peaceful" death but one no less total in its defeat of the will of the demos. Both cases are briefly explored to illustrate the importance of the character of the income-producing assets in a political economy for democratic politics.

Third, it examines the distinct forms of leverage finance relies on in advanced capitalist democracies to get its way. While my broad attention is on the character of income-producing assets and in turn on how finance bears in unique ways on the erosion of democracy and the protection of the wealth of the elite, there are many ways that the financial sector has come to gain a preferential position in formal democratic institutions. I term these three forms of leverage engagement, prominence, and entanglements. The purpose here is to show how deeply institutionalized the political power of finance capital has become. This analysis should demonstrate that a democratic rupture will have to do more than simply get money out of politics. Finance itself has become interwoven into the very fabric of our democratic institutions.

Finally, the chapter examines how the role of the dollar as the global currency might play in the possible democratic exercise of financial power in the US in particular. I argue that though dollar hegemony has been a source of debt and dependence for the Global South, perhaps counterintuitively, it also affords the US state greater room for maneuver, allowing it to enact bold ruptures perhaps even despite the fact that finance's asset power is bearing down on it.

Asset Power

Radical theorists of democracy have rightly identified *capitalist control of productive assets* as the fundamental basis of their power as capitalists. In fact, this control underlies all the forms of leverage that they use in the economy against workers and in formal politics. Without that control, they would not have more organizational, financial, interpersonal-network, and structural resources to push and prod their way through the chess game of capitalist democracy. Neither would the bulk of the demos be dependent on private firms for jobs, which results in workers being less likely to make demands on politics that might hurt their employers.[1] But to gain a deeper understanding of the basis of financial power, and of capital more generally, it is necessary to theorize not only the ways in which power is exercised but also how and under which conditions the context that makes that exercise efficacious can change.

As I showed in Chapter 2, many in the Marxist tradition theorize business power at the abstract level of the mode of production. These theorists analyze classes and their political capacities as abstract ideal types of social relationships; they are stylized simply as *workers* and *capitalists*. There are many questions about capitalist power for which this level of abstraction is entirely appropriate: the private ownership and control of productive assets by a small subset of the population *does* afford capitalists more ways to exercise power, either through intentional and strategic political action or via automatic responses to market signals that have political effects regardless of an actor's intention.[2]

But as I have argued, it is only by examining power at a lower level of abstraction—where variable concrete institutional details and contingent historical factors within capitalist political economies enter the picture—that we can see how changes in the context itself transform the way capital's power is exercised in politics. Businesses own and control productive resources, but the specific character of those productive resources varies considerably. To better understand what is common to all forms of business power, we need to analyze how the assets that capitalists control change, and how this reconfigures the linkages that entangle politics and business. The key issue is the mutable character of income-producing assets.

Asset power concerns the character of the wealth circulated in the process of accumulation itself. For instance, changes in the degree of *asset mobility* (the ease in which that asset is moved around) and *liquidity* (the ease in which that asset is converted into cash) alter the political strategies available to owners of

capital as they seek to defend their interests politically or economically by simply responding to market signals by adjusting their
investment decisions. In contexts where capital assets have lower
levels of mobility and are more illiquid, such as land-fixed assets
like rental properties, mining, and agriculture, capital will be less
able to exit a polity, and the costs of diverting investment elsewhere will be higher. As a result, income-producing assets that
are more geographically fixed capitalist assets always face a
greater risk of being subject to democratic demands for appropriation, redistribution, and even forms of democratic extension and
deepening than assets that are more liquid and therefore harder
for the demos to get their hands on.

Historically, a weak landlord class is an important precondition for the construction of formal democratic institutions. And
where elites have held most of their wealth in illiquid assets fixed
in a political territory, their reaction to movements for political
democracy has been most violent. During the transition to democracy in South Africa, the strongest opponents of democratic
reform came from Afrikaner farmers with assets fixed in the
land.[3] English-speaking elites in the financial and industrial sectors did not spend as significant an effort trying to block
democratic transition because they would be able to move their
capital elsewhere in the event that a new government tried to tax
it, which is precisely what the African National Congress did
when Mandela's government came to power in 1994.[4]

Movements for political democracy have gained traction, and
democracy has been established with less violence in societies
where the elite held most of their wealth in more mobile manufacturing and liquid commercial capital. Peaceful democratic
transitions are far more likely when economies shift from being
heavily reliant on immobile fixed capital assets, such as mining
and agriculture—which are explicitly tied to the land—to more
mobile and liquid forms of capital.[5] Historical and social scientific
evidence suggests that as capital comes to hold more and more
geographically mobile and liquid wealth, it becomes more difficult to tax—and in turn makes the asset holders less resistant to

expanded democratic rights.[6] In such an event, the demos might be formally empowered through democratic rights but left practically worse off because the income-producing assets have been liquidated or relocated to special economic zones and tax havens outside their democratic jurisdiction.[7]

When the income-producing assets that everyone depends upon are more geographically mobile and liquid, it becomes possible for capital to simply exit in order to avoid demands for redistribution and appropriation. But here exit brings with it an indirect punishment of the demos that has been left behind. Capital flight can cause devastating economic crashes. This is a deeply political process, of which elected leaders are keenly aware. In *The Wealth of Nations*, the founder of modern political economy, Adam Smith, even argued that as capital assets become more mobile, the investment environment becomes of greater concern to policymakers.[8]

This threat of exit, either by mobility or liquidity, creates many political obstacles for democratic reformers. States have a far harder time taxing mobile assets, mobility makes the provision of social services more difficult, and labor and social democratic parties find it far harder to win meaningful reform when capital can be diverted outside of a political territory.[9] Capital exit thus means that governments need to concern themselves not only with their own domestic investment environment but also with the global environment, as more attractive opportunities abroad might lead to disinvestment at home.

The character of income-producing assets identified here helps explain historic variation in responses to democratic expropriation across many contexts.[10] Where assets are more fixed, the asset holders must resort to extrajudicial and violent means of defense in the face of democratic demands for expropriation. Just days after taking power in Russia, Lenin and the Bolsheviks passed a handful of decrees, one of which asserted that "the landowners' right of ownership over the soil is abolished forthwith, without compensation." Estates of landlords and land held by the church—as well as associated assets such as livestock and equipment—were transformed into the collective property of the peasantry. At the time, landed elites owned only around 20 percent of all land in regions around the Black Sea in Ukraine and about 7.5 percent of land in central Russia. Yet the peasants remained very much under their thumbs, subject to debts, duties, and forms of taxation that kept them poor and disempowered. It was only in 1861 that Russian serfs won their emancipation. Once formally freed, many of the nearly 23 million serfs in direct bondage traded political for economic subjugation, becoming desperately indebted through inflated land rents to the country's nearly 103,000 landlords. In response to the Bolsheviks' decrees, landlords and the former landed nobility threw their financial support behind the White Army, unleashing a violent terror on the revolutionary government and their supporters in a civil war that lasted until 1923.[11]

There is an analogue in the self-emancipation of slaves in America. In the antebellum United States, elite Southern resistance to abolishing slavery and expanding citizenship and political rights ignited the Civil War. The productive assets of the landlord class overlapped: first were human beings held as private property and second was the fixed asset of the land, which those in bondage worked upon to cultivate the riches of the plantation class. The Reconstruction Act of 1867 promised to reverse the Southern agricultural landlord's political subjugation of slave labor by forcing a ratification of the Fourteenth Amendment and guaranteeing Black people the right to vote in state constitutions. And as W. E. B. Du Bois shows, there was a short period of emancipatory "abolition democracy" that resulted in both the economic and political empowerment of former slaves.[12]

Yet the withdrawal of troops in the 1870s led to a hard reversal in which Black people, now largely subject to new extractive and exploitative relations of debt peonage, were excluded from politics through public violence, fraud, and pernicious legal barriers to voting, such as literacy tests and poll taxes. Murderous violence from the plantation class and their emergent organizations such as the Klu Klux Klan resulted in the reproduction of pre–Civil

War slave relations, albeit under transformed property rights. As Du Bois writes, "The slave went free; stood a brief moment in the sun; then moved back again toward slavery . . . A new slavery arose."[13] Underscoring this violent democratic retrenchment was the asset power of the Southern plantation class, fixed in the land and dependent on the political disempowerment of the Black working class.

Reactive Destruction

With the onset of market liberalization over the 1980s and 1990s, increased capital mobility and the internationalization of the firm became part and parcel of finance capitalism. This has had crucial implications for democracy. The character of the income-producing assets in circulation is clearly not the only political constraint in capitalist democracies. Politicians in office, especially those with economic democracy or anti-elite populist agendas, face multiple political barriers and dilemmas. These include: an institutional dilemma resulting from the congressional or parliamentary constraints faced by lawmakers, which are even more difficult to overcome when a party or fraction of a party holds a minority of seats; an organizational dilemma, which stems from the possible "selling out" of reform-oriented politicians and left parties via what Roberto Michels has termed the "iron law of oligarchy"; and an electoral dilemma, which is the product of the need to appeal to a wide swathe of the electorate and develop cross-class alliances in ways that almost always dilute the program and platform of working class parties.[14] It is beyond the scope of this book to explore each of these—but suffice to say they are structural checks that impose boundaries on policymaking in electoral democracy. But what does a transformation in the wealth in circulation—in particular the increased mobility and liquidity of income-producing assets in finance capitalism—mean for a politics aimed at weakening entrenched economic and political power? Failures of the past offer insights for the future.

When democratic socialist Salvador Allende assumed office in Chile in 1970, his Popular Unity coalition, which included communist, socialist and radical parties, embarked on a radical program designed to fundamentally transform Chilean society. The core of the wealth in circulation when the government came into power was in fixed and illiquid assets, principally in land and copper mines. Allende's program included both profound social changes and redistributive goals. First, it aimed to transform the structural size of capital in the domestic economy by nationalizing copper mining; banking and foreign commerce; strategic industrial firms; and the key sectors of infrastructure, such as energy production, transportation, and communications. Land reform was also a core component, with large capitalist farms to be expropriated and run by cooperatives. Economic development goals had a very strong redistributive character, with higher wages, a shift in production from luxury goods toward consumer goods, more robust social security programs and universal health care, among a host of other reforms.

The short-term results were positive. First, major agreements between the government and the National Workers Confederation resulted in increased average and minimum industrial wage scales and greater worker participation in state-owned enterprises. Second, by the end of 1971, more than 150 industries were put under state control—and many more (those with capital exceeding $1.34 million) were identified by the "Basic Program" for nationalization or transition to being run jointly on a mixed basis. Third, the Popular Unity government also moved to nationalize foreign held corporations in a range of sectors; the largest cases of this were in the US-controlled mining sector, as occurred famously with the Anaconda and Kennecott corporations.

However, the government was soon beset by several economic crises. First, under President Nixon, the American state intervened on behalf of American firms with geographically fixed investments in Chile. The US government and the World Bank gave Chile no new loans after 1970. The economy suffered another serious blow the following year as a result of the drop in the price of copper triggered by recessions in the US and Western Europe, Chile's main export markets. Then in 1972 and 1973, with the economy already reeling, nearly 250,000 truck drivers, taxi drivers, and small shop owners, with financial backing from the CIA, repeatedly shut down their operations in order to make the Chilean path to socialism even harder to traverse. With wealth largely fixed in the territory, the holders of that wealth fought tooth and nail against the Popular Unity government's plans to appropriate it. The economic decisions of these forces were profoundly political, undermining the governing coalition's legitimacy and opening the door to a bloody military coup in September 1973.

Most income-producing assets in Chile's accumulation model were not geographically mobile or liquid and therefore wealth holders, both domestic and foreign, could not simply flee the Popular Unity government's reforms. Their profits were extracted from Chile itself. First, the Chilean bourgeoisie's assets were principally in agrarian, industrial, and financial firms. But these were not separate fractions of capital with distinct interests and exit capacities. Many industrial firms were founded by the landed oligarchy and the banks were typically held by industrial-agrarian groups. This resulted in a heavily monopolized Chilean private sector, controlled by a familial bourgeoisie with deeply fixed commercial ties to the land.[15] Second, until the Frei programs of "chileanization" in 1965, which partially nationalized copper, US corporations Anaconda and Kennecott owned literally all of the copper mines. Iron ore production was principally held by Bethlehem Steel, while nitrate production was controlled by the foreign multinational Laturo Company. These industries made up the bulk of Chile's exports, 40 percent of which went to the US market, on which Chile was dependent for growth.[16] But foreign capital investment extended far beyond just key export industries. Out of all the industrial corporations in Chile, 25.5 percent had foreign holders who controlled 59.9 percent of the corporate capital.

The investment strikes undertaken by domestic and foreign capital in Chile, as well as capital's eventual support for the brutal military coup of September 11, 1973, were exercises in asset power very different from those that undermined the socialist experiment of François Mitterrand in France less than a decade later. Much like Allende's Popular Unity government, the government that was elected to office in 1981 was a coalition of socialists, communists, and radicals. It too embarked on a program of nationalization and income redistribution, as part of its so-called "110 Propositions." It took over two major investment banks, Compagnie Financière de Suez and Compagnie Financière de Paris et des Paribas, both with sizable stakes in industry, as well as thirty-six other separate banks. As a result of the nationalizations, the publicly owned banking sector was poised to control almost 90 percent of total banking deposits. The Mitterrand government also planned to nationalize five major industrial groups and restructure the lending practices of France's largest three banks (which were already nationalized).[17]

Capital's reaction was less bloody in France than it was in Chile, but it was still devastating for economic democracy. France's economy was far more internationalized and its population heavily dependent on imports. Even before the Socialists began to implement their program, instead of being met with the shells and blasts of a coup, they were first subject to an investment slowdown (which also occurred in Chile) but then, even more importantly, they suffered unrelenting capital flight outflows. Ten days before Mitterrand himself was inaugurated on May 21, the Paris stock exchange had to be closed because there were only sellers and no buyers. Billions of dollars of financial assets were moved out of France, and intense speculation in international financial markets caused the value of the franc to plummet like an anchor, bringing democratic socialist statecraft to a staggering halt.[18]

In reaction to the exercise of exit power in France, the government installed capital controls and increased spending as counter measures, but they did both to no avail. The election of a socialist government caused a downturn in the stock market, with investors rapidly exiting the country. A series of severe devaluations forced the French socialist government to turn sharply to austerity; they implemented massive public spending cuts and tax increases. The dilemma was simple—stay the course and risk an even deeper recession or submit to the discipline of capital. Had the Mitterrand administration stuck to its socialist program, it would have had to face down international financial markets by leaving the European Monetary System and embrace a protectionist model of growth build on strong tariffs and the development of its own domestic industry. Such a strategy could only have been successful with a majority of the population fully behind the program and willing to suffer through a "transition trough," the severe economic difficulties that come with making domestic production compensate for the loss of imports.

The failed democratic rupture in Chile in the 1970s and France in the 1980s shows that capitalist constraints on politics operate in very different ways in different places. In France, international investors were able to escape France's socialist experiment because of the mobility and liquidity of the assets that they secured income from, whereas the domestic and foreign capitalist classes in Chile resorted to bloody tactics because their geographically fixed assets left them no other option than to stay and fight to preserve their assets. Both countries, moreover, were subject to international constraints largely beyond their control (global copper price fluctuations in Chile and monetary devaluation in France) that weakened their ability to pursue democratic socialism.

Means of Plunder

In financialized political economies where income-producing assets are more mobile and liquid, capital will leverage a greater amount of exit capacity. But this does not capture the full extent of finance's asset power. This section explores the distinct forms of leverage that this mobility and liquidity activates in politics, showing not only the various ways capital exit works for finance but also the other political processes that combine to establish political hegemony for the financial sector in the countries where Wall Street and the City exert their global dominance. While the popular view of finance has become more critical since the 2008 downturn, its political power has become tightly intertwined with public institutions.

In particular, three main forms of financial leverage are persistent in contemporary democracies and combine to erode democracy itself. These are the sector's structural prominence, active engagement and logistical entanglements. This section explores each with reference to the two centers of global finance, the City and Wall Street. Building on the asset basis of capitalist power, the aim of this section is to both map out the key leverage points in democratic politics conceptually on a general level and specifically with respect to finance.

Conceptually, I make the distinction between sources and mechanisms of political leverage. We can think of a "source" of leverage like a resource, which is purposefully or unintentionally mobilized in politics. Sometimes these sources are actively held by the powerful, but they can also be emergent features of social relations unrecognizable even to capitalists themselves. The power of the financial sector, for instance, is in part solidified because the demos itself generates its own income through privately held financial assets in large pools of finance like pension funds. "Mechanisms" are the way in which those resources generate political capacities or effects in politics. For example, if having lots of money is a political resource in capitalist democracies, a mechanism through which this resource is mobilized could be paying a politician off.

Engagement

The most self-evident form of leverage concerns the way that capitalists actively and purposefully mobilize their resources in politics to get what they want. Termed *engagement*, this power is drawn from two sources: organization and financial resources.

First, capitalists are organized and tied into social networks designed for leverage in politics: through interlocking directorates and business associations. Both means of coordinating interests afford the corporate sector powerful capacities in policymaking.[19] Interlocking corporate directorates generate networks of shared interests for business actors, providing an organizational basis for overcoming collective action problems that might block business actors' ability to develop a shared political purpose.[20] Similarly, by creating networks and spaces for elite deliberation, business associations also develop a shared political perspective and common culture and are therefore better designed to mobilize corporate interests in politics in ways that might overcome collective action problems. As unions have declined and weakened in their capacity to be a countervailing force against capitalist organization, the associational ties that organize the interests of the wealthy in politics have been strengthened in relative terms.[21] The demos is fractured and often unorganized; workers are up against an organizational juggernaut.

Second, the greater financial resources held by capitalists, beyond just the organizational resources at their disposal for overcoming collective action problems, afford business greater capacity for direct spending in politics as a means of exerting influence. A rich social science literature demonstrates that campaign contributions and lobbying are another point of leverage within political institutions.[22] In a context of deep resource inequality, a mechanism of influence for those with significant resources is simply the ability and willingness to pay. The willingness of the wealthy to spend in politics is sharply contrasted by the way that the demos act politically, through a willingness to act collectively.[23] Because the non-elite demos cannot directly pay, their only option for direct leverage in politics is based on their ability to overcome their differences and act collectively.

Considering the global financial sector, both sources of power, interpersonal connections and associations on the one hand and campaign financing and lobbying efforts on the other, are all sources of political leverage. In the City, the key financial-sector lobbying groups are TheCityUK, UK Finance, and the International Regulatory Strategy Group. These lobbying groups are highly coordinated, with significantly interlocked directorates. Wall Street is similarly organized. Groups like the Bank Policy Institute, the American Bankers Association, and the National

Association of Insurance and Financial Advisors pour millions of dollars into lobbying and campaigns. The Financial Services Forum, for instance, is led by the top Wall Street CEOs. Each sits on top of one of the eight largest and most diversified financial institutions headquartered in the US, and five members of the board also sit on the Business Roundtable. A true test of finance's lobby power is that these organizations often do not even need to go to government in the first place; the government comes to them instead. In the US, the Federal Reserve, the Treasury, and regulators in the Security and Exchange Commission and the Commodity Futures Trading Commission regularly meet with the Financial Services Forum for feedback on politics and economic policy.[24] In both the US and the UK, these industry groups are supplemented by a whole complex of their mercenaries, the lobbyist and lobbying firms that do additional political leg work.

Wall Street and the City use this capacity to poach key regulators and outspend those they come against in political and court battles. In the US, between 1998 and 2023, top finance, insurance and real estate firms increased their lobbying by 186 percent from $207 million to $592 million. They have similarly flooded American elections with money. Rich individuals from the financial sector increased their spending on political campaigns an astounding 2,151 percent over twenty years, from $43 million in 1990 to $925 million in 2020. Over just a ten-year period, after the Supreme Court passage of Citizens United in 2010, shadowy soft money groups from the financial sector went from $15 million to $980 million, a 6.533 percent increase. American democracy, for lack of a better word, is literally flooded with bribe money from the financial sector. And this is not a partisan project. The sector hedges its bets politically too. In 2020, the sector allocated $492 million to Republican candidates and $535 million to Democrat candidates.[25]

Prominence
Capitalist firms play an essential role in capitalist economies. The private sector, large corporations, and financial institutions generate the vast bulk of investment decisions that create jobs,

generate growth, and ultimately put money in people's pockets. Capital's privileged ability to decide where and how to invest gives it significant leverage over politics. Both states and the demos are directly dependent on the economic activity of firms for tax revenue and employment. States and the agencies, policy-makers, and bureaucrats that make them up depend on capital to generate growth and provide employment. Both are key to state revenue through taxation and the state's governing legitimacy with the electorate, which makes elected representatives particularly attuned to the needs of business. Critical political sociologists and political scientists have referred to the political leverage that this generates for firms as structural power, though here, in an effort to be more precise, I refer to it as *prominence*.[26]

There are two distinct sources of prominence for capitalists: sectoral size relative to others (i.e., centrality in a given accumulation model) and capacity for investment withdrawal, or exit, from a political territory. Recalling the discussion of asset power above, the former concerns the amount of productive assets held by a firm or sector, and the latter concerns the character of those assets. With respect to size, the prominence of a sector is a position best contrasted with respect to others.[27] Many different degrees of interdependence between the state and capital most broadly, particular sectors, and even particular capitalists are possible.[28] The prominence of a firm or sector is approximated by its size and centrality in accumulation relative to other firms or sectors. At an aggregate level, the prominence of capital itself is inversely proportional to the public sector's relative size; as the latter grows and begins to crowd out the private sector, the prominence of the former dwindles.

Increased size generates a unique mechanism of influence on politics. As social dependence on investment increases not only for jobs but for relatively cheap goods and services—the things people need to survive and live a happy daily life—states and the demos will both be less likely to make demands on business. Why risk hurting the source of what you depend on?[29] If capital alone controls the resources that are critical to everyone's economic prosperity, their position will be privileged in policy without them needing to lobby or make campaign contributions because everyone, to a certain degree, will see their own interests as intertwined with the interest of firms. Capitalist democracy, in this view, will be constrained, through ordinary democratic mechanisms, to create the conditions necessary for capitalist accumulation.

A related, but nonetheless distinct, dimension of prominence is the capacity for exit or divestment from a political territory. This is commonly referred as a "capital strike." Sometimes the investment slowdowns and withdrawals are strategic and intentional, as was the case with the CIA-funded nationwide truck strike in 1972 that hobbled the Chilean economy under Allende. However, these actions can also be spontaneous and nonstrategic and coordinated through the invisible hand of the economy, that is, market responses. The political scientist Charles Lindblom referred to the way popular control of democratic institutions can be quickly devastated by seemingly politics-neutral investment decisions as an "automatic punishing recoil."[30]

As opportunities for profit deteriorate on the market, businesses react by going elsewhere, exiting that market in search of a better one. Capital strikes can therefore be quite distinct from labor strikes, which are not mere reactions to economic indicators (i.e., the dull compulsions of the market) but rather by necessity must be organized by workers who come to have a shared collective purpose and a willingness to take big risks together for a very uncertain collective outcome.[31] While capital strikes often have collective effects, they need not be the result of concerted and intentionally coordinated collective efforts like those of labor.[32] The degree of capital's mobility into and out of a political territory and the liquidity of the income-producing assets that they manage is, however, variable. As I illustrated above, firms with heavy investment in land, plant, and production equipment will face greater costs in exiting than those whose assets are primarily in human or liquid financial capital since the latter can simply fire their employees or sell their assets and move their investments elsewhere.

At a sectoral level, finance is strengthened in politics by both features of prominence. As I showed in the primer (Chapter 3), Wall Street and the City both account for a large share of economic activity in their political economies and are more mobile because of the more liquid income-producing assets under their management. On the one hand, as a share of GDP, finance has grown considerably in the US and the UK, where politicians have become more dependent on the sector for tax revenue and economic activity, and firms in the so-called real economy have become ever dependent on it for flows of credit and business services.[33] Though nonfinancial firms are key agents in the production and distribution of goods and services, finance is fundamental to the allocation of credit, financial services, and investment flows into the circuit of capital. On the other hand, because finance often circulates assets that are more liquid than other sectors, it exerts a greater threat of capital mobility out of political territories.[34] And these shifts in investment can happen in milliseconds. Investment in production often declines slowly, but the buying of financial assets or government bonds and bills can cease on a dime, thus giving asset managers in particular unique political leverage.[35]

In a tightly interconnected world, risk-averse investors fleeing what they perceive as an unfavorable business environment or speculators looking to profit off financial turmoil through derivatives or bond purchases both disrupt politics. In East Asia in 1997 and 1998, a devaluation of the Thai baht generated a quick financial downturn because liberalized electronic trading allowed risk-averse investors to quickly pull out and vampiric speculators to move in and bet on further devaluations. Reactive outflows of capital can destabilize a whole economy. In the UK, since 1945 there have been five sterling crises in which investors dumped sterling and sterling-denominated assets.

But rapid in-flows can be just as economically destabilizing as outflows, driving exchange rate appreciation and asset bubbles.[36] Flight is not the only risk. In some cases, vulture hedge funds have significantly undermined sovereignty and exerted pressure on governments to adopt certain kinds of policies. For instance, Boston-based hedge fund, Baupost, run by billionaire Seth Klarman, bought up nearly $1 billion in Puerto Rican debt at depressed prices. After the devastation of Hurricane Maria in 2017, Baupost pressured the government to install a draconian austerity program that included increasing university tuition, cutting employee benefits and vacation, closing schools, cutting welfare assistance and selling off the Puerto Rico Electric Power Authority, the public energy company. Their effort to push the government to pay creditors instead of spending to help the impoverished inhabitants of the devastated island has largely been successful.[37]

Prominence as a political lever operates via a sector's strategic position in the economy and its capacity to disinvest. Yet even between the two financial sectors in the US and the UK, there are crucial differences in the contexts. Consider the divergent government responses to the 2008 meltdown. In both cases, governments intervened with liquidity, debt guarantees, and recapitalizations for their financial institutions—but did so in distinct ways. There are two forms of bailout: state guaranteed debt (where banks get loans on the market that are backed by the state's guarantee of repayment) or state injected capital (where the state injects liquidity into banks in exchange for shares). Banks prefer the former option because in the latter existing shareholders typically take a loss on their shares and the government becomes a shareholder that can intervene in management decisions.

In the British bailout, the government took on more risk and lost more taxpayer money by subsidizing both unhealthy and healthy banks with state backed loans whereas the American government profited from its bailout by requiring healthy banks to share in the fiscal burden. The US Troubled Asset Relief Program (excluding the auto bailout and mortgage relief) generated an $8 to $10 billion net gain, $4 billion coming from Goldman Sachs, JP Morgan, and Wells Fargo, who resisted capital injections. The reason for this divergence is largely a result of the distinct structural positions of the two financial sectors in their national political economies. Though they were both financial, the particular character of their income-producing assets diverged. Healthy British banks made a much larger percentage of their profits outside of the UK. At the time, HSBC made nearly 80 percent of profits in foreign markets. Healthy American banks, however, make a much larger share of their profits in the US market. Wells Fargo, for instance, is almost entirely US based. This greater dependence on the domestic market enhanced the capacity of regulators in the US relative to that of their British counterparts.[38]

The British bailout's inefficacies show the relative depth of the state's subordination to global finance, while the US's relative success indicates a more robust regulatory sovereignty, albeit one still entrapped within the confines of financial accumulation. Even across this double-planet system, where the two poles of the US and the UK exert their own gravitational force, political power and finance capital are articulated in ways that reflect their unique national contexts and the distinct forms that financial accumulation takes between them.

Entanglement

A similar but distinct form of capitalist power concerns the ways that capital is infrastructurally intertwined with the logistical operations of organizations and institutions beyond itself. I refer to this form of leverage as *entanglement*. For finance in particular, this leverage operates through the sector's entanglement in the governance systems of both democratic institutions and non-financial corporations.

In his work on the state, historical sociologist Michael Mann shows that "infrastructural supports" in civil society enable states "to regulate, normatively and by force, a given set of social and territorial relations."[39] Such infrastructural embeddedness affords states the capacity "to implement logistically political decisions."[40] Consider the myriad ways in which this political power obtains in modern capitalist democracies. Large logistical infrastructures allow states to assess and tax income and wealth, store and access massive pools of information about the residents and the organizations that lie within and sometimes outside of its own territory, and control both digital and physical technologies that allow them to surveil their populations. Yet this power does not only radiate outwards from the institutions of government but rather can be exercised in two directions. Once those entanglements are interwoven, power can then be leveraged against the state by the organizations the state relies on to govern.[41] Finance capital derives additional political capacities from its infrastructural role in *both* political and corporate governance.

Central banks are pivotal to the financial sector's role in state governance. Until the 1980s, central banks like the Federal Reserve in the US, the Bank of England, and the German Bundesbank primarily relied on direct instruments of regulation, such as interest rate controls and credit ceilings. Since then, they have shifted to indirect tools to manage the economy like reserve requirements, standing facilities, and open market operations. In simple terms, modern central banks regulate through financial markets; the overnight interbank interest rate, the specific target of monetary policy, is determined by financial markets. This reliance on financial markets means that providing liquidity involves partnerships between public authorities and private financial institutions. As a result, central banks incorporate practices from the private sector into their own governance arsenals. The logistical entanglements that result have major implications: financial markets cannot be dismantled without also undermining the state's own capacity for implementing its monetary policy. Central banks are not mere regulators of financial markets; they are active participants.[42]

Nowhere is this more illustrative than shadow banking, the credit system that involves activities and actors such as hedge funds or money market funds outside of the regulated banking system. Central to shadow banking are repo markets where loans are made through selling and later repurchasing securities. In these agreements, the borrower sells a security and agrees to buy it back later at a higher price. In the US, the Federal Reserve has used such methods to support financial institutions themselves.

For instance, investment banks like Lehman Brothers and Bear Stearns used these transactions to liquify their mortgage-backed and asset-backed securities to make massive expansions to their balance sheets.[43] Similarly, the European Central Bank (ECB) has used these transactions to lend money by accepting government bonds from European countries as collateral. As political economists Benjamin Braun and Daniela Gabor have argued, both central banks demonstrate how deeply the financial sector is logistically entangled with the state itself. Even after the financial meltdown, which was partly caused by these repo markets, central banks have continued to support shadow banking.[44]

We can extend this focus on finance's entanglement in state governance through central banking to a second form of entanglement—its entanglement with nonfinancial firms. Through its output linkages with nonfinancial firms, finance maintains and manages relationships, goods and services that other sectors of business depend on in their own operations.

For instance, small and medium-sized corporations in the US and the UK carry very heavy amounts of debt. Even before the COVID-19 shock, in the US nonfinancial firms saw their debt jump more than double, from $3.3 trillion in 2007 to nearly $7 trillion by the end of 2019. In the cauldron of the pandemic, that figure further shot up and now stands at $8.2 trillion.[45] With respect to the debt taken on relative to the revenue being generated, it is small and medium firms that are most proportionately in the red. In the UK, by mid-2021, 33 percent of small and medium-sized firms held debt more than ten times their cash balances, more than double the amount before the pandemic.[46] This entangles the financial sector into the basic governance of these firms, who feast upon debt to keep themselves afloat and to finance stock buybacks to appease their shareholders. This zombie meal is called a leveraged buyback.

As the market for private debt since the crisis has grown, it has also diversified. The most zombified firms that cannot access credit from banks have become increasingly reliant on pension funds, insurers, and even individual accounts for cash. Asset managers and investors direct assets to investment vehicles like hedge funds, mutual funds, exchange-traded funds, and collateral loan obligations, which then become a source of cash for firms through private debt or leveraged loans. Issuing debt to the worst-off firms is an almost $2 trillion market in the US.[47]

Why is this entanglement a source of political leverage for finance? When regulators set their sights on business, no business sector is defended by other sectors more than finance in lobbying.[48] Protecting finance is a common project for the capitalist class. Asset managers, banks, and private equity are all vital for managing the credit flows of other firms. The social science finds that though balance sheet indicators of financialization itself are not strongly correlated with lobbying on behalf of finance, financial leverage is.[49]

These entanglements of credit are key to finance's leadership position within business more broadly. It is a source of its hegemony among the other sectors of capital. It helps establish finance not only as the cutting edge of an accumulation model but also the leader among other sectors because of their logistical dependence on it. No other sector enjoys the same degree of business unity that finance does. When regulators threaten finance, other sectors of business are likely to come to its defense. The logistical entanglements finance has with other sectors of business also bring the distinct sources of power of those sectors to bear on politics in its defense. The political levers of finance, its primary *sources* and *mechanisms*, are summarized in Table 4.1.

Anchoring each of these three levers of finance is asset power, the distinctively mobile and liquid nature of the income-producing assets under the financial sector's sway. The leverage finance wields through engagement, prominence, and entanglement stems directly from its private dominion over financial assets. They are not just the source of their profits but also political power. Many of these assets are owned, if not also controlled, by members of the demos itself. Thus, in the face of a democratic rupture, it is imperative to not only curtail each political lever available to finance but also, even more crucially, to build alternatives that

Table 4.1: Levers of Finance

Political leverage	Source of leverage	Mechanism of leverage
Engagement	Interlocking directorates and business associations	Overcoming collective action problems through coordination
	Financial resources	Capacity for direct influence via political payments
Prominence	Size in economy	Dependence on investment reduces anticapitalist demands from demos
	Capacity for exit from political territory	Punishment of polity via divestment
Entanglements	Role in logistical implementation of state policy	State dependence on business through state capacity to govern
	Intra-business dependence for logistical operation	Uncoordinated mobilization of other units of business via their political levers

place those assets under democratic control. Our democratic system has been wrecked anew in the era of finance capitalism, primarily by the political power that radiates out of the assets that they control. The challenge, then, is to reclaim these assets, reasserting democratic governance over what has become a privatized realm of political influence.

Socialism's Black Swan

From the above, it would appear that the political power of finance is overdetermined. With finance so intertwined with the sinews of formal political institutions, how can we even begin to subvert it? The notorious image of a blood-sucking vampire squid is certainly apt as a metaphor for the sector. But there is a critical wrinkle to the conjunctural analysis developed here that tempers its bleak outlook:

the dollar's supremacy in the global market grants the US specific capabilities to counteract the threats posed by finance's asset power.

In short, its weak ties to international creditors and ability to spend more abroad than it earns affords policymakers tools to possibly outmaneuver flight in capital markets. Financialization is a double-edged sword for its power centers. Though it increases the exit threat of financial institutions and other mobile and liquid assets held by capitalists and the ruling-class-managed assets of the demos, states at the center of the global financial regime can also use policy to reconfigure the exit options. Finance depends on those states to enforce the rules from which it profits. The American state is uniquely powerful in this regard.

Most countries are desperate to maintain or achieve good standing in the global financial system because of profound interdependencies that, if broken, would be devastating for them. The centers of finance like the US and the UK draw the liquid assets from other countries into their orbits, exposing those countries to events that throw chaos into financial markets elsewhere—subjecting the demos of countries outside of the US to crises largely beyond their control. The democratic socialist experiment in Chile under Allende had the savage misfortune of experiencing a global bust in copper prices, for example. In a global political economy with such profound interdependencies, downturns out of the control of government can play the part of a black swan for a democratic rupture, stripping an economy of assets and its people of jobs.

The United States does have something of an advantage in the global financial system, since it was constructed largely in that state's interest and to give American business severe leverage over others.[50] First, the US, like other rich capitalist countries, is not bound by tight relationships with external creditors in the same way that developing countries historically have been with agencies such as the International Monetary Fund.[51] There is no international body threatening the US, as the US has done with so many, if it decides to adopt policies that cut against the interests of finance.

Second, and of even greater significance, despite the dollar operating in a regime of floating exchange rates, it serves as the world reserve currency. This position grants the US state significant leverage over the actions of other countries that hold significant portions of their assets in dollars while simultaneously expanding the scope of what it itself is capable of.

To explore the implications of this for finance capital's power, we need to take a brief detour into intricacies of international trade. The global political economy faces a basic question of coordination: How do two countries that use different currencies buy and sell goods to one another? The solution lies in the establishment of an internationally accepted form of currency. Historically, under the Bretton Woods regime, global capitalism resolved this by fixing the value of the currencies it traded with to a third form of money, gold. Since 1971, however, the dollar—not gold—has played this role.

This means that countries have to earn or borrow dollars before they buy things on the international market. The shift to the dollar–Wall Street regime was, as the late Peter Gowan showed in *The Global Gamble*, a "bid for world dominance." At the same time that Allende was initiating Chile's democratic ruptures, Nixon in the US made the decision to sever the tie between the dollar and gold. Now the value of the dollar no longer had to be fixed to gold; it was floating and could be bent by US central bank policy. This policy shift established the dollar as the global standard.

This transition enabled American economic imperialism to extend its reach around the globe more freely and deeply.[52] The first result was the fortification of American capital itself. American banks could more easily create monetary liabilities because of their access to lower interest rate lending from the Federal Reserve, giving them a competitive advantage. Nonfinancial American corporations conducting international business in their home currency also benefitted from cheaper borrower costs and greater ease of access to international financial markets.

The second outcome was that as dollars accumulated internationally, the US could acquire tangible resources in exchange for mere paper currency. This foreign accumulation of dollars effectively provided the US with interest-free loans. The increased global demand for dollar-denominated financial instruments lowered borrowing costs, effectively acting as an interest rate subsidy.

Third, the dollar bestows upon the US state significant leverage over the other countries in the global financial order who trade with dollars. The capacity to grant dollar-denominated loans develops into what the political scientist Jonathan Kirschner has termed "entrapment," wherein foreign users of the dollar cultivate a vested interest in its success.[53] The supremacy of the dollar affords the American state a subtle yet potent means of dominating other countries through its own monetary policy. Nowhere has this been more evident than it was in France under the Mitterrand government, where a Federal Reserve–driven deflation of the dollar and the Deutschmark increased the cost of importing goods, which caused an exchange crisis that sunk the democratic socialist experiment.

For countries other than the United States, a mass sell-off of their debt by foreign asset holders could precipitate a depreciation of their currency, thereby escalating the cost of goods priced in other currencies and potentially plunging their economy into recession. The United States is partially shielded from this process because both its foreign debt and imports are denominated in dollars. Unlike other countries, the US doesn't need to earn dollars in international markets—it can simply print them. The result is that the US does not have the same constraints as other countries. Quite uniquely, it can spend more abroad than it earns abroad.

Though imperialist in its original design and in perhaps all its subsequent applications, the upshot is that the international currency creates significant structural space in the global order for policy experimentation. Political scientist Benjamin Cohen argues forcibly that,

> in the context of monetary affairs, power is all about autonomy. The central issue confronting states, first and foremost, is the distribution of the burden of adjustment to external imbalance. The ultimate foundation of monetary power lies in the capacity

to avoid the costs of payments adjustment—to maintain the state's policy space, as free as possible from constraint. From these roots grow diverse instruments and opportunities for the exercise of influence abroad.[54]

The state's capacity to avoid adjustment costs is crucial. All countries experience monetary inflows and outflows. Inflows are revenues from sales of export goods and services; they are inward capital movements. And outflows are expenditures on imports of goods and services; they are outward capital movements. The summary of inflows and outflows is the balance of payments— all monetary transactions between the residents of a country and the rest of the world. Revenue might be greater or less than expenditures. The former is a surplus and the latter a deficit. Most countries in a deficit cannot print more money to pay for their obligations because their currency is not acceptable to foreigners. Therefore, to finance a deficit, a country must first come up with enough international currency—namely, the dollar—to pay its bills. Poorer countries in this situation must either sell off foreign assets or pile on more foreign debts. In either case, to pay off bills, its net worth will worsen. At some point, though, there are no foreign assets left to sell and international creditors will view the country as having surpassed its borrowing limits. In these cases, the country will often be forced into adjustment, which takes place via one of three ways, devaluation, deflation, or direct controls.

In the case of devaluation, countries have to depreciate the value of their currency, lowering the exchange rate of the national currency and thereby reducing the price of exports. In the case of deflation, austerity politics reduce spending in the economy and reduce imports, prices, and wages and labor controls. And finally, direct controls might be used to limit import volumes with trade barriers and limit outward flows with capital controls and exchange restrictions. These impose profound policy constraints on capitalist democracies that trade in the dollar, both rich and poor. As Benjamin Cohen writes, "In monetary affairs . . . the foundation of state power is *the capacity to avoid the burden of adjustment required by payments imbalance.*"[55] In other words, the issue is *autonomy* in the international economic order.

Wall Street has been built to smash down the walls set up around the social systems of other countries to allow its capital flows to drown local competitors in its waves. The power of the dollar allows the US Federal Reserve to directly control international interest rates, which it does simply by adjusting its own. Its flows of credit undermine democracy elsewhere and reshape economies in the interest of American capital.

But that same power affords the US significant autonomy, in relative terms, to adopt a more just approach not only to its own domestic growth but also in its relationships with other emerging economies around the globe, economies that it has beaten down for so long. It is ironic that the financial system underscoring American empire is the very means of dismantling it. Such a project, however, is only plausible by and through the demos, increasingly constituted on a global scale. It requires economic democracy.

5

Mythologies

Further back, higher than the candelabrum and much higher than the alter, rose the Moloch who was all of iron and had yawning cavities in his human breast. His open wings spread out over the wall, and his long hands reached to the ground.

Gustave Flaubert, *Salambo*

Joining the Maelstrom

Though the dominant financial institutions in society have, for a large part, lost their popular legitimacy, what finance capitalism is and indeed might become remains unsettled. Ours is a time of deep and persistent mythologies when it comes to the idea of "democratizing finance." When it comes to alternatives, we are surrounded by fairytales and fantasies. As Ursula Le Guin once remarked, "Every eutopia contains a dystopia, every dystopia contains a eutopia."[1] This chapter is about financial dystopias and how a subset of bold alternatives to finance capitalism reinforce its oligarchic governing principles.

For many of the advocates of democratized finance today, from each side of the political spectrum, large-scale public ownership via nationalization or state recapitalization, is a proven failure—one that has already been tried and had dire consequences for democracy. In the common anti-centralization view, the more that the political capacity to decide how credit is allocated and at what rates is concentrated in state institutions the more bureaucrats and career politicians will hold power—few want a Gosbank 2.0 where the bureaucrat becomes a banker. This just replaces one set of asset manager titans with another. If democratizing finance doesn't refer to converting financial institutions into public ones run by centralized governments, what might it mean?

The idea of democratizing finance began to circulate in the wake of the Great Recession of 2008 and was most notably championed by Yale finance economist Robert Shiller. In his *Finance and the Good Society*, democratization entailed "the opening of financial opportunities to everyone."[2] For Shiller, increasing access to financial instruments for wealth creation to ordinary people *is* the democratization of finance. Such a view is intended to open up opportunities for wealth creation and preservation in financial markets to more and more people. So, the argument goes, the more people that have access to opportunities to invest their own money in markets that are disproportionately accessed by the wealthy, the more democracy in finance there is. Democracy in the Shillerian view is entirely about access to speculative financial markets for the non-elite.

Shiller's take became the standard narrative, both for those with vested interests in seeing certain stocks go up and brokerage phone apps like Robinhood used and for those with an earnest concern about financial justice and inclusion. One common explanation of the Reddit-fueled short squeeze of the GameStop stock in January 2021, casts the new wave of retail investors in precisely this Shillerian light. In this view, new users were empowered by the gamified investment app Robinhood, which, akin to a tiny voting booth on people's phones, creates a new infrastructure for financial democracy. The app's historical origins, somewhat ironically, began at Occupy Wall Street. The protest spurred the founders, Baiju Bhatt and Vladimir Tenev, to create it. But were access alone the principal measure of democracy, then democracy has had a profoundly negative financial impact on ordinary retail traders. In 2022, after the quantitative-easing-fueled tech bubble of 2021, the average retail portfolio crashed nearly 20 percent. In total, retail investors lost $350 billion of their investments when the bubble burst. Their bags were left jam-packed for trips to the moon that they never took.

This makes clear why the view of democracy merely as increased access to financial markets is less rosy than is straightforwardly presented by some financial economists. Some of the most toxic assets have devastating effects on macroeconomic stability in general and working-class life in particular—as was the case in the junk bond market collapse of the 1980s and subprime mortgage crisis of the 2000s—precisely because they have been more widespread and been made more available. Though the access narrative appears logical when set in front of the background of a market that is always going up, when the investment itself is a bad thing, more of it isn't good.

And, even more fundamentally, mere access overlooks the core concern of this book: power. Our collective capacity to self-govern and have a say in investment decisions that affect our interests is left unsolved by mere access to financial markets. As Chapter 4 demonstrated, finance capitalism is such a threat, not only to workers but to planetary durability, precisely because it has generated specific means of plunder for the richest and their institutions to extract a greater share of value for themselves at the expense of not only the demos but nature itself. This has led to a legitimacy crisis for finance capitalism, an "interregnum" in Antonio Gramsci's usage, in which the finance capital is no longer "leading" in terms of its popular legitimacy but nonetheless remains "dominant."[3] Before turning to my own alternative, public pools of finance governed by randomly selected class- and issue-based assemblies, a brief detour to the alternative vision of democratic finance widely on offer is necessary.

Over the last decade a growing voice for financial democratization has emerged in the world of crypto assets (a term more accurate than currencies), and the public discussion around it has become too prominent ignore. As I show, however, cryptocurrency is not the new world trying to be born out of the old but is rather a "morbid symptom" of the crisis of finance capitalism itself.[4] It is part and parcel of finance capitalism; it's mythological inversion.

Cyptopian Coordination

The political logic underscoring much of experimentation in the world of blockchain technology, a specific subset of the much larger turn to fintech, should be considered in sharp contradistinction to the basic thesis of this book. Even the most publicly minded strata of Web3 premise their experimentations in problem solving in ways that are entirely supplemental to and that lie outside of formal public institutions such as the state. The politics of post-anarchists such as John Holloway pervade Web3, if not explicitly, certainly at the level of its ethos. The aim to "change the world without taking power" is the default orientation.[5] But as I argued in Chapter 2, within capitalist democracies, emancipatory change requires democratic ruptures within the state itself. And broadly speaking, these ruptures have four basic characteristics: they extend formal political rights into the economic sphere; they expand the democratic composition of the economy; they consolidate the body politic along class lines; and they decommodify labor.

Perhaps unsurprisingly, because of its well-documented origins with anarcho-capitalist cypherpunks and Ayn Rand–adjacent libertarianism, the dominant vision for crypto is one that not only renders these aims irrelevant in theory but actively undermines them in practice.[6] In what follows, I consider the two social worlds of crypto, that of the so-called Bitcoin maxis (i.e., maximalists) and the Ethereum Moloch slayers (Bitcoin and Ethereum are distinct blockchains). Both offer unique visions for democratizing finance, which nonetheless converge on the Pollyannaish promise of an exodus from the state and existing financial institutions. Yet in rendering the significance of the state archaic, both ends of the crypto world promote fixes that simply reproduce the core ills of finance capitalism.

Within crypto, this is evident in the very use of the term "currency." There is a pervasive narrative, often associated with the Bitcoin maxis but equally present among those committed to Ethereum, about the possibility of decoupling currency from the state and existing financial institutions. Both proclaim that block-chain technology offers society the capacity to replace fiat money with tokens. In the case of Bitcoin, this is possible, we are told, because Bitcoin issuance is premised on scarcity—a limited supply of no more than 21 million coins—and a public decentralized ledger. This is apparently all one needs for a functioning system of payments. But the distance between appearance and reality here is vast.

Such a vision is fantasy at best, and dystopia at worst. The legal scholar Robert Hockett illustrates this well with a comparison of crypto to the state of money in America in the 1860s, prior to Civil War, when its cash system was principally based on "wild-cat" banknotes.[7] At that time, the notes were denominated in increments of a dollar but were not moderated by a central bank, or any federal government authority, as they are today. The result was twofold. First, there were drastically different actual values across the bank notes. The Billy the Kid note might trade at 50 percent of par while the Wyatt Earp note might trade closer to full. Second, the notes fluctuated wildly in value over time. This led to a highly inefficient system of payments, which offers com-parative insight into the current Wild West of crypto assets. Even if their use in criminal enterprises such as human trafficking and arms dealing were eradicated completely, an almost impossible thing in the regulation-lite context centered in the cryptopian vision of a desirable future, crypto assets would still provide an unsound ground for economic exchange. Because, as Nayib Bukele's authoritarian government of El Salvador discovered when it adopted Bitcoin as legal tender, there is simply too much volatility for it to be reliable.[8] This is because it is a speculative financial asset, not a currency.

The federal government was instrumental in solving the cur-rency problems endemic to the antebellum payments system. During the Civil War, Abraham Lincoln and the Congress passed a series of laws that established federally chartered banks that could all issue the same Treasury-backed note, the "Greenback." Then in 1913, the US government established the Federal Reserve, moving authority from the Treasury to a central bank. The dollar that we use today and that countries around the planet trade in is thus nothing like crypto assets since it is entirely backed by the power of the public and a state that has the capacity to create money and to manipulate its value.[9] To the extent that digital assets follow the trend toward government backing, precisely what the Bitcoin maximalists reject, it will lead to central-bank digital currencies, such as the e-kronar in Sweden, not a proliferation of even more cryptocurrencies, of which there are now well over 20,000.

It is telling that the libertarian cypherpunks who came of age in the 1990s tech boom envisioned a future for their crypto assets where governments wouldn't have the capacity to back their own money. They adopted a vision of the future reminiscent of the table-top role-playing game *Cyberpunk 2020*, in which formal states would decay under tyrannies dominated by private corporations who were the *de facto* pseudo-governments. As Brunton writes in *Digital Cash*,

> Their money, like all money, was built of the promise of a future. Their anticipated future was one in which the collapse of existing systems into some combination of tyranny, decadence, and anarchy would force a return to sources of "objective value" and the validation of their philosophy.[10]

Such a view found a home in camps as divergent as seasteaders and the new anti-woke populist right focused on the neofeudal power of liberal financiers. In this *Blade Runner* version of the future, the libertarian strand in crypto aims to build private counter-powers that will reside outside of the existing system of nation states and corporations on chain.

There is also a collection of blockchain technologists concerned with more progressive ambitions, such as reversing climate change and creating public goods. They are, in the main, associated with Bitcoin's main competitor, Ethereum—whose chain has allowed for a flourishing of new tokens and Web3 projects.[11] The Ethereum community leading the turn to blockchain projects that aim to solve real-world problems principally operate through DAOs, blogs, podcasts, and even conferences, such as ETHDenver. For DAOs in particular, decentralized autonomous organizations (originally called DACs—decentralized autonomous corporations), there have been, in the words of one keen commenter, "an explosion of network-native organizational creativity."[12] Sometimes going by celestial monikers like solarpunks or lunarpunks and donning a neon-colored rave aesthetic, the new public-minded cryptopians communicate through white paper debates and new experiments in governance, which often swirl around Ethereum co-founder and default boss Vitalik Buterin. Similarly allergic to the formal powers of the state and dedicated to modes of experimentation external to it, it is not surprising that they speak very little about democracy per se. Instead, armed with the tools of basic game theory, much of the debate concerns coordination.

One public-facing manifesto at the center is *GreenPilled: How Crypto Can Regenerate the World*, self-published by GitCoin founder Kevin Owocki. At the living heart of the vision of these self-described "chaos magicians of the internet of money" is the concept cryptoeconomics.[13] In short, informed by basic game theoretic models, they use blockchain-based incentives built on the Ethereum chain to design "new ways to fund, design, develop and market applications and digital assets" with a public purpose.[14] For Owocki and others the aim is to change people's internal criteria for what they deem good or bad investment, to transition from #degen (degenerative) finance to #regen (regenerative) finance. Anecdotally, he finds that many "regens" follow a distinct path in the Web3 community to public-minded concerns: I bet I could make some money in crypto → down bad → finds community → joins DAO → starts contributing → WAGMI ("We all gonna make it").[15] It is telling that the most progressive elements of crypto take a strategy strikingly similar to the most conservative financial reformers in mainstream finance found in business schools across the globe, projects such as ESG investment guidelines, which reproduce the basic dimensions of finance capitalism.

The core object of their social critique does not involve giving voice to the powerless or increasing the collective capacity for decision-making over investment (i.e., economic democracy) but rather coordination failures in the creation of public goods. They refer to a coordination failure, somewhat confusingly, as Moloch, the bull-headed Old Testament god of the Ammonites who demanded child sacrifice. This association became popularized through a 2014 post, "Meditations on Moloch," on the now defunct Silicon Valley rationalist blog, *Slate Star Codex*. Like many things in the crypto world, Moloch is simpler than he seems—it is merely a situation in which people would be better off working together but fail to do so because they act alone in what they perceive as their own self-interest. It is the collective action failure, classically conceived. The beast represents the situation illustrated by the famous Prisoner's Dilemma developed by RAND Corporation social scientists in the 1950s. In fact it is the direct inspiration. Yet within the subculture associated with making and building on the Ethereum chain, Moloch has come to take on a larger-than-life quality, becoming the object of DAOs. "Slaying Moloch," for instance, is one of the ambitions of MolochDAO, which offers grants to blockchain projects. The seventy-member group controls millions of dollars in funds.

Another, GitCoin, a grantmaking DAO that uses quadratic funding (i.e., it offers matching grants to funded projects), has even released a series of comic books popularizing the vision of a slain Moloch, resulting in a perfect society free of states and problems. One, "Anon Vs Moloch: The Greatest LARP Has Begun," opens with an illustration of a mesmerizingly sleek and clean "Quadratic City" located "somewhere in the not-so-distant-future." The architecture, perhaps plucked from Dubai, is surrounded by lush green growth. The comic copy reads, "At first glance, Quadratic City looks like a Utopia, but we all know there's no such thing. But with the rise of coordination technologies in recent decades, life here has come as close as you can get to one. It started simply. Funding public goods on the blockchain, driven by what the people want. Crowd-funded grants for public problem solvers, curated by the people they serve. All of it quickly evolving to create what we have here today, what became known as the Quadratic Lands."[16]

The crytopians that build on Ethereum believe that crypto is valuable precisely because it coordinates people better than previous coordination mechanisms throughout history and those available to the state today. Their ambition is for people to opt out of states and into blockchain-based projects and then to solve social problems through them—that is, principally through the goodwill of donations in crypto. Ameen Soleimani, founder of MolochDAO, describes the vision of crypto as an "Olympics of belief"; all around the world new projects and currencies are available for anyone to believe in and buy into and those that win do so by virtue of people's convictions.[17] For a project to succeed, all it needs is belief, expressed explicitly by how much the believer is willing to buy.

While those in Web3 might describe coordination failure as Moloch, Karl Marx used the god of child sacrifice to personify finance capitalism. Marx wrote in *Theories of Surplus Value* that

> the complete *objectification, inversion* and *derangement* of capital as interest-bearing capital—in which, however, the inner nature of capitalist production, [its] derangement, merely appears in its most palpable form—is capital which yields "compound interest." It appears as a Moloch demanding the whole world as a sacrifice belonging to it of right . . .[18]

In one account, collective action failure is the metaphorical threat to humanity, in the other it is the insatiable thirst for financial returns.

The intellectual hub for reimagining governance systems in crypto revolves around Glen Weyl, an economist and Microsoft researcher; the organization he leads, RadicalXChange; and Ethereum's Vitalik Buterin, a board member of RadicalX-Change and its principal financial supporter. Though the language of decentralization and more recently pluralism pervade the intellectual space, theirs is a vision most fundamentally hitched to markets. The ideas of Weyl and Buterin are particularly influential in providing direction for organizational experimentation in Web3, with practitioners adopting new design mechanisms to test the latest idea from the brain trust. Weyl became prominent through his 2019 book with legal scholar Richard Posner, *Radical Markets*.[19] At the heart of their experiments is a reconceptualization of voting and systems of resource allocation.

Posner and Weyl's development of the notion of quadratic voting has been uniquely influential for DAOs. In short, quadratic voting brings markets into the politics of governing tokens and Web3 projects. Individuals are allocated a certain number of credits, and they are allowed to spend whatever amount they like on votes. I might, for instance, spend all my credits on voting x and none on voting y, because x is more important to me. The procedure turns voting into spending; the amount a person spends indicates how much weight they put on the importance of a certain decision about that topic relative to other possible options.[20] Quadratic voting has been taken up by GitCoin in their system of funding, whereby open source blockchain projects that are funded are given matching grants, which incentivizes funding in the first place and rewards those that have the most support within the DAO.

Buterin has toyed with the whimsical idea of making governance rights in DAO a nontransferable NFT (non-fungible tokens) tied to the individual. The notion, which he terms a "soulbound" token, is inspired by the legendary looted items in the massive multiplayer online role playing game (MMORPG), *World of Warcraft*. When a specific character picks up a legendary item, it becomes tied to that character in the game. These soul-bound tokens might enable a DAO to mitigate Sybil attacks (when one person impersonates many to make changes) and make the leadership of DAOs more responsive to their members, dynamically shifting as the composition of the community itself shifts. Recent work by Buterin and others emphasize the need to shift toward coordination mechanisms that promote intergroup coordination and pluralistic diversity.[21] Gitcoin has implemented this through pairwise quadratic funding, which allow the DAO administrators to reward plurality by making matching funding adjustments on the basis of how much the contributors already do or do not cooperate.[22]

Others have also put new market-governance mechanisms into place in DAOs as well to make them more responsive to DAO participant needs. A participant by the name of Tracheopteryx (from the DAO Coordinape) developed a system of constrained delegation for distributing income—or, as they call them, "gifts"—to developers for their labor. Every month, the DAO runs gift-giving ceremonies where each member is given a set number of tokens. Members then gift those tokens to people based on the value they think they have added to the DAO. This is their means of distributing income, by dividing the monthly income budget according to the amount of tokens held at the end.[23] As if taking a page out of Marcel Mauss's *The Gift*, there is an attempt to create social obligations and norms through the practice of gift giving.[24]

The vast bulk of the solutions for coordination on offer within Web3 aim to solve rational actor coordination problems by creating incentives to get otherwise selfish people to act in the interest of the common good and to create public goods in the process. Much is based on simple assumptions about human behavior found in the introductory level game theory courses you might take as an undergraduate in economics or political science. But in practice, even the most innovative spaces in Web3 offer a logic of reform that is strikingly market oriented. The bulk of DAO projects are little more than investor clubs with governance structures dominated by those that hold the most tokens. Underneath it all, they are plutocracies.

Even the mission-driven DAOs are in the main self-serving. The BuyTheBroncosDAO was set up, for instance, to buy the Denver football team, and ConstitutionDAO was created to buy the American constitution. Some DAOs have emerged for specific social ends. After the Russian invasion of Ukraine, several emerged to raise donations for the Ukranian war effort. UkraineDAO, in particular, raised more $7 million in just three days.²⁵ Yet most of the significant mission-driven DAOs are set up to solve problems within the blockchain community itself and provide funding to developers working on improving specific projects. They are not designed to solve problems for the 99 percent of the world completely outside of cryptocurrency—which is, perhaps, odd given that so many in the crypto space were explicitly activated through involvement in projects seeking to take on the 1 percent, such as Occupy Wall Street. You have to squint, quite tightly, to see how these can be ratcheted up to solve the macro problems in finance capitalism more broadly.

Cipher Decay

For the most part, the experiments in crypto all have major drawbacks and fail to redress the dilemmas of finance capitalism. Instead, they deepen them. While I am not ruling out their usefulness in inspiring "design mechanisms" in other spheres or even those attached to a blockchain, in the main they have been beset by five major problems that make them unable to democratize finance in a way that is desirable, achievable, or durable. And worse, on their own terms they deepen the intertwining crises of the conjuncture.

First, crypto reproduces and deepens finance capitalism's tremendous inequality and capitalist democracy's undemocratic mode of governance. Most of the governance models in Web3 are plutocracies by design. Though projects for decentralizing finance are often advanced under the banner of democratization, theirs is a deeply impoverished vision of democracy. Far from democratizing finance via opening up access to crypto markets, equality of access in principle has, in practice, become an astounding concentration of ownership. A National Bureau of Economic Research working paper on Bitcoin ownership finds that the top 1 percent of holders hold 27 percent of all Bitcoin.²⁶ And Ethereum boss Buterin himself acknowledged that, even within the diverse ecology of DAOs built on Ethereum, the model of voting and governance for Web3 projects is that of a plutocracy because the majority of projects are governed by the principle of "one coin, one vote."[27]

Thus what determines the capacity for one's influence in these seemingly new "democratic" organizations is neither the liberal principal of equality, such as one person, one vote; a rationalist method of deliberation that allows for curation of good judgements; or a radical theory of democracy that gives voice to the margins. Instead, it is one that is strikingly similar to the governance of the capitalist corporation itself. Perhaps what we are viewing is not an evolution in democratic design but rather a new instantiation of the plutocratic corporate capitalist firm: from joint stock companies to limited liability corporations to DAOs. Crypto more represents a possible evolution of the existing corporate tyranny than a promise of economic democracy. Like the private firm or the typical asset manager board, DAOs typically function like private tyrannical governments.[28]

Second, instead of democratizing finance, Web3 financializes democracy, tying the principles of organizational governance to financial asset management and value maintenance and expansion. The crypto assets tied to blockchains are even more speculative than the market for stocks. At least in the case of stocks, we can tie them to the fundamentals of the corporation and the firm's underlying cash flow. Thus, when a company has a particularly gloomy quarterly earnings report, fluctuations in the value of its stock price are the typical response. As already mentioned, this dynamic in and of itself leads to speculative bubbles and Ponzi-like schemes within financial capitalism. But the Minskian bubble dynamics for crypto assets, which are entirely speculative and tied to people's fleeting beliefs and hopes, are even more prone to Ponzi pump-and-dump schemes than are corporate stocks, which are at least connected to a firm's potential and cash flows. It is an "Olympics of belief" built on quicksand.

In the main that is exactly what the large bulk of crypto is, a Ponzi-scheme. There are currently over 20,000 cryptocurrencies, the majority of which are built out of unregulated schemes for financial fraud. There was a huge burst in ICOs (initial coin offerings) between 2020 and 2023, when pump-and-dump schemes from Elon Musk's online cheerleading of Dogecoin to inflate his own earnings to so-called rug pulls, offering a coin and immediately selling everything you have for a quick profit, dominated blockchain activity. And all, again, are entirely detached from some underlying value (as a stock is tied to a firm's performance) and free from state regulation.

Other blockchain assets, such as CryptoPunks and Bored Ape Yacht Club NFTs, have principally attracted speculators searching for rapid wealth windfalls. While some of the early and more well-known art NFTs, such as Beeple's piece *Everydays*, will probably retain their value because they are now recognized by art insiders as part of art history, there has been an outrageous spread of copycat NFT launches; at a certain point you are no longer buying a Marcel Duchamp—you are just buying a urinal.

The speculative frenzy around blockchain assets has resulted in incredible financial volatility for them. Even Bitcoin, the established token on the block, is far more volatile than the other financial assets commonly traded and is more volatile than even the world's most volatile currencies. This is due to the fact that their value is derived from their ability to hype up crowding-in rather than from their ability to add any actual value to people's lives. DAOs are principally responsible for managing these blockchain projects. Thus, to the extent that they are viewed as sites of democratic experimentation, of community, and of civic engagement, this aspiration is nonetheless attached to the management of a purely speculative asset tied to a financial logic in its purest sense; it is not public-minded, nor can it ever be.

Third, and fundamentally, they have not genuinely produced public goods and it seems unlikely that they can durably address our social and climate crises in a way that is sufficient to the scale of the problems. What's striking is how poorly they achieve their own missions, even after they have raised massive amounts of funds. And much like capitalist markets themselves, they impose persistent and dangerous externalities on publics entirely outside of Web3. As mentioned before, the mode of public-good funding offered here is entirely based on changing the moral calculus of individuals to contribute toward funding out of their own virtual wallets. This is the normative premise underlying Sam Bankman-Fried (SBF) and FTX's trivial embrace of the principles of effective altruism, which are most prominently defended by liberal moral philosophers like Will MacAskill (who served as an advisor to SBF's Future Fund).[29] It turns out, of course, that SBF was financing politicians and causes out of people's deposits in his exchange. But it is also the normative premise underlying explicitly #regen projects, such as Gitcoin. Across crypto, public goods, to the extent that they are produced at all, are the result of charitable giving not binding collective decision-making about what we need to fund together. Much hangs on this fundamental distinction. Crypto, much like the finance capitalism of today's major asset managers, relegates the demos to the outside of investment politics.

The reasons for why this generates profound deficits in funding for public goods are already thoroughly documented. Capitalist markets, like crypto, are designed principally to capture profits; they struggle to produce public goods at the scale at which they are needed socially because, once a good is public, it is impossible to monetize and capture profits from it. Public goods, by definition, are things that are difficult to exclude anyone from consuming once they have been produced so there is little incentive in capitalist markets to produce them. This problem also extends to private goods that produce "positive externalities." It is not surprising that despite being flush with cash, the crypto world has failed to fund any truly public goods like public education, health, or even more mundane things like public infrastructure, parks for sports, or public centers for art making. Instead, this world funds the renaming of stadiums, like the Crypto.com Arena in Los Angeles and SBF's FTX Arena in Miami, or Superbowl ads. It is a capitalist money-making operation that wins through crowding in more and more users. It is quite simply a dead-end proposition that finance capitalism broadly, and DAOs specifically, could ever produce public works or empowerment of the demos, given that both are designed from the start to generate a profit.

Instead, blockchain technology produces significant "negative externalities" for those not involved Web3. Unlike a positive externality, in which benefits from the production and consumption of a good flows to a third party even though they were never involved in the transaction itself, a negative externality occurs when third parties suffer the cost of transactions they are not involved in. There are two principal ways in which blockchain projects do this: their anonymity and energy consumption. The anonymity has led to a massive number of financial frauds and scams and the financing of some of the darkest criminal activity, such as human sex trafficking. And because it is a profit-driven system situated in unregulated markets, it doesn't account for its own environmental negative externalities. In a year, the energy consumption of crypto mining exceeds that of a country the size of Argentina or Australia.

The existence of cryptocurrencies raises a host of thorny questions about our planetary future. How might we invest in projects that are nonprofitable and costly in the short run, such as green renewables and infrastructure? Can finance provide positive externalities, such as a livable planet to future generations? How do we invest in projects that are rarely profitable, such as public education or social housing, but nonetheless provide the positive externalities of having more educated citizens and less vagrancy and street suffering? Decentralized finance offers no solution to these real coordination problems because its funding of public goods is premised on the hope that very rich people will act altruistically, which of course they never have.

Fourth, they do not consolidate the body politic along the antagonistic class lines that are at the root of our social and ecological problems but rather render social difference, in its many dimensions, invisible. Instead, decentralized finance promotes the creation of anonymous transactional identities in governance and justifies this move with the apolitical view that "code is law."[30] As anthropologist Anna Weichselbraun has noted, the underlying techno-logic in Web3 is that "governance will replace politics."[31] The empty hope is to destroy politics, that is, the realm of power and domination, with contracts. Yet governance sans politics will deepen the atomization of political identity in capitalist democracy more broadly, the atomization that finance capitalism and the financialization of the wealth of the demos has already produced as investor selves.[32]

Nicos Poulantzas has argued that deep social-structural ine-qualities and differential access to power is reproduced through capitalist democracy in part because "its elective institutions all involve the atomization of the body-politic into what are called 'individuals'—that is juridico-political persons that are the sub-jects of certain freedoms."[33] This splitting up of people, into "equivalent monads," who then express individual preference via their vote during election cycles applies the liberal logic of free equivalents in the market to the space of politics. And in presenting itself as the concentrated expression of the nation, lib-eral state institutions reproduce the conditions underlying the political atomization that the financialization of everyday life merely accelerates and deepens.[34]

Core to this book's theory of democratic rupture is the chal-lenge to reorient this atomized political world as one of antagonism between classes. It is, as sociologist Dylan Riley has noted, "to make the 'noumenal' realm of the [class] structure converge with the 'phenomenal' realm of civil society."[35] This requires a recon-stitution of the political, not an effort to render it invisible through contracts. Yet blockchain governance draws politics in the opposite direction since its anonymity occludes people's identity not simply as members of classes and class fractions but even as individuals embedded in multivariate, overlapping political com-munities. This represents a deepening of finance capitalism's most pernicious cultural effects. Identity is so obscured that the entire DAO ecosystem is beset with concerns over, and actual examples of, so-called Sybil attacks, in which a single actor makes governance power moves by creating the false impression that they are in fact multitudes.

Yet politics is not simply governance, it requires open conflict (what I will later call agonism), and the degree to which it is submerged in crypto renders democracy an even more unlikely outcome. Moloch has already emerged as finance capitalism; fail to confront him directly and he will continue to cull for sacrifices. We must replace this demon with the demos.

PART III

RUPTURE

A Plan for Radical Democracy

6

Class Logics of Reform

There's more than one way to skin a cat.
proverb

Responding to Plunder

A peculiar condition of the current conjuncture is the widespread acknowledgement of the mess we are in, with hardly any shared sense within the demos about what to do about it. And the problem isn't partisan. Even within traditional political camps and parties, there is prickly disunity about how to solve the layered crises. Ours is a time of deeply fractured possibility. On both the left and the right, people understand that finance capitalism has run amok. But there is no clear path beyond its crises with some broad popular agreement, or even competing coherent agendas from the main political parties. Therefore, the political terrain of capitalist democracy today combines a legitimacy crisis with a lacuna, where an emergent alternative might otherwise be. To develop a desirable solution to finance's erosion of democracy and underfunding of socio-environmental goods, as a first step this chapter aims to understand our fractured politics of the possible. It does so by exploring the different financial reform strategies being proposed as well as their underlying emancipatory logics.

Perhaps surprisingly, there is very little conceptual work available on the modes of financial transformation accessible to insurgents, reformers, and technocrats. As a result, we lack a coherent means of both categorizing the reform ideas at the ready and identifying the conditions under which reform might disrupt and reallocate financial power. This chapter takes up the first task to develop a framework for classifying different projects for business reform, again focusing specifically on the crises unfolding because of finance capitalism, which were elaborated upon in the primer chapter. It draws from recent reform proposals in the centers of global finance in both the US and the UK as a means of showing the varieties of financial reform projects in circulation and how they relate. These reforms operate in four broad modes: normative, regulatory, supplemental, and control. After exploring the basics of each, I show how the modes rest upon distinct class logics. Like the mythologies spun out of blockchain, several of the reform paths only deepen the crises of finance capitalism. Others are insufficient without meaningful democratic participation and involvement of the demos. Only by democratically controlling finance can an alternative path of financial allocation be carved out.

Normative Reforms

The most common strategic response to the legitimation crisis of finance capitalism, advocated by many in the financial sector itself, is a normative one. This response operates at the level of individual and institutional moral calculus to inform, and ideally shape, the economic behavior of key financiers and asset managers through discourse intended to alter their worldview. Here moral entrepreneurs in glitzy venues like the World Economic Forum and the UN's Conference of the Parties urge business to engage in forms of self-regulation by challenging the knowledge regime in which economic decisions are made and by reshaping business actors' future expectations. They do this, not through coercive legislation or building alternative institutions, but through relational ties that are scaled up across organizations through firm-NGO and public-private partnerships.[1] This is perhaps the oldest response to the predation of capitalists, their own effort to self-present in the context of crises as progressive.[2]

This normative response to financial plunder is by far the most pervasive. It is broadly concerned with corporate social responsibility

(CSR) to stakeholders both inside and outside the firm. As Black-Rock CEO Larry Fink wrote in his annual 2018 letter to the world's major CEOs, "Companies must ask themselves: What role do we play in the community? How are we managing our impact on the environment? Are we working to create a diverse workforce? Are we adapting to technological change? Are we providing the retraining and opportunities that our employees and our business will need to adjust to an increasingly automated world? Are we using behavioral finance and other tools to prepare workers for retirement, so that they invest in a way that will help them achieve their goals?"[3]

Within the financial sector, CSR is expressed in institutional advocacy for environmental, social, and governance (ESG) investing by responsible investing think tanks like Ceres in the US and ShareAction in the UK. The aim here is an epistemological and rhetorical break with University of Chicago economist Eugene Fama's efficient market hypothesis, which argues that the stock price of a company is a true reflection of the value of that company.[4] With respect to responding to financial and ecological crises, the institutional and activist movement for ESG investing aims to establish alternative investing criteria that would inform new "best practices."

The United Nations Principles for Responsible Investment (PRI) now has over 3,800 signatories that include a wide range of global asset managers and financial services providers. The UN PRI promotes the incorporation of ESG criteria into investment analysis and decision-making. It promotes active ownership, ESG disclosures by institutional investors, the promotion of ESG within the investment industry, collaboration on implementing the principles, and reporting on progress toward implementing ESG goals. Some of the world's largest financial asset managers have signed on, including CalPERS; the New York City Employees' Retirement System; the Dutch public sector employees' pension fund; the Dutch health care employees' pension fund; and the world's largest pension fund, Japan's Government Investment Pension Fund. A total of 330 large sovereign wealth funds and pension funds have signed.[5] The UN PRI's relational work is the means through which financial actors reassess the morality of their own economic actions.

Finance capital has led to money management practices that are increasingly driven by daily valuation in stock markets and quick investment turnaround. Quarterly earnings report decision-making has led to investment churning and spurred volatility in stock prices, and it cuts against patient, longer-term, active investing. Unlike prior efforts to promote "mission-based" investing, ESG initiatives have argued that investors incorporating ESG concerns into their investment decisions won't simply better impact stakeholders, they will also be more profitable over the long term, explicitly challenging dominant investing ideas and investors' expectations of future returns.[6]

But Moloch is in the details. What counts as ESG? Much of the investor interest is in firms that are viewed as long-term environmentally friendly or give a greater voice to shareholders in corporate governance questions. Tesla, for instance, receives ESG investor praise despite its dependence on an anti-union labor regime built on systematic speedups. Social questions, such as unionization, workplace democracy, wages, and benefits, receive scant attention from the power centers of this investment trend. And nobody promoting ESG doubts that the people with say over how financial assets are invested should be the ones already doing the deciding. While some propose a more substantial incorporation of social factors into ESG investing standards, it's not clear why investors would do that on their own without regulatory enforcement, which violates the principle of moral self-regulation underlying this response.[7] Investors understand well that union representation often increases costs for firms and negatively bears on stock value over the long term.[8]

As an information campaign aimed at changing how investors think about investment, ESG has thus far been a failure on its own terms and offers no reasonable path to weaken finance's power. First, despite a huge number of signatories to the UN PRI, financial markets remain governed by the profit motive, with investors mostly giving lip service to the ethics of their investments. Despite the repressive character of the Saudi regime and the negative long-term implications for environmental sustainability, Saudi Arabia's state-backed oil company Aramco made a record-breaking $100 billion in orders in its April 2019 international bond sale.[9] Well-known signatories of the UN PRI, like Goldman Sachs, BlackRock, and HSBC, have been key players in the Aramco IPO. Second, even if implemented in its more watered-down "EG minus S" form, behavioral approaches to financial reform like ESG are blind to issues of class power. Since on its own it offers no program for challenging any of finance's power sources, it is unclear how ESG might confront the zero-sum interests at play between an economics for the many and one for the few.

Regulatory Reforms

In sharp contrast to the commitment to voluntary action of normative reform, regulatory responses to plunder direct finance to take specific actions, impose restrictions on certain actions or direct the sector to self-regulate to achieve mandated outcomes by means the firm or industry itself can decide. It is also principally the result of actions taken by political actors in governmental agencies and branches. Here the state enters in with binding, nonvoluntary enforcement mechanisms. Along these lines, today many progressives in the US pine for Roosevelt's New Deal regime. In the UK there is a parallel nostalgia for the welfare state principles embedded in the 1942 Beveridge Report, which laid the groundwork for the Atlee Labour Government's (1945–51) robust extensions in social welfare, public education, and economic nationalization. Advocates for regulatory reform, politicians like Democratic senator Elizabeth Warren in the US and Labour's chancellor of the exchequer Rachel Reeves in the UK, don't aim for nationalization though. Instead, they want stronger regulations to curb bad financial behavior, such as the "Robin Hood Tax" on speculative financial transactions. They implicitly point to a historical moment, circa the 1960s, when finance had not been so out of control.

Regulation can take one of two forms: means-based and ends-based regulation. Means-based regulation forces businesses to take particular actions to achieve certain ends. This more traditional approach to business regulation, sometimes referred to as "command-and-control" regulations, issues government mandates to achieve specific ends through specific means. Ends-based regulation, on the other hand, mandates a particular outcome but allows the firm to decide how to achieve it. In an ends-based regulatory approach, the government specifies what must be achieved but grants business actors flexibility in choosing how. The end goal might apply to the economy as a whole, to a given sector, or to a particular firm. For example, with respect to environmental regulation, a particular firm may be tasked with reducing its emissions to a certain output, or an industry could be tasked with achieving a certain emissions target through market mechanisms such as carbon trading. Since 2008, financial firms and the sector have been subject to renewed political debate about regulatory reform.

A large bundle of regulatory reforms circles the world of white papers and policy shops, far too many to review here. In the US, there have been repeated calls to revive regulations in the Banking Act of 1933 (also known as Glass-Steagall) by politicians such as Senator Elizabeth Warren. Excessive bank debt and lack of transparency were key causes of the mortgage crisis. A combination of trillions of dollars in loans from the Federal Reserve, billions in direct investment from TARP, guarantees from the FDIC, and the maintenance of low interest rates has ensured that the debt-driven model of banking has survived.[10] Progressive economists associated with Economics for Inclusive Prosperity have argued that a key means to reverse this debt-based system of banking is to remove safety nets for banks and revise the tax and bankruptcy codes that encourage excessive use of debt funding.[11] Others point to the distinct problem of bank malfeasance. In Australia, a 2019 report by the Royal Commission uncovered widespread misconduct in the sector, which had been somewhat sheltered during the global downturn, including fraud as egregious as charging fees for services never provided. They propose a systematic set of regulations on how banking services are offered to customers.[12]

Post-crisis proposals by policymakers have also focused on macroprudential regulation, which aims to make finance less volatile by addressing and mitigating the spread of compounding booms and busts.[13] In the wake of the 2008 downturn and the unexpected collapse of giants like Lehman Brothers, the policymakers in the G20 prioritized thinking about implementing counter-cyclical policies and enforcement of rules over institutions critically important to the systemic health of the economy. Broad problems identified have been excessive risk-taking by financial institutions and increased concentration of the financial sector into monopolistic banks and asset managers. Very few rules have been added and most have only been layered onto the existing regulatory system, such as the capital requirements for banks that have been slowly reversed. In all, the weak regulatory reforms that have passed seek merely to stabilize the finance-led model of growth, which is itself intrinsically prone to Minskian crises.[14]

Part of the macroprudential approach includes antimonopoly proposals that take on finance capital's banking structure. Like in the UK, the US banking sector is heavily concentrated. The six largest banks in the US control over $10 trillion in assets equal to approximately 54 percent of GDP. They have a total exposure that exceeds 68 percent of GDP. In October of 2018, the tenth anniversary of the bank bailout, Democratic senator Bernie Sanders introduced the "Too Big to Fail, Too Big to Exist Act" to the Senate to break up any financial institution with exposure in excess of 3 percent of GDP ($584.5 billion). There are currently six banks that fit this definition: JP Morgan Chase, Citigroup, Wells Fargo, Goldman Sachs, Bank of America, and Morgan Stanley. Overseen by the Federal Reserve, banks would have two years to restructure to get under the cap. Three months after an institution is given the "too big to fail" designation, it will be prohibited from accessing Federal Reserve discount facilities and from using insurance deposits.

Supplemental Reforms

Supplemental responses to financial predation aim to fill in niches in the market with alternative financial organizations governed by states. These are not merely experiments in alternative finance: a key aim for those that advocate them is to respond to financial plunder by leveraging state power against dominant financial actors and institutions in order to serve those that are marginalized in the dominant mode of finance capitalism. However, supplemental proposals do not directly require or prohibit financial actors and institutions from engaging in certain practices, as is the case with regulatory ones. Instead, they aim to reform their behavior indirectly by redesigning the action environment in which they are situated. Supplemental responses do so via the market, through their direct competition with existing financial institutions with whom they intend to complete with their own financial services and investment. Providing better services and investments would theoretically allow them to crowd out the bad practices and institutions with state-governed ones.

For example, in the US some have advocated a plan for the creation of a Post Bank, a public banking option housed in post offices around the country, for household financial services and deposits.[15] With respect to its logistical capacities, such a public banking system would be housed in the United States Postal Office where there are 5.5 times the number of branches as that of Well Fargo, the largest bank branch network. A Post Bank is similarly under consideration by financial reform activists in the UK.[16] The aim of such an approach is to challenge explicit inequality in the financial system and to achieve financial inclusion.

Under the plans, private lenders that charge exorbitant, predatory fees and rates of interest to the un- and underbanked would lose their market share if a public bank were offering similar services for better rates. According to the logic of supplemental strategies, it is through the mechanism of market competition that private financial actors would be impelled to reform some of the dysfunctional aspects of the financial system. And more and more people would be able to access the benefits of financial services and wealth growth.

A public bank need not be solely aimed at providing financial services for those excluded; it might also play an investment role in the economy. In this respect, state development banks like the Bank of North Dakota (established 1919) or the German Kreditanstalt für Wiederaufbau (KFW, established 1948), direct economic activity. The former does so by financing the agricultural sector, and the latter with loan programs for developing countries. In the UK, the Labour Party proposed the creation of a national investment bank that could take on both inequality and climate change. With a coordinated network of regional development banks under it, Labour's now-defunct plans were to raise and manage a £250 billion fund to increase research and development (R&D) to 3 percent of GDP by 2030 and reallocate 60 percent of energy investments into renewables and zero-carbon sources.[17]

Through policy briefs released from the Roosevelt Institute, the economist Lenore Palladino calls for the establishment of a "public asset manager" to offer an alternative to the finance capitalist asset managers who manage the savings of the demos.[18] A public option would work for pooled funds, especially public pensions, by enabling them to opt out of the existing private system of asset management. Her plan sets up a public asset manager subject to guidelines to direct worker savings into investments that meet socio-ecological criteria in addition to financial ones. Palladino, our most brilliant contemporary critic of the shareholder primacy myth, explores the means to determine what the real value of an investment is and concludes that it best be determined by our political institutions rather than the market forces that allow these assets to be controlled by extractive financial institutions.[19]

Another supplemental proposal is the creation of sovereign wealth funds, which are similarly run by states. Globally, the more than fifty countries that operate sovereign wealth funds control more than $11 trillion in assets. China's sovereign wealth assets are collectively the largest; its five funds control over 30 percent of the global total.[20] Together, Middle Eastern funds control nearly half of total global sovereign wealth assets. Saudi Arabia, Kuwait, and the United Arab Emirates have notably large funds. The single largest fund, however, is Norway's oil fund: it holds an average of 1.3 percent of every publicly listed company in the world and has over $1.6 trillion in assets.[21] Some policy activists call for the establishment of sovereign wealth funds that might issue ownership and potentially voting rights to every citizen and entitle them to the regular distribution of a "universal basic dividend" from the returns on the fund's portfolio.[22] Again, the principal aim is financial inclusion.

Finally, in 2019 an International Monetary Fund (IMF) working paper titled "The Return of the Policy That Shall Not Be Named" heralded the comeback of a once-abandoned approach to development: industrial policy.[23] The pandemic revival, or at least demystification, of state financing of different sectors of capital transformed the political viability of industrial planning in advanced capitalist countries.

In the US, the new supply-side progressivism has resulted in a $369 billion energy-and-climate-policy package to support green energy technology and infrastructure and geopolitically significant sectors, such as microchips, to generate greater comparative advantage for US manufacturing and its exports. Under the Biden administration, the Department of Energy's Loan Program Office lay at the center of the clean energy industrial strategy. There a swaggering bureaucrat, Jigar Shah, was given the authority through the Inflation Reduction Act to arrange $400 billion in loans for clean energy technology.[24] Shah became a heroic figure for those on the left committed to the long march through the institutions. One think tank researcher described him as "the world spirit."[25]

Similarly, the European Green Deal, approved in 2020 by the European Commission under the reign of Ursula von der Leyen, adopts an industrial planning approach to a green transition as well. The new state-led developmentalism has laid to waste the neoliberal myth that governments should, or even can, stay out of markets. For at the moment, this appears to be the new Washington Consensus, with governments around the world falling over each other to come up with their own industrial strategy packages.

It has spurred on incredibly bold new proposals. Law professors Robert Hockett and Saule Omarova have recently argued for the creation of a National Investment Authority, which would act as a "public option" for investment. The National Investment Authority, according to the proposal, would create an ecosystem of investment funds financed by the state in its capacity as sovereign issuer of currency. It would be staffed with experts with in-house ability to identify development goals and the ability to translate those goals into investments. The new Washington Consensus falls far short of proposals such as these. The National Investment Authority promises to take the industrial strategy logic to its fullest potential—a fully empowered state-investment body, in part modeled on the New Deal–era Reconstruction Finance Corporation.[26]

While bold, each of the supplemental proposals explored here contain a crucial limitation. Public banks, a public asset manager, sovereign wealth funds, and a national investment authority to supercharge the new industrial strategy need not, in and of themselves, be pursued in the interest of the demos. Because they are run by states, in each case, their investments will be allocated in ways that reflect their politics and the functioning of those very states. In the case of sovereign wealth funds, some of the world's most successful directly bolster authoritarian regimes with their returns. While it is true that some sovereign funds are more transparent, politically accountable, and concerned about responsible investment standards (Norway's and New Zealand's stand out), like public banks, industrial planning, and the public sector more broadly, they reflect the character of state politics.[27] Finance capitalism itself has degraded and eroded democratic institutions, especially in its centers in the US and UK. Given that the demos is already excluded from governance, without careful reincorporation, we should expect or at least have the strong suspicion that states will govern on behalf of those who already run them.

Control Reforms

A final subset of responses aims to enliven the excluded demos to exert control over finance and flows of investment. Control reforms work either through the mechanism of direct seizure by the demos or government of existing financial institutions or through a more gradual transition of ownership and control. These proposals operate at distinct scales. This section explores five varieties of control reforms debated in the centers of global finance: creating democratic public banks, adopting inclusive ownership funds, democratizing workers' pensions, democratizing central banks, and nationalizing finance.

First, community organizers and democratic socialist elected officials have proposed establishing public banks governed democratically. In the US, most vibrant attention to the issue of public banking has been at the municipal level in the state of California. In 2019, the state passed AB-857, the Public Banking Act, to charter up to ten local public banks. Activists across the state with the California Public Banking Coalition are working to construct them for the demos. For instance, Public Bank LA (PBLA) is working to charter one in Los Angeles. PBLA is a coalition that includes SEIU 721 (the largest public sector union in Southern California), Inclusive Action (a community development financial institution), and ACCE (a multiracial community organization focused on economic and racial justice).

In Los Angeles, the public bank would take and insure city deposits, create liquidity, and fulfill municipal banking needs. Additionally, the bank could be mandated with making targeted loans in the local economy by financing projects such as public infrastructure, renewable energy, affordable housing, and small businesses in historically financially marginalized neighborhoods. Organizers at PBLA, academics, and think tanks such as the Public Banking Institute and the Democracy Collaborative propose that democratic assemblies make the decisions, setting mandates for public banks.[28]

But democratic banks have not been a concern limited to the local in the US. At the federal level, congresswomen Rashida Tlaib and Alexandria Ocasio-Cortez submitted The Public Banking Act of 2023 to the United States Congress, which also includes democratic provisions. The bill provides a framework for establishing public banks and loose guidelines for how they should be governed. For banks with more than $500 million in total assets, it requires that they be governed by a democratic assembly, like the plan for public banking in Los Angeles, composed of people randomly selected from the demos. Such a democratic bank has precedence. The highest decision-making body of Costa Rica's Banco Popular y de Desarrollo Comunal (established 1969) is a 290-person Worker's Assembly, which draws its members from the key social and economic sectors of the country. As the public banking expert Thomas Marois notes, democratization of the Banco Popular forces the institution to "internalise popular demands and operational oversight in legally binding and public interest ways."[29]

Second, at the level of the firm, radical think tanks such as Common Wealth located in UK have proposed the adoption of inclusive ownership funds (IOFs) by private companies employing more than 250 people. These funds would allocate new shares of the firm to the firm's workers, which would afford them greater say in the firm's management though their growing share of the ownership.[30] Claims on firm returns and economic democracy lie at the core of the inclusive ownership fund plan. This is quite distinct from simple ownership of the firm through stock options. This is already somewhat widespread in the US, where there are almost seven thousand employee stock ownership plans (ESOPs) that house more than $2 trillion in assets. With respect to returns, by the fifth year of the plan, British workers would receive about £5 billion a year in dividends from the IOFs. To guard against deepening inequalities in the workforce, dividends received by workers will be capped at £500 per year. The remainder would then be distributed to a public fund to be used for social investing in public goods. In the UK, 10.7 million workers, approximately 40 percent of the private sector workforce, would initially be covered by the plan.[31]

Inclusive ownership funds and pension funds operate at geographic and institutional scales quite distinct from the funds proposed, but only partially realized, by the Swedish labor movement in the 1970s. But they similarly aim to put financial control into the hands of the demos. The Meidner Plan proposed the establishment of wage-earner funds installed by a gradual transfer of ownership of eligible Swedish companies into sector-based funds controlled by the unions. Unlike the inclusive ownership fund, the wage-earner funds would have been financed by a share levy on profits of 20 percent per year rather than a fixed percentage of equity. According to the plan, Swedish companies would issue new company stocks to their employees or pay hefty taxes. In his 1978 book *Employee Investment Funds*, Rudolf Meidner suggested that with an average profit margin of 15 percent a year the funds would have a majority ownership of Swedish firms within twenty-five years.[32] As the founding legislation stated, the funds would give a "greater measure of participation and workers' influence in economic life."[33] The experiment of wage-earner funds in Sweden played out quite differently though. The plan's most ambitious features with respect to transfer of ownership were drastically rolled back because of a counteroffensive from Swedish capital. The funds eventually became financially defunct, brought down by an asset price bubble in Swedish property. Yet, by 1991, the wage-earner funds did become Sweden's eighth largest shareholder group, holding 2.6 percent of total Swedish stock value. While they performed well financially relative to other investors prior to their collapse, the funds ushered in very little in terms of the democratization of firms their original designers intended.[34]

Third, union organizers in both the US and the UK aim to exert democratic voice over the finance workers themselves own but that others control. The largest unions have capital stewardship programs that not only aim to develop and implement responsible investment techniques but also train union activists on how to use their pension funds to exercise shareholder voice in corporate governance. Again, the principal goal is control. There are already large pools of labor's capital in retirement funds that some see as "labor's last best weapon."[35] The AFL-CIO and the SEIU in the US and the UK's largest union, UNISON, have large capital stewardship programs that aim to democratize this worker finance. Controlling workers' capital is hardly a post-crisis idea though. In the US in 1923 the Amalgamated Clothing Workers of America founded its own bank to offer workers affordable credit. And two years later the American Federation of Labor's Samuel Gompers established an insurance company (today called Ullico) to offer financial services to union members.[36] Since then, however, unions have focused most of their attention on pension funds because of their massive size (over $38.4 trillion in assets under management by asset managers). What if these pools of investment were controlled by the workers whose money are in them?

The fourth reform concerns central banks, such as the Federal Reserve and the Bank of England. In the midst of massive plunder through monetary policy, some think tanks such as Positive Money in the UK, propose their democratization. As both activists and researchers argue, to mobilize the central bank authority for public ends requires the elimination of so-called central bank independence by making central banking subject to collective input about the use of seigniorage to fund social investment. It would subject the way monetary policy complements fiscal policy to public debate and democracy.

Central banks might begin by disentangling their monetary policy from the shadow banking sector to embrace more direct policy mechanisms like interest rate control and credit ceilings.[37] And more fundamentally, they might shift away from monetary policy more broadly to support fiscal and industrial policy instead. Support from the lender of last resort might be critical to any financial reform agenda, which is precisely why in 2015 Jeremy Corbyn developed the later-discarded "People's QE" program to use the money-creating power of the Bank of England to finance a public investment bank and social investments. Corbyn noted, "One option would be for the Bank of England to be given a new mandate to upgrade our economy to invest in new large-scale housing, energy, transport, and digital projects: Quantitative easing for people instead of banks."[38] With respect to banks, they currently allocate their most risky activities through wholly or partially owned subsidiaries such as hedge funds and private equity funds. Democratic control of these institutions might contribute toward the elimination of this shadow-banking system.[39]

Finally, some even advocate for the socialization of the investment function entirely, either through wholesale nationalization by way of state recapitalization plans or by transforming banks and asset managers into public utilities. Nationalization sits somewhat awkwardly in my quintet of reform types. On the one hand, it is aimed at state control of existing institutions and is therefore not supplemental. But on the other hand, that control will be subject to the same limitations of all the supplemental proposals. The value of the public (the state) taking over the private is almost entirely dependent on the democratic character of the state, which within capitalism is always partial and disjointed but also open to extensions and deepenings. Suffice it to say, this contradiction is the concern carving through every corner of this book. But as they have been the cornerstone of the democratic socialist experiments in Chile under Allende and France under Mitterrand explored in this book, let's turn to nationalization, keeping this categorical ambiguity in mind.

Briefly very popular in midst of the 2008 downturn, even momentarily supported by Federal Reserve chair Alan Greenspan, this approach has been advanced in the US and UK more recently by radical activist think tanks in the US such as the Democracy Collaborative.[40] Nationalizing banks subjects the governance of financial institutions and the allocation of their credit and services to political mandates. If instead of being broken up, if those banks were subject to public ownership and democratic control, they could do much of what a public investment bank might do but potentially on an even larger scale: fill gaps in the credit market, allocate investment into social projects, finance new green technologies and projects, underwrite government bonds for social purposes, and ultimately shape the direction and form of social development.[41]

There are, of course, detractors both on the right and left to nationalization schemes. In the wake of the 2008 downturn, when the notion of bank nationalization was peaking in popularity, progressive economist Robert Pollin argued that nationalizing banks would lead to problems of "crony capitalism" and corruption in their political management. Pollin argued that there is a significant chance that in the US and the UK, which unlike Japan, France, and Germany lack a rich history with public banking, the daily management involved in public finance would prove too great a bureaucratic burden to governments. Pollin worried that the long-run result would be costly breakdowns in the public banking system that would fall on the shoulders of taxpayers, perversely undermining the longer-term goal of developing a larger public role in the financial system.[42] In short, he argued, while perhaps good in theory we lacked the political and institutional capacity to actually run financial institutions converted to public utilities.

These are serious concerns. Nationalization comes with deep contradictions, pitfalls that can bedevil socialist governments. Not least of these, as we have already shown, is that public ownership does not necessarily translate in practice to meaningful control by the demos. Nowhere is this more evident than in the large pools of finance that workers and their families already own in the US and the UK. Though they came to own nearly 25 percent of all US corporate equities in the 1970s, pension funds were invested by corporate-controlled boards in ways that drove down labor standards, contributed to deindustrialization and the modern wreckage of cities like Detroit and Pittsburgh, financed leveraged buyouts during the merger wave in the 1980s that led to firings and asset stripping, heightened financial risk and global turbulence, and weakened the unions that had fought to win them in the first place. And despite such profit-driven destruction, pension funds have often underperformed relative to the assumed rate of returns calculated by their fiduciaries. Between 1966 and 1976, banks averaged just a 4.4 percent rate of return on pension fund investments, 33 percent less than the rate of return for the S&P 500 index. The development of institutions of worker finance such as pension funds underscores the need to develop forms of governance that aren't simply reliant on the existing institutions of representative democracy in the US and UK. Market forces will no doubt impose constraints on public finance in ways that might subvert its public aims, as Pollin warns. Therefore new mechanisms of democratic control need to be identified and designed to empower the demos against the power of finance capital in both the economy and democratic institutions themselves. These strategic responses to finance's legitimacy crisis are summarized in Table 6.1.

Table 6.1: Varieties of Reform

Mode	Mechanism of influence	Empirical examples
Normative	Self-regulation via work of individuals and organizations to change the moral calculus of financial actors	Corporate social responsibility, ESG investing, UN's Principles for Responsible Investing
Regulatory	State regulation by means/ends-based legal mandates	Glass-Steagall, macroprudential rules, breaking up banks "too big to fail," oversight for malfeasance
Supplemental	Indirect by crowding out bad practices through market competition with state-run institutions	State-run investment banks, public asset manager, public household financial services via a Post Bank, sovereign wealth funds, national investment authority
Control	Direct control by seizure or gradual transfer of decision-making power to publics tied to the demos	Democratic public banks, inclusive ownership funds, pension fund control, wage-earner funds, central bank democracy, bank nationalization

Submerged Class Logics

As a regime of accumulation, finance capitalism is caught in a political feedback loop with no clear exit. On the one hand, realizing profits has required ever stronger means of political plunder, which is part and parcel of the sector's loss of popular legitimacy. On the other hand, while the loss in legitimacy has opened the door to a new fiscal approach to state-led manufacturing in the form of the new industrial policy, it has not resulted in the creation of an alternative political regime with a weakened financial sector. Finance still rules. The arsenal for political plunder that finance has built up overrides opinion shifts within the demos and industrial policy experiments. The politics of financial accumulation appear to be at an impasse.

The projects that have emerged in response to this loss of legitimacy offer four stylized paths to move beyond it. However, the extent to which such an exit is possible is highly varied across the normative, regulatory, supplemental, and control responses. In this section, I consider each with respect to their hidden class logics. I argue that these logics become clear when the responses are set against two fundamental criteria: first, their capacity to reconfigure class power relations in politics—that is, the means of plunder available to finance; second, their capacity to overcome the deeper crisis of underinvestment in the socio-environmentally desirable projects that finance capitalism starves of resources. I argue that these response strategies vary across criteria and hide four distinct class logics: reproductive, restitutive, redistributive, and hegemonic. The findings for each logic are summarized in Table 6.2 below.

While normative projects may in principle alter investor behavior at the margins, they do not bear upon the means of plunder available to the financial institutions that advocate for ESG, nor do they offer a plausible path to counter underinvestment. In fact, they more subtly reinforce finance's hegemony by perpetuating the myth that the sector is responding to our planet's core crises rather than being a principal driver of them. They are the ideological

Table 6.2: Class Projects

Strategies of response	Socio-environmental underinvestment	Means of plunder	Form of class project
Normative	Does not alter investment incentives	Actively reproduces existing relations of capitalist politics	Reproductive
Regulatory	Seeks to restore prior macrofinancial regime	Does not alter existing relations of capitalist politics	Restitutive
Supplemental	Aims to reallocate investment to underdeveloped areas and marginal groups	Indirectly alters existing relations of capitalist politics	Redistributive
Control	Prefigures new mode of accumulation by allocating investment power to subsections of the demos	Downward redistribution of the means of plunder within capitalist politics	Hegemonic

veneer for the Wall Street consensus—the status quo finance capitalism that has been greenwashed.[43] As an information campaign aimed at changing how investors think about investment, for instance, ESG is unconcerned with the domination of the political realm or the investment slump in socio-environmental goods produced by capitalist markets. On ecological downturn, it offers no Green New Deal. Instead, normative strategies reinforce the very causes of ecological devastation, macroeconomic instability, and upward-driven redistribution through political plunder. In this respect, the normative project is largely *reproductive* of finance capitalism and the ills we have already laid out. It is, as senior fellow at Common Wealth Adrienne Buller pointed out, largely the "alchemical pursuit of turning 'green' into gold."[44] ESG should be better understood as a façade for finance's self-preservation.

The regulatory proposals to respond to financial predation, such as the restoration of Glass-Steagall Act, the use of macroprudential rules such as capital requirements and the demand for greater banking oversight for malfeasance and transparency, address meaningful proximate problems in finance capitalism.

But like normative projects, they aim to do so in ways that neither meaningfully redistribute the means of plunder available to finance nor redirect investment. Though they dominate formal political discourse, it is perhaps surprising that in neither the US nor the UK have any of the major proposals resulted in meaningfully robust regulatory transformations. In fact, with exception to stronger enforcement of antitrust rules by Lina Khan in the Federal Trade Commission, there has been regulatory backsliding since the post-2008 responses enshrined in the Dodd-Frank Act in the US.

The allure of regulatory reforms lies in their promise to restore a bygone era of global capitalism. They therefore rest on a peculiar logic that I term *restitutive*.[45] Most of the regulatory responses to the Great Recession and the Corona crash aim at reestablishing the financial system to its former glory. With allusions to the golden age of postwar capitalism, advocates seek restoration of the macrofinancial regimes that were obtained prior to their official end in the 1990s, when the regulatory scaffolding that only governed them in principle was dismantled. But the ambition of reviving the political economy of the past fails to address the underlying condition that led to the disappearance of regulation in the first place: underinvestment into socio-environmental goods, which simply do not generate a high enough return for financiers. This nostalgic pursuit of the past not only fails to address our moment's biggest challenges—the power of finance and the underinvestment in socio-economic goods—it also rests on a romanticization of the past for which the conditions today simply do not exist.

Supplemental responses produce a *redistributive* class logic because they aim to allocate new investments into areas and communities that are resource- and investment-starved and have been historically marginalized. They are governed, in other words, by the aim of distributional justice to right historical wrongs. These injustices have been, in the main, the underinvested goods, services, and sectors such as green infrastructure, retrofitting, and clean energy in communities that are largely excluded from financial services, such as the poorer working-class communities of color excluded from banking services and channeled into usurious relations of extraction at pawn shops and check-cashing outlets. These so-called alternative financial services operate as shadow banking for the poor.[46]

These plans aim to counter profound problems related to uneven economic development and the material grievances that result from it. With respect to power, they may have the longer-run effect of empowering the worst-off communities economically and politically in relative terms. In the short term, however, they do not alter the dominance of finance in our formal democratic institutions because they fail to confront asset manager control over financial flows— that is, finance's asset power—and leave the demos sidelined with respect to decisions over how investments themselves should be allocated. Because of their heavy reliance on the state bureaucratic corps and governmental experts in their proposals, they do not prefigure a new model of accumulation beyond finance capitalism. At their most robust their aim is to create emboldened governmental agencies and bureaucrats that can be power players in the financial system to redress inequalities within finance capitalism. This is clearly desirable as an alternative to our current model, but it rests on too tight a distinction between the private and public spheres. These spheres have become deeply imbricated at the expense of the demos.

Control responses offer a path of a different sort that might serve as a catalyst for the democratic ruptures laid out earlier. They are the radical approach to financial reform in the quartet, directly homing in on the question: Who should have asset power? These alone respond to both deep underinvestment in socioeconomic goods and financial plunder in a way that also prefigures an alternative. With respect to finance's means of plunder taken together, control proposals more directly upend them than do normative, regulatory, or supplemental approaches. If adopted, for instance, democratic public banks, inclusive ownership funds, and democratic pension funds could all afford particular subsections of the demos greater say over how resources should be invested.

If democratic investment as a source of stability and growth were enlarged, and existing and new pools of finance made sufficiently democratic, they could weaken the engagement, prominence, and entanglements of finance capitalism into the formal institutions of the state.[47] If large enough, these pools of democratic finance could work like a war chest for the demos, to be allocated to offset the social costs of disinvestment, capital flight, or a disciplinary international financial order. There are two distinct ways democratic finance might be used in this defensive manner. First, finance could be allocated to areas that are being divested from by reactive finance. Regional capital flight, for instance, might be met with regional public investment and job programs. And second, democratic finance (whether through pension funds, banks, or asset managers themselves) might use their ownership positions as shareholders in companies to exercise voice to shape corporate governance decisions in the interest of the demos. Both, however, would require a very large development of the democratic sector in order to compete with private finance capitalism or even state capitalism, with respect to their own structural prominence. Democratic finance needs to be big.

Financial radicals, whether in groups like the California Public Banking Coalition, Common Wealth, or campus-based antiwar activists who have launched divestment campaigns aimed at their endowments for a ceasefire in Gaza, have all made their target the asset power of finance. The various plans to control finance are constitutive of a larger *hegemonic* project. Only through control might the demos extend and deepen democracy into the economy, in turn creating countervailing powers that run against the asset power of finance that prefigure an alternative model of accumulation dependent on the role of the non-elite in decisions about the allocation of productive investment and credit.[48] They help articulate a new "general economic interest" composed of differentiated publics drawn from the demos—be they workers or residents—making investment decisions in ways that might serve the socio-environmental good over the private good.[49] We are, in many respects, in an interregnum where the crises of financial capitalism have led to a loss of legitimacy and deep political uncertainty about the future of capitalism and democracy.[50] Control responses offer a hegemonic project for the demos to reconfigure state power relations and democratize investment. But this leads to the next question this book takes up. If control is the answer, what form should it take?

7

Minipublics

> If the drawing of lots appears to our "democracies" to be contrary to every serious principle for selecting governors, this is because we have at once forgotten what democracy meant and what type of "nature" it aimed at countering.
>
> Jacques Rancière, *Hatred of Democracy*

Our Gordion Knot

The restorative, restitutive, and redistributive class logics embedded, respectively, in the normative, regulatory, and supplemental reform proposals on offer come with profound limitations and are unable to meaningfully challenge the core dilemmas of finance capitalism. If control is preferred because it offers a hegemonic path, this chapter asks, what *kind* of control? The answer is deceptively simple: democratic.

But there are few concepts more contested than democracy. And as was demonstrated in Chapter 5, democracy is not only contested but is beset by conceptual confusions and rhetorical misdirection when it is applied to the so-called economic sphere. This chapter will explore how democracy, understood traditionally as collective say over public policy, might be applied to finance. It aims to discover a means of coordinating democratic activity to control finance that is more desirable than the alternatives. It answers a question for the proposal of democratic rupture of finance: If people should have a greater say over investment how should decision-making power itself be organized?

Democracy isn't simply about participation in financial markets, but more robustly concerns decision-making power about and deliberation over how credit and investment is allocated. This chapter considers some mechanisms for coordinating people into deliberation over financial flows moving from the representative modes of parliamentary and congressional deliberation of the present and ending with a promising peculiar ancient Athenian technology of the distant past, the *kleroterion*. I will argue that one of the most auspicious modes of coordinating participation into democratic finance, what I term minipublics, would draw on this ancient technology, the lot, to make possible democratic governance of finance.

Many would agree that a democratic society is one in which its people share an equal access to the means of participation in governance and to decision-making about which values and goals are prioritized over others. Its etymological meaning, after all, is "rule by the people." Yet this capacity to "rule" has a dual character rooted in a common principle, the power of people to have a say over the things that affect their own lives. On the one hand, democracy includes the freedom of individuals to make choices that affect their lives on their own, independently, and without constraint of legal restrictions or community approval. But on the other hand, it also includes fairness in access to participating meaningfully in political decisions that affect both ourselves and our larger communities. This means that people not only have formal political equality to participate as stipulated by the law and constitution. More fundamentally, for democracy to work, people need to be empowered to meaningfully participate and have their participation actually bear on public choices. Democracy, therefore, is neither anti-social atomism nor anti-individual collectivism but a careful and necessarily contested dialectical dance between the two.

This leads to a central conundrum for all democracies (and many of the political theorists puzzling through this form of government): How are we to draw the line between decisions left to the "private" sphere (i.e., individual freedoms) and those made by the "public" (i.e., subject to policy)? This has been a core fault line of disagreement in the history of global political justice that extends up to the present. If the planet remains inhabitable, this boundary problem will likely persist for generations to come due to its intrinsic ambiguity. It is therefore the central puzzle of democracy, its Gordian knot. And it traverses the politics of science, religion, economy, the human body, and even our personality and sense of self. What is governed together and what is governed alone?

Advocates for the decentralization of finance largely err on the side of "private" decision-making, but for both moral and instrumental reasons we should be suspicious of this tendency. Is it democratically desirable that flows of credit and investment be in the main left to private financial institutions and investors? We might solve this boundary problem with a simple intuition: decisions that meaningfully effect our collective fate and shared interests should be subject to democratic decision-making processes. Those that don't should be left to individuals and communities to decide without engaging formal political procedures that ensure fairness and equal empowerment. If we are meaningfully affected by a decision, we should have meaningful say over it.[1]

Even with the intuition, we can still quibble about what goes into one bucket or the other, and large tomes have been dedicated to carefully delineating the normative foundations of what should be subject to democratic deliberation and what should be left up to individuals. But few things impact our collective fate more than the direction that credit and investment flow. This much should be plainly obvious to anyone, even without logic proofs. Where we invest directly determines our social and natural reality, our capacity to live free from acute want; allocation gives life to the conflicts that persist on a global scale and across the neighborhoods of a city and explains why some children are hungry and others well fed. It is undeniably the most important factor constraining and governing our individual, community, and collective life goals, and yet it is left entirely to private actors who happen to control large amounts of investable assets, on occasion without even owning them. And whether you have the capacity to determine those investment flows or not depends almost entirely on your location in the capitalist class structure. By virtue of their location in that structure, the demos simply does not have decision-making power.

This suggests, as political theorist Carole Pateman has written in *Participation and Democratic Theory*, that a democratic society "requires that the scope of the term 'political' is extended to cover spheres outside national government." This wider definition forces us, in Pateman's view, to recognize "industry as a political system in its own right."[2] Writing in the late 1960s, at the dawn of deindustrialization in rich capitalist democracies, Pateman concerned herself principally with the workplace traditionally conceived. Yet she acknowledged that the call for democracy and participation "can be applied to other spheres."[3] We might add to Pateman that, in the era of finance capitalism, democracy be applied to financial institutions themselves.

Herein lies the crucial problem of finance capitalism that a more robust democratic system would need to address. A large bulk of decisions about the allocation of credit and investment are made by private financial institutions or investors seeking to maximize their own individual or corporate gain. They are not subject to collective decision-making and public participation. Advocates for DeFi and Web3 leave this basic feature of finance capitalism undisturbed. Their core ambition is to increase the scope of people who might make those decisions privately. But even if more people are drawn into the electronic herd, they would be doing so as individual investors not as participants in a process of shared decision-making. And as individuals, they would be incentivized to allocate their own capital in ways that prioritize returns not the production and maintenance of public goods. This would either reproduce or worsen the status quo in which public goods are already battered and beleaguered.

Democracy

Democratizing finance aims to make credit allocation and financial markets accountable to a deliberative demos. To realize this rhetoric in practice, any project for democratizing finance would need to be specifically attentive to the kinds of democratic institutions that might be installed to activate and reproduce popular engagement and the influence of the ordinary. If not via escape, as we showed with Web3 experiments in DAO governance, how might publics participate?

First, I discuss what we might mean by democracy itself, moving from the weak Schumpeterian view to the strong Pateman view. Then I discuss three distinct modes for coordinating public participation that might be pursued in a democratizing finance agenda: representative, direct, and minipublics. These modes of engagement vary on two dimensions: the degree to which participation is voluntary or mandatory and the degree to which preferences are expressed through representatives or active deliberation.[4] One emerges from the discussion more promising than the rest. As to which, you can probably guess from the title of this chapter: minipublics.

Schumpeter's *Capitalism, Socialism and Democracy* has been influential in establishing the basic minimal definition of democracy. There it is defined as a "political *method,* that is to say a certain type of institutional arrangement for arriving at political— legislative and administrative—decisions."[5] In the Schumpeterian view, democracy is simply a means for selecting political leadership through competitive elections where potential leaders (typically selected from among the elite) struggle against one another in an effort to secure votes from the electorate.[6] Implicitly, it is this working version of democracy embedded in most of the Web3 experiments as well as the formal institutions of capitalist democracy they seek to escape. But this understanding is profoundly limited and largely produces oligarchic results in practice. It is perhaps a bit ironic that advocates for cryptopian futures simply reproduce it.

Schumpeter's criteria, crucially, does not require participation or deliberation. Not only does the Schumpeterian view make the American form of democracy the democratic ideal, but it also comes strikingly close to the conclusions reached in antidemocratic arguments. Returning to the words of Pateman,

> No longer is democratic theory centered on the participation of 'the people', on the participation of the ordinary man, or the prime virtue of a democratic political system seen as the development of politically relevant and necessary qualities in the ordinary individual; in the contemporary theory of democracy it is the participation of the minority elite that is crucial and the non-participation of the apathetic, ordinary man lacking in the feeling of political efficacy, that is regarded as the main bulwark against instability.[7]

But if participation and deliberation are the crucial elements of democratic governance, what kind and how much? A stronger view suggests that democratic participation should both be extended beyond formal political institutions and deepened within them. The political theorist Archon Fung has shown that forms of direct participation vary along three distinct dimensions: who participates, how participants communicate and make decisions, and the authority and power that those participants have over the policy outcome itself. Along each dimension we find wide variation for the design of democratic institutions. Is participation open and voluntary or restricted to a small ruling elite? Do participants passively receive messages from officials or do they actively deliberate? Are the decisions that are made by participants taken under advisement or are they binding, as participants directly govern? Fung's exploration of the varieties of participation along each of the three dimensions produces a useful analytic tool—a *democracy cube*—that maps stronger and weaker versions of democracy along multiple dimensions.[8]

How might representative, direct, and minipublic modes of democracy hold up with respect to the degree of effective participation of the demos in decisions concerning financial allocation? In particular, how do each of these vary with respect to who participates, how decisions are made, and how much authority the public has in setting policy? Following Pateman's critique of Schumpeter, I will argue that representative mechanisms offer the democratically weakest mode of popular governance for finance and deliberative minipublics the strongest. Direct democracy, it will be shown, fails for reasons of feasibility. Though its ideals are lofty, direct democracy is simply not possible on anything beyond a very small scale.

Representative

The most common means of exerting democratic control over existing pools of finance or newly created ones is through governing boards made up of experts that are either elected or appointed by elected representatives. This Schumpeterian solution has become the axiomatically obvious one for most people on the progressive end of the political spectrum. When we refer to democracy, surely, we must mean voting for politicians to represent us—so the default thinking goes. And because the current mode of participation in public decision-making is voting for representatives who act on behalf of the demos, why not simply extend it to finance? The reality, however, is that representative elections are not democratic at all and in and of themselves require democratic deepening and reform to be worthy of the name.

Two major limitations, which are only made more difficult to navigate in the digital age, have emerged with representative democracy, and both weaken the quality of participation via voting and the power of voters themselves in setting policy: motivated reasoning and principal-agent problems. As far as democracy goes, voting is one of the weakest tools available to the demos. We would be better off with another way to participate in collective governance.

First, we now have a large amount of experimental evidence in social psychology demonstrating that a person's prior political or social views heavily shape and condition their reaction to new political information especially if it is provided or signaled by partisan pundits or politicians. Whether it be views associated with their own identity, group status, or party affiliation, atomized members of the demos are often motivated to reason in ways that confirm their preexisting biases. This is what social psychologists term "motivated reasoning."[9] This problem has worsened as partisan divisions have deepened and party signaling such as the use of racial dog whistles on campaigns and in governing are more common.[10] The result is a democratic nightmare. Large sections of the electorate, both left and right, simply ignore facts or consider them in a highly selective way and in turn process information in ways that reinforce biases; they do not use that information to facilitate the discovery of more accurate views. Highly atomized voting without deliberation, which appears in many instances to be the default, has impoverished the basic inputs of representative democracy. But even worse than these inputs are its outputs.

Second, even if motivated reasoning were overcome and voters were rational and open to new information and views—which, as long as they are socially atomized or organized into reactive solidaristic groups by elites, they are not—there remains the more fundamental principal-agent problems between the electorate and the elected that would nonetheless persist.[11] Principal-agent problems are typically considered problems specific to economic contexts where an owner of an asset is different from the one that manages that asset. The problem arises when there is a conflict of interest between the owner of the asset, the principal, and the one delegated to manage it, the agent, over their priorities for the asset. Yet principal-agent problems are a critical matter for popular ownership of financial institutions because ownership need not mean control. Sometimes control decisions can run counter to the interests and desires of the principals who own the asset, as longstanding debates in the study of corporate management illustrate quite well.

Consider, simply, the governance of a publicly traded firm, which has direct implications for the governance design of public finance. In *The Unseen Revolution*, the mid-century management guru Peter Drucker argued that, "if 'Socialism' is defined as 'ownership of the means of production by the workers'—and this is both the orthodox and only rigorous definition—then the United States is the first truly 'Socialist' country."[12] Drucker came to this bold conclusion because of the widespread dispersal of stock holding in the US by the mid-1970s. American workers came to own a significant share of American capital through their pension funds. They became, in some significant sense, owners of American capitalism. By the time Drucker was writing, nearly 25 percent of all US corporate equities was held in the pension funds of American workers.

But managerial studies of corporate governance going back to the 1930s cast serious doubt on Drucker's view. Simply put, *ownership does not equal control.*[13] Not only do a firm's shareholders rarely have a say in the daily control of a firm, but the managers (or those with daily operational control of firms) are also not accountable to them. That's the classic principal-agent problem and one of the main rhetorical justifications for the rise of the principle of shareholder value. As a result of this, managers have directed corporate strategies in ways that run contrary to what the owners prefer.

Electoral democracy works in a similar way. The elected (the agents) often act in ways counter to the interests of the electorate (the principals). In fact, in countries such as the US and the UK, they do so systematically, as if it were a design feature of our democratic institutions. There are several reasons why the separation of ownership and control is important for public finance projects governed by elected representatives. Most proximately are the informational disadvantages that the demos confronts when it comes to developing the opinions that will inform its votes. The demos faces significant barriers, related to time, capacity, and the urgency of their own concerns, to collecting relevant information on the issues, especially ones as inaccessible to nonexperts as policy concerning investment and credit allocation. And they are meant to do this entirely on their own without support and guidance about how to find and consider information.

Once politicians are then elected, there is also no clear way for the public, news junkies excepted, to monitor what the government does, especially regarding its administration of programs and its development of policies that are off the radar of the popular press and out of the public eye. Even in the ideal representative democracy, if an elected official or party fails in its tasks, they don't get voted out until the next election cycle. So in addition to the informational issue, there is a temporal one with respect to the ways that information can actually be used to shape policy. Given these information asymmetries, the demos will likely face deep disadvantages in their ability to adequately assess the performance of policymakers in their management of public finance. A simple "public" solution like nationalization doesn't circumvent this problem at all.

Additionally, research in comparative politics demonstrates that the practice of representative democracy is far less democratic than the theory; much happens without the knowledge or input of the demos. It is in these areas of "quiet politics" that elite and business-group influence governs freely.[14] Therefore, even in the ideal of a well-functioning representative democracy where people understand the issues and vote with their perfectly formulated and real preferences front of mind, if deliberation and decision-making is left to state managers who act as trustees of the public interest, the financial interests that we laid out in Chapter 4 will likely hold greater sway in the policy arenas subject to less popular scrutiny between elections.

The result is the deep weakness of existing institutions of representative democracy with respect to their own democratic accountability and functioning. Here is the revelatory reality: these are not democratic institutions at all but aristocratic ones. America's founders were explicit in this design when they set up the republic to be governed by elites rather than ruled by the people. Who is chosen after all? Those who have the most money to campaign and are the most charismatic. Though problems of disproportionate elite interest cut across the capitalist world, American democracy is particularly insulated from the preferences of average voters. Even in cases where the demos does have a strong preference in a policy area and therefore the lack of information is not a concern as it was above, research suggests that these preferences have at best a weak relationship to actual policy outcomes.[15]

Here is the kicker though. Even if the voting demos did have considerable sway and we lived in a fantasy land in which Citizens United had never passed and in which politics were drained of money and power, the election of representatives would *still* fall short of democracy. As political scientist Bernard Manin writes, the mechanism of election is, "an aristocratic or oligarchic procedure in that it reserves public office for eminent individuals whom their fellow citizens deem superior to others."[16] Again, democracy is not merely about the formal right to participate, as embodied in the vote, but about the empowerment of the demos in ways that meaningfully enable them to have a say in the decisions that bear on their own lives. Representative democracy does not produce this capacity; instead, by virtue of its aristocratic procedure, it produces an oligarchy—rule by the few (with money).

Together, these problems should cast overwhelming doubt on any public reform proposal that doesn't specifically include mechanisms that empower the disenfranchised majority. Therefore, the degree to which a government-run public finance project is democratized should, in significant ways, reflect the democratization of the state itself. Representative democracy is too democratically weak to be our North Star; we should be fleeing it, not moving toward it. Though its design appears to provide significant public input via the vote, the outcome it reproduces consistently and everywhere, when it is left unchecked by strong countervailing working-class organizations rooted in civil society such as unions or labor parties, is rule by the elite.

Direct

Elections don't work. So what else is in our democratic arsenal? Another mechanism of coordinating popular participation removes the formal representative entirely and subjects issues of public policy to popular deliberation in public fora open to all (or as many as can fit). Here, the demos directly determines policy outcomes. We can term this method direct democracy.

The most famous example of the direct approach to democracy are the participatory budget experiments, modelled in Porto Alegre, Brazil, but installed in dozens of countries around the world.[17] Though there is variation in the form these experiments take, participatory budgeting happens when the residents in a community are brought together, often into a district-level assembly, to negotiate, deliberate, and make direct decisions about the allocation of public money. In Porto Alegre, the experiment has been useful in diverting public money from patronage payoffs to useful public services and projects, such as fixing potholes on roads. Participatory budgeting experiments were installed after a left coalition lead by the Workers' Party won municipal government in 1988 to combat the siphoning off of social expenditures to party machine corruption. Their Orçamento Participativo reform created a Regional General Assembly within each region of the city that met twice a year to settle the budget.[18]

Their model of coordinating participation through direct and open access to anyone has been replicated in other contexts, noticeably for this book in the Zuccotti Park encampment of Occupy Wall Street, where direct democracy operated on a loose principle of consensus, expressed by the participants in an assembly by the twinkling and snapping of fingers. Is this coordination principle best suited for determining mandates for investment and credit flows for pools of public finance as it was used for the surplus of the Porto Alegre budget?

This mode of participation is ill suited to the task of democratizing finance in four crucial ways. First, a core limitation of direct democracy is the built-in self-selection bias with respect to the way it coordinates participants. The people who show up do so because they want to be there and have the time to come. Though it appears to be the deepest open-public-square form of democracy, in practice it reproduces a core problem in Schumpeter's weak version found with the simple vote: participation is not necessary. A simple smell test for any institution that goes by the name democratic is: Can it continue to function normally with less and less involvement from the demos? If most of the demos is able to opt out and yet it continues on normally, it hasn't passed the test. This is a major problem for direct democracy, which even in robust forms opens a clear path to aristocratic backsliding. In some cases of direct democracy, participants are disproportionately drawn from older and wealthier communities, who have both the time and resources to spend doing democracy. In others, the democracies have been captured by small sub-groups with a deep interest in their outcomes.[19]

Second, even if direct democracy were able to overcome participant self-selection problems, it might still be fail because of democracy fatigue. Few people have the stomach for sustained participation in political meetings. Because the cost of participation, at minimum, is time, those that show up are likely to do so out of a strong sense of civic engagement or strong individual-level or community-level interest in a given issue, which is unlikely to be widely distributed across the entire pool of possible participants (i.e., the demos). In representative democracies many people do not vote, but in direct democracies many more won't come to meetings because of the even higher participation cost that is entailed. And many of those eager ones who do initially participate will experience burnout eventually.

Third, direct democracy is impossible at larger scales. Though active deliberation and participation are crucial for democracy, they are not feasible beyond small groups of people. This is why today it is principally the elite who deliberate. A deliberative process of thousands or even millions would be logistically nightmarish, too time-consuming, and cognitively impossible for people to manage. Even the most sophisticated technology available for ratcheting up deliberation between groups to larger numbers falls far short of complete direct democracy at scale. At Stanford, James Fishkin has developed a "deliberative polling" technology that gathers 500 people for multiple day deliberations, but even here, they are broken down into smaller deliberative subgroups of about fifteen people. And MIT's Mark Klein's technology, the Deliberatorium, uses a digital platform for deliberation but can only expand the number of participants to a few hundred. The direct participation promise is simply one that cannot be kept at scale in an all-inclusive way. To the extent that our best and brightest have solved this problem, they have done so through deliberation with smaller units of participants from the demos.[20]

Finally, deliberation presumes a reflexive and adaptive political agent with unfixed preferences who seeks the common good. The deliberative process itself is one in which it is assumed that the confrontation of various points of views changes and sharpens one's own preferences.[21] And this will help to generate an outcome, especially in quasi-consensus contexts, in which the "right" view will win out through that deliberative exchange. A rationalist ethos underscores much of the discourse within deliberative politics and theory in general, which depoliticizes key questions and renders meaningful social cleavages invisible. It also offers a political agenda that is politically decentered from the political organizations that tend to be the conduits of collective interests, such as parties, unions, and social movement organizations and other associations and clubs. Here, there are only the participants and the experts that provide them information to act upon.[22] Democracy should, however, draw out the underlying economic and social cleavages that so much of electoral democracy renders invisible through elite rule. It should be, as the political theorist Chantal Mouffe suggests, agonistic. There is no structured way for direct democracy to solve this problem. Minipublics, as discussed below, will solve for the limitations of fatigue and of marginalizing the already underrepresented that inhere in direct democracies, but alone they will not necessarily produce agonism. In the next chapter, however, I will address this directly.

Minipublics

Another possibility, and the one that this book advocates for, is the management of financial flows though people's assemblies that are filled by lot. This is possible at various geographic scales through representative bodies chosen at random or through stratified random selection from the relevant affected constituency to ensure demographic and other forms of diversity or an over-representation of certain groups, as I will argue for in the next chapter. The groups that deliberate are intentionally small but also representative of the relevant demos. And therefore, we might term them "minipublics."

The random selection process is referred to by different names, such as sortition or lottocracy. Once this lottocratic means of coordinating participation has gathered participants together, they are given information and questions to answer or mandates to create and then enter into a process of deliberative decision making. For set terms, akin to the citizen juries common to every town across the US and UK, these bodies might serve as trustees for the demos with respect to the investment-mandate agenda setting and operational management of public finance. There is a better technology than the election booth, the public square, or the blockchain that we might turn to when considering how to coordinate democratic participation through random selection, an ancient one—the *kleroterion*, which was once used in classical Athens to govern through small groups chosen by lottery. While it dates back to an old society, random selection from the demos has been used in different democratic experiments ever since, nearly always as a direct result of class struggle on the part of the demos against oligarchic rule.

Kings and tyrants ruled in the early days of the ancient Greek city-state (polis). The fifth century was the age of democratization. Large numbers of Greeks owned little property and no slaves; they were the commoners, the non-elite. Collectively, these people were referred to as the demos. In its original use referring to the non-elite, demos was born as a class category.

Democracy itself was a form of agonistic class rule meant to undermine the power of the elite. It emerged through a mass action, the Athenian revolution of 508–7 BCE, which turned aristocratic class rule upside down. Democratization was sparked by a large-scale three-day-long class riot against the aristocratic *boule*, the agenda-setting Council of Five Hundred that ran the city and excluded the poor and working classes. King Cleomenes I and his Spartan troops had occupied the center of Athenian power, the Acropolis, but during the uprising, the dispossessed and disenfranchised working classes laid siege to the Acropolis, forcing Cleomenes and his men out. The uprising of the demos not only forced Sparta out of Athens, it also undermined oligarchic rule within it and led to the statesman Cleisthenes devising a new constitutional order that gave permanent voice to the demos.[23] These reforms gave the common people a place in the sovereign assembly, the *ecclesia*.

In 462–1 BCE rule by the working classes, democracy, extended further. Under Pericles the voice of the non-elite was extended into the *dikasteria*, the jury court system. The boule itself, the Council of Five Hundred, that ran the daily affairs of the city was also democratized. In the period that follows, we find that much of the selection for governance in both the assembly and the courts is done through lot. There also emerged the practice of paying citizens for their political work, which enabled even the poorest to play their own part in civic life and the juries. These reforms greatly expanded political participation, and historians of the ancient world refer to this period of government as the *radical democracy*.[24] With the exception of military leaders, who were elected, under the radical democracy, lot became the most common way to select public officials.

Little from this ancient arrangement still exists today in places like the US, although an exception is the jury system. But class rule in Athens—that is, a jury of one's peers—was extended well beyond criminal justice. As Aristotle notes in *The Athenian Constitution*, the creation of deliberative and administrative bodies for governing reached every nook of life, from the market magistrates to the temple repairers and festival planners and to the administrators responsible for ensuring that "the girls that play the pipes, the harp and the lyre are not hired for more than two drachmae" when market demand began to outstrip the supply of sufficiently talented harpists.[25]

Citizens, the free common men of the polis (women and slaves were excluded), added their own names to lists, and these lists were then used to draw names randomly. And while there was self-selection in the pools of those who might be chosen, the cultural norms for participation in Athens were so strong that few slacked on their civic duty. The contemporary English word "idiot" can trace its etymological roots to the ancient Greek word "ἰδιώτης," or *idiotes*, an ancient epithet reserved for a person who refused public office.

At first random selection was achieved by drawing beans from an urn. But the Athenians eventually designed the kleroterion, a Rube Goldberg–like contraption intended to perfect the allotment of citizens into governing bodies by removing, as much as possible, the ability of the selector to use any discretion.[26] The selection processes became a complicated democratic orchestration. Consider Aristotle's description of the jury system:

> There are ten entrances to the jury-courts, one for each tribe; twenty allotment-machines, two for each tribe; a hundred boxes, ten for each tribe; further boxes, in which the tickets of the men picked as jurors are placed; and two water-pots. Staves are placed by each entrance, as many in number as there are to be jurors; accords are placed in the water-pot, the same number as the staves; and on the accords are inscribed letters (beginning with the eleventh, *lambda*), as many in number as there are courts to be manned.[27]

Radical democracy proved surprisingly durable to internal threats in Athens. The demos defended it against major efforts to reestablish oligarchy. During the Peloponnesian War with Sparta, Athens briefly fell into oligarchic rule. The oligarchy of the Four

Hundred, installed in 411 by the wealthiest Athenians, lasted or only four months. In 404, the oligarchy of the Thirty was installed by the Spartan commander Lysander. The oligarchs reestablished elite rule in the boule and created a whip-bearing police force of 300 to do their bidding. To suppress the demos, they ruled through violence. As Aristotle notes, "Within a short space of time they had killed no fewer than fifteen hundred."[28] They exiled people and disarmed them. But the working classes again protected democracy. The demos from Phyle mounted the Athenian resistance of 403 and eventually re-democratized Athens via the lot. Radical democracy in Athens survived until 322 BCE, when it was crushed by the Macedonians after the Lamian War and transformed back into an oligarchy.

One skeptical view of the lot suggests that minipublics are only workable under conditions of profound human oppression and exploitation, as obtained in the ancient city-states of Greece. In Athens, no urban economy sustained the cities; instead wealth was overwhelmingly drawn from the countryside where slaves helped to cultivate and harvest goods like grain, oil, and wine. These slaves were the polis's key economic resource and pervaded every aspect of Athenian society. And they were incredibly numerous. In the fourth century BCE, the ratio of slaves to free citizens was three to two (it was even higher in Sparta).[29] And non-slave Athenian women had no political rights or public voice; never allowed to govern, they were governed by men via the kleroterion. Did minipublics work in Athens because it was a society where only a few had the leisure to do politics? The answer here should be clearly not, as under the radical democracy pay for service enabled large numbers of the lower and working classes to participate. Some might also conclude that it is a mode of coordinating political participation that is simply unadaptable to complex and liberal contemporary democracies.

But there are many historic illustrations of effective lottocratic governance in more complex societies. Participation in governance in the ancient Roman Republic depended on property ownership; it was a timocracy. But lot retained a significant role in determining tribal voting in the *Comitia Tributa*, the tribal assemblies.[30] Lot played an even larger agonistic role in the Italian commercial communes that emerged in the eleventh and twelfth centuries. In the late fourteenth century, radical democracies, of the sort that developed in Athens, similarly resulted from working-class struggle.

In 1378, textile workers in Florence overthrew the governing elites in a revolution known as the Ciompi Revolt. At the time Florentine politics were based on a guild system. Constitutional changes in 1293 had made guild membership a condition for political rights. But the majority of the working classes and poor were excluded from these guilds and therefore had no decision-making power. The outbreak of the bubonic plague in 1348 killed approximately half of the city's inhabitants. A few decades later a severe financial crisis hit. As a result, wool workers, who were among the poorest paid in the city, were thrown into crisis and deepening poverty. With the aristocracy internally divided, they rose up alongside other craftsmen who were excluded from the city guilds and corporations, seized the Signoria, the government, and hung the public executioner by his feet at the Palazzo Vecchio. Workers overthrew the government and installed a radical one of their own, demanding the right to a guild and to say over production.[31]

The Ciompi Revolt was short lived, crushed within two months in a massacre that left many dead. But it helped install a radical democracy that lasted until 1382. The Ciompi Revolt established new guilds and weakened the power of the aristocracy. It resulted in the extension of guild membership and therefore political rights to approximately 10,000 people in the poor and working classes, the *popolo minuto*. These members were in turn granted access to magistracies and to the *Signoria* through the lot.[32] A lot of the demos lasted until 1382, when the old elite was able to abolish the guild system as a source of dangerous working-class rebellion and, using the rhetoric of unity an consensus, to reestablish an oligarchy.[33]

In another wealthy commercial Italian commune, the republic of Venice, an aristocratic form of sortition was also used. Venice was run by a series of governing bodies that used a combination of random selection and secret ballot to choose governing participants. Though their evolving constitutional pyramid structure changed, the General Assembly; a Great Council; The Forty and the Senate; the Ducal Council, and a head of state, the Doge of Venice, were all at least partially filled by random selection. The lottocratic system brought aristocratic stability; the Venetian republic practiced one version or another of lot until its 1797 fall. As medieval historian Frederic Lane writes in his definitive history:

> Drawing lots prevented a few men, those best known on account of achievements or family, from being the only ones to obtain the honor and power that went with office-holding. It also prevented election campaigns which would intensify rivalries, hatreds, and the organization of fractions.[34]

Perhaps the Dogecoin should be replaced with a randomly selected Doge of Finance.

Minipublics used to govern public finance offer several advantages over both representative and direct modes of participation. Some even argue for sortition to completely replace elections in democracies.[35] Others prefer more bicameral systems, where lottocratic selection supplements elected bodies.[36] I will leave these debates to the side, instead focusing on sortition into minipublics at a more general level. There are several reasons to find minipublics promising. They offer both procedural advantages in decision-making processes and broader political advantages for concerns about democratic power and equality. Though these are profoundly intertwined issues, I separate them here for ease of presentation.

Knowledge Discovery

Sortition brings with it surprising power in validating good or bad conclusions in deliberative processes. It is, in other words, epistemically useful. First, democracy in complex capitalist societies requires divisions of cognitive labor. Any individual at any given time simply cannot know what is best regarding all decisions across all areas of governance. Representative governments of elected professional leaders are one attempt to solve this, albeit through a mechanism that favors aristocratic and elite selection. A politician is elected to govern on behalf of others and then takes up the task of governing. Their constituents largely go about their lives. But representative democracy has failed to generate informed democratic decision-making because of confirmation bias in voting and the principle-agent problem we pointed to above. Lot solves this coordination problem by assembling ordinary people together. Provided with clear evidence, they then learn about an issue or set of options and deliberate on the key questions posed to them in order to produce collective judgments. Their smaller size allows for deliberation but also the development of adequate knowledge on a given topic to deliberate meaningfully and govern.[37]

Second, deliberation with randomly selected people reduces top-of-mind bias in judgement and decision making. Capitalist democracies are beset by elite-driven, popular divisions that result in a hyper-sensationalized political culture. Finance capitalism's deepening economic polarization and loss of legitimacy following the Great Recession has led to a contradictory political conscience in popular politics. Though the legitimacy crisis has opened up the political space, popularly known as "the Overton window," for political innovations and even democratic socialist politics, the crisis has also entrenched the demos in political camps that are dependent on party cues, which worsen bias in political judgement.[38] Yet even without such party cues, in our atomized political culture where all but the elite lack organizational ties to sources of political education, such as movements or unions, which contribute to preference formation, top-of-mind bias and directional motivation in politics remains endemic. Simply put, voters actively ignore facts and double down on preexisting positions.

The deliberative process in a minipublic has two effects that run counter to the directional reasoning endemic in capitalist democracy. On the one hand, the individual participants themselves often come to new understandings of issues and therefore new political perspectives through processes of discussion and deliberation. The act of engaging with factual evidence to openly discuss issues results in a change of perspective. Therefore, and this is key, political preferences are not simply top-of-mind impulses but in some cases, especially those obfuscated by technicality or cultural polarization, must be discovered. People don't always already have concrete policy positions worked out in their heads, which they then simply express when asked or, even worse, vote for. Deliberation is therefore the means of discovering what one thinks about an issue.

On the other hand, and as fundamentally, social scientific evidence suggests that this mode of judgement creation holds more weight with the broader public when conveyed to them than does messaging from experts, interest-group organizations, or political organizations.[39] When the broader public is presented with the findings and recommendations of minipublics, they tend to view them with less skepticism than they would if the information were coming from a politician. When ordinary people know decisions are made by other ordinary, randomly chosen people, they see it as having greater democratic legitimacy. Therefore, deliberative minipublics can be a better source of improved knowledge for the demos as a whole than typical party signaling or interest group messaging. We want democratic institutions that both deserve and earn people's trust; minipublics offer us up that possibility. They offer a means to create a politics that has legitimacy.

Finally, there is an additional important epistemic reason for prioritizing deliberative minipublics in decision-making for financial flows: they generate better political judgements. The notion of collective intelligence, which is an emergent property of a group, is particularly illustrative in minipublics. Cognitive research suggests that group intelligence is not merely reducible to the individual intelligence of people within a group but also a function of the group's composition. Groups of people with different ways of seeing the world and different personal experiences are collectively able to make better decisions. Differences in perspective, interpretation, heuristics and predictive models, when combined, can lead to higher-quality problem solving than decisions made by people who are cognitively similar, even if the latter group is composed of people who are individually more intelligent.[40] This is precisely what underlies the intersectional feminist Audre Lorde's vigorous defense of difference, as "a fund of necessary polarities between which our creativity can spark like a dialectic."[41]

What a democratic revelation! As political theorist Hélène Landemore writes, "all things being otherwise, deliberation among more-inclusive groups is likely to produce better results than deliberation among less-inclusive groups, even if those less-inclusive groups include smarter people. In other words, it is epistemically better to have a larger group of average but cognitively diverse people than a smaller group of very smart but homogenously thinking individuals."[42] Thus minipublics offer a more efficient way to make deliberative decisions than rule by a socially similar elite—that is, a representative democracy—does.

Against Oligarchy

As I indicated above, neither elections nor direct assemblies give the members of the demos from different class and other demographic backgrounds equal chance to participate meaningfully in governing. The most potent political feature of minipublics is that by their very design, they can produce political equality or fairness. These are potentially two different outcomes, but each is conceptually possible depending on how one chooses to design the selection process. Sortition-based procedures for participant selection in governance can be designed in such a way that they explicitly mirror the demos (equality) or oversample certain groups that are deemed historically disenfranchised, by, for instance, class (fairness). We will discuss this selection process in greater detail in the next chapter, but unlike elections and direct procedures for selection, sortition at least provides the possibility for political equality and fairness.[43] This is why Aristotle writes in *The Politics* that "it is thought to be just that among equals everyone be ruled as well as rule, and therefore that all should have their turn."[44]

With democratic inputs such as these, we might expect more democratic outputs with respect to the policy concerning allocation of credit and investment. As suggested above, representative mechanisms for selecting governing bodies in politics not only produce oligarchic results, but they were also explicitly designed to produce those results. Because of problems of self-selection in direct democracy, it is unclear how such unequal outcomes in policy creation can be overcome. And even if they could, because direct democracy is not scalable in any meaningful sense, it is not a viable process to deal with any but the most local concerns. In either case the problem of capture of democratic institutions persists in both representative and direct forms of democracy. And perhaps as important, the problem of the constitution of the body politic as undifferentiated individual monads or political solidarities constituted by the elite is also left unaddressed by either participant coordination mechanism. In the case of sortition neither are the participants selected based on their wealth or ability to secure wealthy donors (as in representative democracy), nor do participants voluntarily opt in because they have free time or are especially motivated (as in direct democracy). Instead, minipublics filled by lot offer a much stronger institutional design for guarding against capture by oligarchic subgroups, which would undermine their democratic aim and in turn produce policy that benefits the already advantaged.[45]

Further, because selection can be stratified and minipublics can be constituted in ways that reflect broader social-structural inequalities, democratic institutions can also help constitute the body politics in ways that break with the rationalist individualism of liberalism. I will address this issue in greater detail in the next chapter, by showing how lot can also be used to create class-based and issue-based governing bodies within financial institutions to empower the historically disempowered.

Riding the Wave

It helps that the time is right. Lot as a mechanism for coordinating political decisions has the winds of history at its back. Increasingly, governments around the world are turning to deliberative minipublics to take on complex and highly polarizing political problems. The OECD has even described the batch of popular assemblies, over 500 and counting, as a "deliberative wave."[46] The first permanent popular assembly was established in 2019 in German-speaking region of Belgium, Ostbelgiem. It has the power to create one-time citizen assemblies to take up issues and concerns and them bring them to Parliament.[47] Others have followed, noticeably the Paris Citizens' Assembly established by Emmanuel Macron's "Great Debate" following the anti-elite upsurge of the Yellow Vest Movement, perhaps a modern-day Ciompi Revolt. There is the Toronto Planning Review Panel, a lottocratic assembly that provides feedback to government on urban development projects, and the DemoLab in Bogotá to incorporate greater gender diversity and popular participation in local government. And many others.

Though assembly experiments have limited and toothless advisory roles—few politicians want to give up the ability to set the agenda—that need not stifle our emancipatory imagination for their potential. Claudia Chwalisz, founder of the lottocratic political action group, DemocracyNext, argues that, "While citizens' assemblies today are largely advisory and complementary to our existing electoral institutions, it is not impossible to imagine a future where binding powers shift to these institutions—or where they perhaps even replace established governing bodies in the longer term."[48] There is prefigurative power in the experiments underway today around the world too promising to ignore. Drawing from them, let's now turn to our cookbook for democratic finance.

8

Plebeian Recipes

> As the king-in-council succeeded the king by grace of God, so in future democracies, the toleration and encouragement of minorities and the willingness to consider as "men" the crankiest, humblest and poorest and blackest peoples, must be the real key to the consent of the governed.
>
> W. E. B. Du Bois, *Darkwater*

Design Principles

In response to a French critic of his masterwork, *Capital*, volume 1, Karl Marx wrote in the postface to its second edition that its purpose was not to write "recipes for the cook-shops of the future" but rather, and exclusively, to provide a thorough "critical analysis of the actual facts."[1] Out of exasperation that his critic would quibble with confining himself "merely" to the capitalist mode of production and not what might lie beyond it, Marx wrote, "Imagine this!"[2] But as is evident from Marx's writing elsewhere, to have a robust political imaginary, having at least one foot in the cook-shop of the future is necessary.[3]

In this chapter I aim to lay out the basic steps in the cooking process of one such recipe: a democratized pool of finance. Though I will talk very concretely about the design principles and processes that could animate a democratic public bank, drawing upon innovations in critical political theory and on recent examples of democratic experimentation around the planet as inspiration, the principles of design can be applied to *any* democratic pool of finance—whether it be investment funds, pension funds, or sovereign wealth funds. These principles are largely agnostic about the type of financial institution as long as the institution is a public one and not, say, a private institution or individual account. Investment decisions extend well beyond banks, in fact most happen far outside of them. These ideas may additionally be relevant for other financial institutions, such as central banks. The control central banks have over the interest rate through their open market operations with other banks is a private maneuver with massive implications for the demos. But I will leave it to others to consider the application more fully.

The four democratic design principles I lay out below are affected interests, subsidiarity, agonism, and extension of the democratic economy. They are intended to cast some light on what I consider to be the core participatory and deliberative features of a democratized financial system. Taken together, they are meant to serve as a practical set of guideposts for the design of concrete democratic financial institutions. I introduce these principles as a means of answering four key questions: Who has a say? At what scale are decisions made? How are participants selected? How are the pools of finance themselves financed? After reviewing each of these principles, I unveil a design for a democratic public bank. I then conclude the book, showing how democratic finance would fulfill the basic requirements of a democratic rupture and that it should thus be a core aim for anyone committed to radical democracy.

Affected Interests

What overarching *general* regulative principle for participant selection in democratic finance might we use? What considerations should guide our response to the question, "Who has a say?" This is the problem of "constituting the demos."[4] Who is included in the demos, broadly conceived, and who is not? Who are the inputs to draw from to create minipublics? It turns out that even though this is perhaps one of the most fundamental questions, it isn't one with an obvious solution. And for many decades, there was "a silence at the heart of democratic theory" with respect to it.[5] Schumpeter even went as far as to suggest that what constitutes the demos doesn't really matter—it should be left to the *populus* to define *for* itself. "A race-conscious nation may associate fitness with racial considerations. And so on."[6] But this anything-goes view of the demos is horribly flawed for our purposes. Such a view would justify, at least on procedural terms, the exclusions of slaves and women from the lottocratic governance of Athenian society.

Instead, the pool of possible participants in democratic decision-making should be composed of people whose interests are most directly and deeply affected by the activities of the organizations we hope to subject to democratic procedures. In democratic theory, this is referred to as the "all affected interests principle."[7] We might be conservative and offer a narrower conception of the relevant demos to argue that individuals should be empowered to influence organizations if those organizations are involved in activities that regularly and deeply affect their ability to live flourishing lives.[8]

Imagine we were democracy maximalists and believed that all institutions of public importance should be subject to democratic input. When applied broadly to all organizations, this principle constitutes a sharp break from the single citizen in a single nation-state framework for thinking about democracy. Instead, each person would have many organizational memberships, which would overlap, intersect, and evolve dynamically based on what those organizations did. Such a compass point for democracy does not only include formal political organizations, but also, in principle, many traditionally conceived private organizations, such as businesses, unions, school boards, and so on. In the ideal I defend here, democracy should not be concentrated in a singular institutional entity but rather an intersecting network of democratized organizations.

One reasonable reaction to such a principle is that every decision effects everyone to some even miniscule degree, therefore, with respect to finance, the only way to have a truly democratic institution would be a democratic world bank in which the planetary population is available for random selection. Such an arrangement—that is, a global financial institution for coordinating global financing needs—might in and if itself be essential. But such an arrangement would necessarily sacrifice depth of influence, which requires a smaller demos, for scope of influence, which requires a very large demos.[9]

For democratic finance, the principle I advance here attempts to balance these two design concerns to give members of the demos a reasonable chance of participation. The likelihood of anyone being selected out of a global demos to participate in a small assembly body even if they occurred often and regularly would likely hover somewhere very close to zero. Therefore, we should design a system of democratic finance—concretely, in this case, a system of democratic pools of finance—that operates at different geographic scales and with different investment foci. This would mean that there would be multiple demoi in which individuals would simultaneously have membership in multiple democratic financial institutions. Returning to a concept from the previous chapter, one would be eligible for inclusion in a variety of minipublics, ranging from perhaps a local green bank to a planetary green transition fund.[10]

Subsidiarity

Now that we have a rough model for an overlapping system of democratic financial institutions in which participants for deliberation are selected on the principal of affected interests, how should we think about how to allocate financing power? A diverse spectrum of models is possible here. If financing influence is distributed across geographic scales, should it be evenly distributed, concentrated at the top and centralized, or spread out at the bottom and decentralized? Or should some other distributional logic guide investment power by minipublics? Based on the principle of affected interests alone, it is clear that a planetary system of democratic finance must be multiscalar, but what principle should guide its design? The answer I give here is subsidiarity.

The concept is an old one, albeit not as old at lot. It was first laid out theoretically in 1603 by Johannes Althusius, a Calvinist jurist from Germany.[11] The principle of subsidiarity is quite simple: all other things being equal, tasks should be carried out at the lower institutional scale. There are many institutional and geographic scales—planetary, regional, national, state, city, and even hyperlocal scales like the neighborhood (consider the neighborhood association)—at which we can imagine building democratic financial institutions responsible to a distinct demos. Subsidiarity suggests that authority over particular issues should be allocated to the scale most effective at governing that particular issue. When different scales would be equally effective, the smaller of the scales should be chosen.

Applying this principle, some democratic pools of finance would have wider jurisdictions than others because of their financing focus. For example, to be truly effective at mitigating climate change some democratic green banks may need to be planetary in scale. The combination of the scale of the climate problem, the planetary nature of a solution to it, the planetary interest in reversing it and the planetary scale of the positive and negative externalities that such a reversal will have may simply make a planetary green bank the most functional solution to the problem of reversing climate change. But an investment fund with a unique focus on small-business development or the financial inclusion of historically excluded groups by definition works at a more localized level and would therefore need to be organized at a more appropriate scale.[12] The scale matters, in other words, for what problem the democratic pool of finance is aiming to address—it is not pregiven.

Subsidiarity cuts against decentralization for the sake of decentralization, which you find in much of rhetoric associated with Web3. But it also runs counter to the simple nation-state nationalization model, often treated as axiomatically good among socialists and others on the left. The centralization versus decentralization debate is thus confusing as it presents the two ends of one spectrum as the only options available when there are in fact many possible ones. This binary runs not only through debates about finance but indeed through emancipatory theory itself.[13] Subsidiarity offers a different view about the scale at which emancipatory change occurs.

Building on the affected interest principle above, a system of democratic finance designed through the principle of subsidiarity would produce many polycentric and federated circles of inclusion for possible participants and would be a source of legitimacy for projects viewed as bound to specific geographies by the inhabitants of those places.[14] This polycentric system, in which smaller governing institutions are subsumed under larger ones, can coexist within the federalist one. To imagine a planetary system of democratic finance fully realized, a unionized worker in Bangladesh would be a possible participant in multiple assemblies and commissions in their local, regional, national, hemispheric and planetary democratic financial institutions, albeit with a decreasing likelihood of selection with each additional expansion of geographic scope and the widening of pools of possible participants.

Agonism
So far, I have considered only general principles that are theoretically applicable in all times. Yet we are situated in a particular historical context and want to design democratic finance to address the conjunctural problems I laid out in the second part of this book. There are two fundamental unrealities that mainstream political liberalism take as truisms: 1) if people are allowed to express opinions rationally and through open discourse, the correct consensus view will emerge in politics; and 2) ordinary people in capitalist democracies are free and legally equal, and therefore have no systemic advantage in politics or policymaking overtime. Both of these views are demonstrably false when applied to the context of capitalist democracy. The principle of class agonism provides a design alternative.

As we discussed at length in the last chapter, the best mechanism through which we should select possible participants is sortition. Relative to the two other selection options available, representative and direct, sortition is best suited, if designed correctly, to promote political equality and fairness, to block the capture of institutions by the elite, to promote good problem solving in policymaking, and to ensure that democratic decisions have popular legitimacy. Thus, even on its own, random selection is an advance on the weaknesses of the democratic processes that we already have (elected representatives) and what many activists most strongly wish we did (direct forms of democracy). Lot, again, points to a different means to emancipatory change.

Yet as with other purely deliberative models like direct democracy, left completely on its own, sortition has a significant weakness. It is beset by liberal assumptions about the likelihood of consensus in politics via rational deliberation. It therefore renders meaningful and durable social divisions invisible and in turn presumes that on balance people are reflexive and adaptive agents willing to work toward the common good. It treats democratic politics like a Habermassian rational public square where, it is assumed, if people are able to participate freely and as equals, the best and most rational choice will emerge from the exchange. This depoliticizes key social cleavages in society. Instead, capitalist democracies create social oppositions between groups over zero-sum policy questions.

As this book has shown, however, finance capitalism entails a particular class politics that results not only in oligarchic capture of dominant political institutions but in dominance by finance capital as a system of income generation. To challenge and transform it, an alternative hegemonic class politics has to *be built*. It is Pollyannaish to assume away class politics in class-divided societies in our democratic designs. Developing alternative class politics that redistribute power downward on the class hierarchy, attuned to the ways that class is differentiated horizontally and vertically within the conjuncture, is the political content of democratic ruptures.

Therefore deliberation and collective decision-making alone should be treated with a heavy dose of skepticism. In politics there are winners and losers, Schmittian friends and enemies, and therefore power is always afoot.[15] That capitalist democracy depends upon these fundamental antagonisms has been most forcefully argued for by left populists such as Ernesto Laclau and Chantal Mouffe. Indeed, this isn't simply their view of what politics is; it is part and parcel of their strategic orientation to politics—that is, what politics *should* become. Laclau writes in *On Populist Reason*,

> populism requires the dichotomic division of society into two camps—one presenting itself as a part which claims to be the whole; that this dichotomy involves the antagonistic division of the social field; and that the popular camp presupposes, as a condition of its constitution, the construction of a global identity out of the equivalence of a plurality of social demands.[16]

The aim of politics, in such a view, is "the discursive construction of an antagonistic frontier."[17]

Part of the principle I lay out here, agonism, has been sharply developed by Chantal Mouffe, who argues that politics always operate through conflict.[18] Mouffe reasons against the rationalist view that all democratic institutions should facilitate this agonism and moved in a more liberal and non-Schmittian direction; opponents are not life-and-death enemies but mere adversaries.[19] As Mouffe writes, "Proper political questions always involve decisions that require making a choice between conflicting alternatives. This is something that cannot be grasped by the dominant tendency in liberal thought, which is characterized by a rationalist and individualist approach."[20] Our democratic financial institutions should not try to diffuse the underlying socio-economic cleavages that create the differentiated sets of interests that bring politics to life but should instead provide a context for those opposing views to enter into adversarial combat. Politics entails disagreement.

How might we apply this general agonist view of politics to the politics of democratizing financial capitalism today given that the financial elite actively and indirectly capture political institutions and, in effect, render the voice of the demos completely absent. As

I showed in detail earlier in the book, capitalist democracy is already profoundly biased in favor of the rich and the owners of—especially financial—capital. These few dominate the many, who are politically disempowered through finance's engagement, prominence, and entanglements in democratic politics and institutions from the outset. In the face of the asset power of finance and in the absence of the countervailing institutions that once existed, such as unions or strong civil rights organizations, the demos has lost its political capacities. If there is one liberal claim that we should reject decisively, it is that there exists a sovereign people, composed of free individuals who all share the same political liberties and formal rights under the law, among whom no group enjoys any systematic advantage in politics over any other. This is the liberal democratic delusion. Therefore, the key to any attempt at democratization should be the distribution of power down the class hierarchy.

Here, I build on the principle of agonism with insights from the new "plebeian republicans," who aim to use lot to create anti-oligarchic, class-based political institutions.[21] Much like the working classes today, in the Roman Empire, the plebeians, or plebs, were excluded from the political institutions controlled by the aristocratic patrician class. In rebelling against this outsider status, they were eventually able to achieve political inclusion. The story is not unlike the working classes today. After achieving significant forms of political power in the first half of the twentieth century, the working classes in most advanced and developing countries have been crowded out of politics via a post-1980s oligarchic backlash. The ordinary people today are much like the plebs of ancient Rome. Simply by virtue of being a non-elite one is by default a second-class citizen.[22]

The writings of Machiavelli are influential in this return to plebeian political institutions. In the *Discourses on Livy*, the Renaissance Italian argued that plebeian tribunes were the key institution responsible for the Roman Republic's durability and success.[23] And Machiavelli himself had a lottocratic plan to empower magistrates drawn from ordinary citizens, the *proposti*, who could attend sessions of the Signoria, veto offices dominated by the elite, and play a role in the citizens assemblies. He saw these as having an advantage over the tribunes, who could often be bribed or intimidated by the nobility.[24] Machiavelli's political philosophy was principally agonistic and presumed a foundational socio-ontological impasse between ruling elite and the plebeian masses. In his view, the conflicts this impasse would produce if allowed to take expression in formal politics would be the source of political liberty and stability.[25]

The principle of political agonism aims to make the unequal equal so that our political and economic institutions can define their purpose and determine what is socially held as the basic guideposts of human flourishing through a deliberative process that clarifies our social divisions rather than render them invisible. This was, as I mentioned in the previous chapter, a core aim of the textile workers in the Ciompi Revolt of 1378. Machiavelli recounted one of their agitators, putting it in these terms before they were massacred,

> Do not let their antiquity of blood, with which they will reproach us, dismay you; for all men, having had their same beginning, are equally ancient and have been made by nature in one mode. Strip all of us naked, you will see that we are alike; dress us in their clothes and them in ours, and without a doubt we shall appear noble and they ignoble, for only poverty and riches makes us unequal.[26]

The political theorist John P. McCormick restored this Machiavellian idea of democracy by proposing the constitutionalization of a "People's Tribunate" in the US. Excluding the top 10 percent of wealth holders using the most recent US census data, he argues that it should be filled by lot from the rest.[27] The tribunate, according to McCormick's plan, would be composed of fifty-one members who would serve year-long nonrenewable terms for which they would be fully compensated. McCormick suggests that inequalities not directly reducible to class should also be addressed, altering the pool from which lots are drawn "to give

African American and Native American citizens a greater chance of serving as tribunes."[28] They would come together on a full-time basis to study and discuss the business of the government. In McCormick's blueprint, the tribunate could call referenda, initiate impeachments, and have certain veto powers over specific legislation and Supreme Court decisions. They would only be allowed to make such interventions once during their term.

Some plebeian republicans challenge wealth exclusions on the basis of feasibility (i.e., they are unconstitutional in liberal democracies that are based on political equality) and arbitrariness (wealth can fluctuate from year to year and so might not be a great measure of class).[29] Additionally, even without formal exclusion, random selection is likely to produce class-based institutions because the ruling few by definition would always be a minority. Still, I argue that there is a discursive and cultural purpose to making class-based institutions drawn from the demos: the creation of class consciousness and working-class solidarity that explicit inclusion and exclusion along class lines make possible. As will be shown below, using a mix of truly randomly selected people's assemblies and more restricted class-based and other issue-based standing commissions, I offer a hybrid approach to class-based governing bodies for democratic finance.

A recent constitutional innovation by the political theorist Camila Vergara offers a means to bridge the principles of affected interest and subsidiarity with the aims of the new plebeians. As opposed to simply having a single tribunate, as in the McCormick plan, Vergara argues for a "sovereign network of local assemblies" that would operate as a "bounded system, gathering information, processing it, and sending political signals throughout the network."[30] As in the principle of subsidiarity, these are not merely federated but are rather equal and stand-alone parts of a whole. The assemblies, composed of residents from districts sized between 450 and 600, deliberate on issues that affect them. We might further apply the principle of subsidiarity to Vergara's constitutional idea for local lottocratic assemblies and have additional governing bodies at higher levels of scale if those levels are most suitable to solve certain problems. Although in Vergara's plan there are local councils on the one hand and a tribunate at the level of the republic on the other, in the case of democratic finance, we might have a wider range of financial institutions at different levels of political and geographic scale: local, metropolitan, region, national, hemispheric, planetary, and so on.

There are several advantages that creating agonistic financial institutions would produce. Principally, they are anti-oligarchic because they provide a way to empower ordinary people, the demos, and disempower the powerful in decision-making processes. Not only does this create a check on the power of the elite, or in our case finance capital, it also gives meaningful political agency in finance and questions of development to sections of the population entirely excluded from the rooms where such decisions are normally made. Political institutions built on the principle of class agonism also represent a hard break from the liberal construction of "the people" as a monolithic whole, in which rational citizens are interchangeable with one another as the constitutive mass of the nation.[31] And crucially, they can help constitute the body politic along class and other socially significant, but politically underrepresented, lines.[32]

Fundamentally, it is not merely class consciousness that plebeian institutions can help generate but class solidarity—which is necessary to overcome pro-elite interest-based modes of reasoning and collective action problems that favor capitalists in the long run.[33] Many argue that class-based democratic institutions will therefore produce better and more egalitarian policy outcomes.[34] In the case of allocation of finance, there is sound reason to expect lottocratic plebeian institutions to more fairly allocate finances in a way that benefits everyone.

Enlarging the Democratic Economy

The most radical class-based tribunician proposals in circulation have a common limitation, however. Their sole concern is with the exclusion of the demos from the formal democratic political institutions captured by elites. But focusing just on formal politics creates blind spots to the workings of capitalist politics. As I showed earlier in this book, the engagement of the elite in politics is only one source of their power within the formal political institutions where public decisions are made. But outside of these parliamentary, congressional, and judicial institutions, as much, if not more, happens that influences the decisions ultimately made within them. The prominence and entanglements of capital in general and finance in particular are other sources of political power located outside and away from formal political institutions. It is therefore a key conclusion of this book that efforts at extending democratic processes into spheres beyond the formal institutions of the state, in particular those of the economy, is a crucial way to make society as a whole more democratic and accountable to working class people.

It is here that I come to the fourth and final principle of design for democratizing finance: enlarging the democratic economy via ownership transfer. If a crucial source of oligarchic power in the financial sector is its structural prominence in society and its entanglement with government and nonfinancial businesses, then it is crucial to transfer a meaningful portion of that activity to the democratic public domain, to the demos. This bears centrally on the question of how we supply democratic finance with resources to function—that is, how we finance it.[35]

The public banking advocate Thomas Marois shows that there are many ways to finance a public bank, each of which should be relied on to a greater or lesser degree depending on considerations about both their desirability and feasibility in political terms. First are direct government allocations. We might have special government funds that can help finance the initial capitalization of our pool of public finance as well as annual allocations into it. We might also use indirect financing for guarantees of returns on investment for certain kinds of lending programs. Similarly, public contributions might be drawn from essential services, infrastructure, and public pensions. Certain types of pools of finance (such as commercial banks) can accept deposits as part of their

retail services, which can in turn be used in programs and projects. And finally, democratic pools of finance might rely on
certain forms of borrowing to finance operations.[36]

But a democratic rupture requires going beyond building
power in the interstices of finance capital to dismantle and redistribute investment capacity. Here we need forms of ownership
transfer to help finance our pools of democratic finance. One
means of transferring ownership is through levies. The government can consider an ongoing financial transactions tax on
private financial institutions and retail traders. In 2016, the
public economist Dean Baker calculated that a 0.1 percent tax
on bond trades and a 0.2 percent tax on stock trades could generate 0.6 percent of GDP in revenue, or around $120 billion.[37]
Similarly, for the large asset managers, the government could
impose higher levels of taxation on the management fees charged
to manage the funds. Or more directly, the government could
take over the assets of distressed private financial institutions in
times of crisis, as they have so many times before, and use them
to further fund democratic pools of finance instead of auctioning
them off to private financiers in FIRE sales. Regardless of the
mix of funding sources—and practically speaking it would need
to be a mix—a key principle is that the expansion of democratic
finance should be financed through a transfer of ownership from
the private to the demos.

Ingredients for Democracy

Randomly selecting people to decide how to allocate finance
probably strikes most as strange. Class-based political institutions might sound even stranger (even though that's *already* what
we have). And suggesting that this is how *most* investment should
be allocated beyond a few localized experiments in public investment perhaps sounds otherworldly. But let's be frank, its
otherworldliness is a selling point. In a time of such profound
overlapping crises of finance capitalism there is an urgent need to
experiment with what might first be viewed as absurd. It is in that

spirit that I now turn to my recipe for democratic finance. My recipe offers one means of institutionalizing the power of the working classes. It is also a plan that might consolidate the politically dispossessed, out of their differentiated starting points, into a solidaristic block of the body politic.

Building upon my design principles and drawing upon recent experiments in democratic governance, I propose the establishment of a democratic public bank composed not only of ordinary financial experts and operational divisions but of a series of people's assemblies and standing commissions that can help bring to life the four democratic design principles laid out above.[38] These design proposals build upon recent experiments in democracy that are already ongoing all around the world. As you will see, this book proposes a recipe, but the cookshops for democracy are already fired up and baking. For each key governance design area in the bank, I will show that a similar democratic mechanism is already being put to work elsewhere in the world. The proposal might be otherworldly, but every component has been tried and proven at a local scale.

The design I propose is meant as a suggestive heuristic not as an airtight prescription. I am highly skeptical of anyone that presents themselves as having all the answers to questions of future design, so have no intention of giving the reader the impression that is my own disposition. But I am convinced, and I hope that after getting this far into the text, you are as well, that such an effort in democratizing finance is a necessary next step for a downward redistribution of power. A democratic pool of finance, as part of a growing network of democratic financial institutions designed on the principle of subsidiarity, is the possible step this book champions. But the exact design need not follow the one I am about to lay out precisely, and other pools of finance might be deemed better to democratize, or more feasible, than that of a public bank. Below I ask: How can we subject circuits of finance tied to an investment bank to democratic processes such as democratic deliberation, participation, and decision-making?

Here, for the sake of simplicity, we will use the example of a mission-led investment bank. Similar mechanisms, however, can be applied to the pools of assets that asset managers control, such as pension funds, investment funds, sovereign wealth funds, and other pools of investable money. A democratic investment bank will require a governing board of experts and regular operational divisions, much like any private capitalist bank. That governing board might be filled by a general election, the findings of a minipublic, political appointment, or a randomly selected hiring commission. And the operational divisions would largely be managed and hired by the governing board. Left at that, the bank might still function like a typical public bank. But mechanisms are available to not only imbue the bank with democratic legitimacy and mandates but also to create a democratic dynamism that can be reproduced in governance cycles. Below, I consider some recent innovations in democratic governance and explore the main democratic institutions of our bank. Figure 8.1 is a diagrammatic depiction of the end result (p. 200).

The People's Assembly

The city council of Bogotá, Columbia, set up the Itinerant Citizen Assembly for sequenced deliberation with citizens selected through a representative civic lottery through the organization DemoLab.[39] These permanent bodies run simultaneously and consider different issue areas. And their members change through citizen lotteries. Their purpose is to develop collective recommendations to the city council in order to better integrate ordinary people into the management of the city. In December 2020, the assembly was put into action for the first time; 110 ordinary citizens, selected through a stratified sample, participated in the first assembly and were tasked with identifying broad objectives for the city's urban planning. In the second round in October 2021, sixty citizens, eighteen of whom participated in the first assembly, were brought together to turn those ideas into actual recommendations. For both assemblies, citizens spent two weeks engaged in learning activities and then two days on deliberation.

We can take the innovation of an assembly and make it the highest body of our democratic pool of finance and the core

Figure 8.1. A Design for Democratic Finance

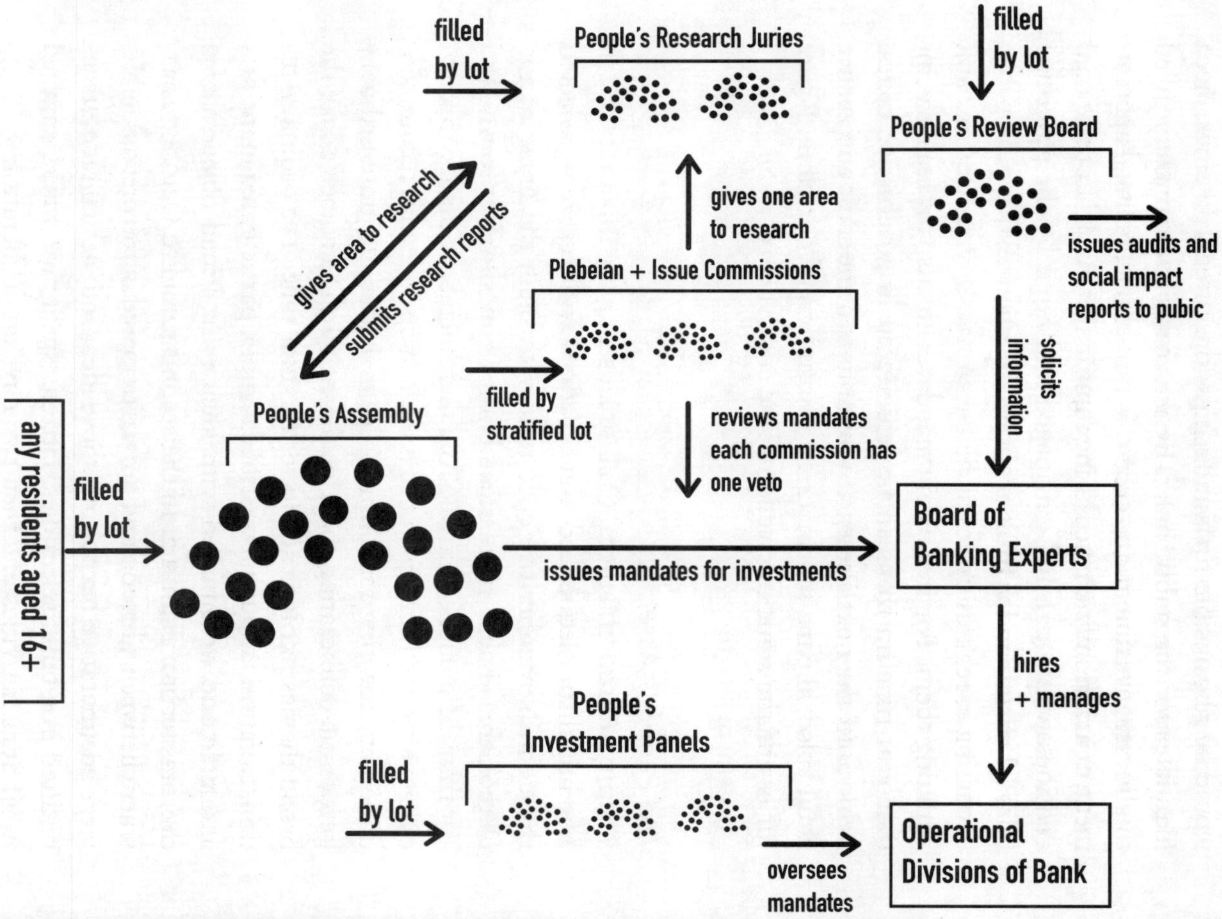

People's Review Board — filled by lot

issues audits and social impact reports to pubic

solicits information → **Board of Banking Experts** — hires + manages → **Operational Divisions of Bank**

People's Research Juries — filled by lot

gives one area to research

Plebeian + Issue Commissions — filled by stratified lot

reviews mandates each commission has one veto

issues mandates for investments

People's Investment Panels — filled by lot

oversees mandates

gives area to research

submits research reports

People's Assembly

any residents aged 16+ — filled by lot

mandate-generating layer of a public bank. Our People's Assembly would be composed of ninety-nine residents selected by lot (stratified sampling to ensure demographic representation) and would be responsible for establishing the three-year investment mandates for the public bank. By selecting broad priority areas to allocate investment and credit, it would set the bank's investment mandates which would then guide the board of governors and the operational divisions of the bank in managing its portfolio of assets and liabilities. We can imagine this process as occurring in regular cycles of deliberation, setting mandates and pursuing them. For instance, these priorities would be made on four-year time horizons and would set the broad mission of the bank until the next People's Assembly convenes. The assembly would also, in part, set the agenda for optional People's Research Juries and the mandates for the operational divisions and People's Investment Boards.

People's Research Juries

The populist Gilets Jaunes, or Yellow Vests, protests erupted in France in November of 2018, most proximately reacting to gas price increases but more fundamentally agitating for political reforms and reductions in French economic inequality. In response the next month President Emmanuel Macron tried to address the unrest by initiating the "Great National Debate," an exercise in lottocratic deliberation to discuss specific questions within four broad themes: ecological transition, state services and organization, taxation, and democracy. The result of the experiment was about 10,000 townhall meetings all over France and in some overseas territories that produced 18,847 grievance books. Somewhere between 500,000 and 1.5 million people participated in the large deliberative experiment. These nonbinding initiatives resulted in a tepid series of measures announced by Macron on April 25, 2019.[40]

As part of this great debate, in 2019, thirty Parisians selected by lot were tasked with convening, deliberating, and making recommendations about ways to improve citizen involvement in governance in Paris itself. The group recommended the creation of a permanent Assembly of Parisians, which the city council voted for in September of the same year. Paris' assembly was kicked off November 27, 2021, making it the first major city with a permanent standing citizen's body.[41] The design element of interest here in Paris is their citizen jury. As part of its charge, Paris' citizen assembly can initiate one-time citizen juries that are tasked with answering a question set by the assembly over a three-month period. The purpose of the jury is to produce recommendations for further consideration of the assembly at its next convening.

People's Research Juries can play a similar role for democratic finance. Here the People's Assembly may identify poorly understood areas of possible interest for investment. Say that, for instance, significant concern arises about lead water pipes in the city in the assembly process. But the conveners of the assembly and prior citizen juries did not anticipate this topic being discussed, and thus assembly members have only poor documentation and evidence to set a mandate. In such an event the citizen assembly issues a request for a research jury to investigate the area, commission studies, and generate recommendations for the convening of the next People's Assembly. The research juries would run between the second and third years of the four-year cycle. Their recommendations and the findings of their commissioned studies would then be deliberated at the beginning of the next four-year investment cycle by the newly formed People's Assembly. Research juries bring democracy to bear on the informational inputs available to the general assembly process.

People's Investment Boards and Review Board

Ostbelgien in Belgium has set up a *bürgerdialog*—a citizen dialogue process using deliberative minipublics. Much like the Parisian assembly, the Belgians set up a permanent citizens' council with agenda setting power.[42] However, it also has the mandate to create up to three citizens panels to address specific issue areas.

These panels, which consider popular proposals in depth, are composed of between twenty-five and fifty people through lot.

With respect to our democratic bank, our People's Assembly would form specific people's investment boards, much like the Belgian citizen panel, to oversee specific parts of the mandates for the bank. These twenty-five-person standing boards would rotate people in and out over the course of the four-year plan. The purpose of these investment boards is to oversee actual investment allocation in given mandate areas. They would be in charge of monitoring the portfolio to ensure that the operational divisions are fulfilling their charge. This mechanism is a key step to ensure that principal-agent problems don't arise within the democratic financial entity. There might be, for instance, a worker-owned-cooperatives investment board, a housing investment board, a clean energy investment board, a financial inclusion and community-wealth building investment board, and so on. The actual content of the mandates is an issue of democratic deliberation, thus it cannot be predetermined. Their purpose, however, would be to work with the governing board and the operations divisions to deliberate over key questions in specific investment areas. They would then issue short reports on their mandate area to the People's Review Board.

Upon receiving mandate-specific audits by the People's Investment Boards, a People's Review Board can review the financial entity's entire operation to make sure that it is achieving its overall mandate. This similarly sized board would then issue public facing financial audits and social impact reports to the demos as a whole to ensure that those members of the demos not part of its operation have clear information as to its functioning. Like the other deliberative minipublics, these panels would be filled by lot. Though they would be standing panels, they would not meet continuously over the four-year cycle. Instead, the review panel would meet the second and fourth year of the five-year-plan cycle to provide assessments. In the second year, the panel would produce a report for the public about the bank's progress. And in the fourth, in addition to the public report, it would produce a report for the next citizen assembly to help guide the creation of new mandates.

Class and Issue-Based Commissions

For our final set of democratic institutions, we take greater inspiration from the class-based political institutions of the past such as the tribunate of the Roman Republic. Here we might include standing commissions that are determined by the demos via referenda to ensure that certain viewpoints and social fractions are represented in the determination of the investment policies of our financial entity.

As an example, I propose the creation of five such commissions: a workers commission, a clean energy commission, a racial justice commission, a tribal commission, and a cooperative ownership commission. Each of these commissions would consist of thirty-one lottery-selected participants from specific subsections of the demos. Combining the affected-interests principle and the agonism principle, these standing commissions would ensure the inclusion of historically excluded groups and would therefore be filled by politically underrepresented groups.

The workers commission should not only exclude the wealthy and political elites but also the upper-middle and managerial classes. First, we would make John McCormick's selection restriction even more restrictive, excluding members of the wealthiest 20 percent of families. Second, and crucially, we would employ a more relational understanding of class to exclude certain occupations. The current mood in political theory accepts the gradational stratification approach and theorizes class as merely the quantity of wealth or income a family commands. While there is considerable overlap, class is not fundamentally about what one has but rather what one has to do to survive and how those survival strategies are dependent on the survival strategies of others. So in addition to our wealth exclusion requirement, which will by definition include mainly workers, to ensure that nobody in an employer or manager role is selected for the workers commission, we will include an authority-based exclusion and exclude anyone that exercises employment or managerial authority over one or more other people in the workplace.[43] Similarly, our clean energy commission will only select from ecological experts and green social movement organizations. Our racial justice commission would only select from racial justice social movement organizations. Our Indigenous commission would only select from tribal communities and Indigenous social movement organizations. And finally, our cooperative commission would select from experts on cooperative ownership and democracy in the workplace, as well as worker cooperative social movement organizations.

Our commissions would play an agonistic role in setting the mandates and would have two basic powers. First, they would review the initial mandate recommendations of the People's Assembly. They would be able to approve those mandates or be able to veto only one of them. Second, they would have the power to initiate one area for a research jury to investigate and make mandate recommendations for the next people's assembly process. This way, particular class-, ecology- and historic-injustice-based interests would be fairly represented in the democratic public bank. The composition of these commissions might be restructured dynamically over time as social and ecological life changes through assembly votes. Yet the guiding principle should be that however qualifications are changed, there will always be a hard limit on participation by the wealthy and those in exploitative capitalist class positions. The commissions must remain plebeian and working class in spirit and form.

9

Democracy on Fridays

We are, in short, surprised, even stunned, to discover that something so old could be so sophisticated.

Stephen Jay Gould, "Up Against a Wall"

Contradictions

Capitalist property relations, whose basic feature is the private control of the investment function in the hands of the few, generate systemic barriers to human flourishing and democratic life. These include ecological destruction, inequality and precarity, and chiefly for this book, high concentrations of political power for those with the capacity to make decisions about productive investments. These crises have been recurrent ever since what we know today as capitalism began to be implemented about 600 years ago with the initial wave of enclosures that "freed" the peasants from the land. That gave the new capitalist landowners control over how to cultivate that land and what to invest in and what not to. At its core, our major crises are the result of a basic design feature: capitalism shields investment decisions from democratic input. Though I have warned against abstractionist approaches to capitalist politics, the persistence of this simple structural parameter is strikingly durable. Indeed, were a social system to deviate from it, by definition it would cease to be a capitalist one.

In his book *Finance Capital*, the Austrian economist and finance minister Rudolph Hilferding wrote, "The problem of property relations . . . attains its clearest, most unequivocal and sharpest expression at the same time as the development of finance capital itself is resolving more successfully the problem of the organization of the social economy."[1] The finance capitalist conjuncture raises the crises of capitalism in normal times to brave new heights. It is a deepening of capitalist contradictions. Our conjuncture is one which is, to draw from the philosopher György Lukács characterization of crisis, "no more than a heightening of the degree and intensity of the daily life" of normal capitalist societies.[2] Finance capitalism, which maintains a shielded protection of private control over financial flows, compounds crises.

In this book I discussed debt and financial insecurity, underinvestment in socio-environmental goods, macroeconomic instability, and climate catastrophe. Solving those crises, however, amounts to a world-historic financing challenge. We know that human flourishing requires financial security, safe housing, decent jobs, an ecosystem in relative balance and decision-making power for the demos. Where will the money come from if competitive financing markets oriented around the bottom line continue to divert cash away from these goals? The short answer is democratic financial institutions.

Democratic finance, as I have laid it out here, is a way to steer investment flows toward goals that are determined through popular participation and deliberation rather than through the existing ecology of private institutions and individual investors whose principal aim is securing a financial return. The financial oligarchy will not save us; it will bury us. With the backing of governments (who can raise funds through a mix of taxes and fees, voluntary contributions, fiat money creation and other mechanisms), democratic finance creates the institutional capacity for imbuing finance with a socio-environmental purpose.

There is no reason to anticipate the concrete decisions of a democratic process prior to actually running it. But we might imagine three plausible lending outcomes. First, public finance could offset housing crises by investing in deeply needed affordable housing units. Such money flows might help finance new construction to increase the supply as well as finance low- and moderate-income mortgages to allow homebuyers to take advantage of the new supply of homes. It might also be designed to finance public housing or housing cooperatives commonly owned and maintained by their residents. Or it might even lead to the creation of a public acquisition fund to purchase sites for the development of affordable housing.[3] These are questions best left to the demos.

Second, democratic finance could be a means to financial justice through wealth creation for working-class communities that have been left out to dry. This is not a mere matter of financial inclusion, such as access to banking services like financial literacy coaching, credit lines and savings accounts, which has often been the focus of Postal banking advocates. Instead, our democratic bank might focus on genuine wealth building for working-class communities. We might finance small cooperatively owned businesses as well as help convert viable businesses into worker-owned enterprises by financing the purchase of single-owner firms for the acquisition of their employees. Such efforts are already underway in places like Cooperation Jackson, Mississippi, which was founded in 2014 to help incubate and build out a solidarity economy.[4] Unlike our dominant financiers, democratic pools of finance might support cooperatively owned enterprises, helping them not only survive but thrive. We could thus have a program for targeted business loans that would help firms transition to being worker owned and run. It might also be a means to non-workplace wealth creation, such as capital investments into education, community centers and parks, and infrastructure upgrades.[5] Again, in our shift away from atomistic approaches to finance, democratic finance might orient us toward collective and shared wealth, rooted in the organizations we participate in and the physical infrastructure we navigate.

Third, and perhaps most pressing, reaching carbon neutrality is the most existentially urgent need for our planet, but finance capitalism offers no means for the large-scale investments in the new generation of clean-power sources and infrastructure that are needed anytime soon. And while welcome, the gestures in this direction from the emergence of the new industrial policy in the Inflation Reduction Act and the CHIPS and Science Act are a mere drop in the bucket. Again, democratic finance offers one promising path if pursued at a robust scale. Democratic finance might allocate investments into community solar and wind projects that can replace dirty energy sources on the grid, it might prioritize the expansion nuclear, or it might opt for some combination of all the above. The particular composition of the energy matrix in a green transition is a highly debated issue within the environmental movement. It is one particularly well suited to the kind of deliberation minipublics are conceived for. Let the demos decide.

Along these lines, a truly democratic system of global finance might be the funding mechanism needed to build a clean transnational energy grid. It might be used to gain control over key sectors that are highly reliant on fossils in order to hasten a green transition through public ownership and control, invest in public systems of transit to wean ourselves off carbon emitting vehicles, and create democratically mandated programs to provide funding for retrofitting buildings so that they are green.[6]

Democratic processes and experiments themselves must be left to work out the details of the lending programs the different democratic financial institutions at different scales might pursue. Again, our ambition should not just be to create one democratic financial institution but a whole global network of them organized along the principle of subsidiarity. We can—and *should*—come up with recipes for the cookshops of the future, but we can't predict how people will decide which meals they want to make. The recipes offered up in this book, in any case, are premised on a commitment to not only the value of democracy, but also its promise in practical terms. Democracy is worth defending not just in itself but also a means to a better, less crisis-addled, life. Rule by the few has been part and parcel of the resource extraction and human dispossession at the center of our throes. It's time we gave democracy a try and trusted in the deliberative judgements of ourselves and our peers.

After Rupture

Finance capitalism and the new industrial policy bubbling up around the world appear to have very little in common. If finance capitalism has negatively defined our conjuncture, perhaps industrial policy is offering up something of an inflection point. As this book has shown, the former directs flows of investment into speculative physical and financial assets and the titanic accounts of the wealthy and the smaller personal accounts of workers that mimic them. It has thrived in a post-Volcker world of monetary policy where the blunt instrument of interest rates are used to spur economic activity, the cost of which appears to be of little concern to the central bankers at the helm. Governments are beginning to embrace a more active role in channeling investment flows into industrial policy, as we have witnessed with the passing of the Inflation Reduction Act and the CHIPS and Science Act in the US. The aim, both stated and implied, is to attack the problems of finance capitalism at the point of the supply-side. The new policy mood, what a 2019 IMF paper termed "the return of the policy that shall not be named," harkens back to the decolonial era of state-led development, which questions the free market as a means to development. Yet there is no agreed upon path for the new industrial policy; it represents a large-scale coordination problem.[7]

But despite all that distinguishes these approaches to solving the coordination problem that all societies face, finance capitalism and the new industrial policy both rest on a fundamental similarity: in practice both have been suspicious or outright dismissive of democratic processes, democratic demands, and the demos in general. Both, in their own way, operate upon a technocratic promise: the smartest people will be set to the task of solving our problems because they, and they alone, have the chops for the job. Finance capitalism presumes that the smartest guys in the room are the asset managers and venture capitalists making the bulk of investment decisions about financial assets whereas the new industrial policy presumes them to be talented government bureaucrats and appointed experts. In both cases, the demos is missing. This is because, from the boardroom to the agency, the demos is feared as irrational and dangerous.

This problem is a deep one spanning the vast bulk of the debate about the trade-offs between the so-called private and the public. For those two categories to be of any use, we need to add a third, the demos, which the argument advanced here emphatically prioritizes. The theory of democratic rupture advanced in this book radically departs from this suspicion of working people's governing capacities. The only way to meaningfully reverse finance capitalism's rot is to salvage together a better world out of the ruins of the existing one *through* democracy not around it. It's not just the desired outcome of the institutional designs on offer here, it's the means for neutralizing and reversing societal and ecological decay. This entails a transformation of the private and political institutions that wield investment control into ones that empower a working-class demos, differentiated vertically in the class structure and horizontally along factors such as race, gender, and citizenship.

Democratic ruptures, I have argued, involve four key transformations: they extend formal decision-making rights into the economic sphere of life; they expand the democratic composition of the economy; they consolidate the body politic along class lines; and they decommodify labor and work. The theory that this book advances should make plain that democratic ruptures are not limited to the democratization of formal politics and political institutions. They are not a means to better transparency and rebuilding the legitimacy of our dominant political institutions. Such gripes about contemporary politics are premised on a haunted view of the past, one that was rosy and good and had healthy and democratic political institutions filled with lost potential. Alas, our liberal pundits that tell this story are masters of mythmaking. It is little more than a legend. Instead, democratic ruptures are breaks that reconfigure dominant relations of power in capitalist politics and institute real democratic processes in these politics.

Capitalism is in part defined by its dynamism. "All that is solid, melts into air," Karl Marx remarked. The social forms and institutions that accommodate the private control of the means of investment and production and facilitate a dogged pursuit of profitability are remarkable in their scope and complexity. Capitalism's intricate apparatus is constantly transforming and developing, from one era to another, one conjuncture to the next. It develops in combined and geographically uneven ways. It undergoes anabolic and catabolic shifts—build up and break down, growth and crisis—all along evolving out of its dynamism new forms of production and politics that accommodate its dominant modes and leading sectors. It is in the punctuated equilibria and dynamic disruptions, in other words the contradictions, that capitalism can't help but to point beyond itself in every new conjuncture. In every new hell, there are glimpses of heaven. Because power is so systemically skewed in the favor of its own reproduction, the collective agency is rarely willing, available, or able to move beyond it. But in those moments of historic rupture, working-class political agency has imprinted itself upon politics and selected new tracks along and within which capitalist dynamics develop. This book is about a junction where we might jump from one such track to the next, putting the demos in the conductor's cab.

There is no certainty that the democratic ruptures proposed here for our time of finance capitalism will work. The masters of finance will certainly draw from their reserves when it comes to keeping the ruptures from happening. They won't give up allocation control over investment without a tooth and nail fight. This book itself has laid out a host of barriers to the achievability of its own proposals in simple policymaking terms, finance's means of plunder: engagement, prominence, and entanglements, all activated by the mobile and liquid character of their assets, their asset power. And the ruptures proposed are not without risk and potential setbacks. But the sector's grotesque swelling points to a crossroads; either we seize upon the possibilities the conjuncture throws up or we will be swallowed up by them anew. There are two options, jump the track or stay secured, rupture or renewal.

Modernity Caving In

The popular writing on Paleolithic cave art once took for granted a gradualist theory of its subject, arguing that our earliest ancestors did very simple and rudimentary drawings and sculptures that became increasingly complex and realistic over time as the artists themselves became more complex and cultured. Surely the height of artistic accomplishment is that of the moderns, for whom most of what came before leads progressively to their distinction. This often implicit view was the gold standard for decades. Italian photographer and director Mario Ruspoli summarized it well in his book of color plates and illustrations *The Cave of Lascaux*: "From the earliest images onward, one has the impression of being in the presence of a system refined by time . . . The development of Paleolithic cave art can be summed up as 15,000 years of apprenticeship followed by 8,000 years of academicism."[8]

But an excursion in December 1994 would come to upturn this gradualist interpretation. In the southeast of France near the commune of Vallon-Pont-d'Arc, three speleologists (scientists who study caves) found and explored the Chauvet-Pont-d'Arc Cave. What they saw in the Chauvet was remarkable: hundreds of animal paintings produced by artists employing a wide range of sophisticated techniques that produced subtle and realistic flair. Deep in the Chauvet were perhaps the most realist cave paintings ever discovered. Yet these were not paintings at the height of prehistoric refinement and stone age distinction. Dating techniques reveal them to be not the most recent but the most ancient prehistoric cave art known, perhaps 32,000 years old.

It turns out that the gradualist principle about the transformation of prehistoric compositions was little more than a bias about our poorly understood ancestors—a prejudice that implied a less intelligent, less refined, and cognitively simpler prehistoric human, the sort once depicted hunched over, grunting with a club in kid's cartoons. What was revealed in the expeditions of Chauvet were prehistoric perspectives quite similar to our own, the kind we can even *feel* when we see them; it is as if we can sense precisely what the person behind their creation felt. Despite living in vastly different times with radically divergent societies and cultures, we are, after all, fundamentally the same. Zoologist and popular science writer Stephen Jay Gould commented on the discovery with his usual clarity. Comparing us (moderns) and them (prehistorics), he remarked, "Human bodily form has not altered appreciably in 100,000 years."[9] Though in vastly different social and cultural contexts, they were, cognitively, biologically, and perhaps even emotionally, as we are—a link in an unbroken chain of the history of our species, *Homo sapiens*.

If we began this book with the end, a vignette about a possible democratic finance of the future, why have we now ended with our human beginnings? In the sense that we once viewed prehistoric art techniques and technologies as more rudimentary and our modern techniques as more sophisticated, we continue to view ancient governance techniques and technologies in the same way. Our assumption is that they are ill suited for contemporary problems, but this presumption is just a prejudice.

If we are ever to have a democratically enriched future, modern democracy must allow itself to be humbled by the past. Like a vampire's meal, we have been glamoured by the theory of pluralism and representative government. But uncomfortable facts have piled impossibly high and reveal two devastating truths about the impoverishment of our existing democratic institutions in the rich capitalist world.

First, capitalist democracies are beset by profound biases that lead them to govern on behalf of elites and in the centers of global finance such as the US and the UK where financial interests hold unique sway. Policy is chiefly the product of elites. The notion of pluralism—that while there are winners in capitalist democracy, capitalist politics don't produce systemic advantage—is perhaps an ideal, but as a description of reality, it is American political science's worst contribution and largest failed export. It is more Cold War saber rattling about the supremacy of American political institutions than an actual scientific finding about how those democratic political institutions work in reality. An example of democratic backsliding, in theory, has contributed to our complacency about democratic erosion in practice.

Second, representative government is not a more complex democratic advance beyond the simpler direct forms of government of the past. It's neither more sophisticated nor more democratic. In fact, it has worked precisely as intended from the outset, to provide members of the non-elite, such as workers, with a voice but barely any control at all when compared to the political capabilities of the rich. It's a massive principal-agent problem gone awry. One needs mountain gear to climb the summit of facts in the social sciences that demonstrate the uncomfortable but now undeniable truth about our most modern of governance innovations, representative democracy: it has failed.

Let's not be moderns anymore. There is an ancient technology available that points to even greater democratic sophistication than the rudimentary and gerrymandered ballot boxes used to allocate positions to the wealthy in contemporary democracy: the kleroterion. It offers a simple but profoundly effective and democratic mechanism, random selection. Here lies a means of democratic governance that allows us the capacity to have equal say, a deliberative democratic exchange, and the ability to ensure that the work that is involved in democracy, when we get the call, is compensated. We don't need to be in an endless meeting; democracy on Fridays through sortition will suffice.

Nowhere today is the installment of lottocratic class and issue-based institutions more needed than in the case of finance. It is the time of the financier. But they are dancing on the backs of sleeping dragons.

Notes

Preface

1. Edward Bellamy, *Looking Backward: 2000–1887* (Boston: Ticknor & Co., 1887), 102.
2. Ibid.
3. Jessica M. Kim, *Imperial Metropolis: Los Angeles, Mexico, and the Borderlands of American Empire, 1865–1941* (Chapel Hill: University of North Carolina Press, 2019), 2.
4. Ibid., 31.
5. Audre Lorde, *The Master's Tools Will Never Dismantle the Master's House* (New York: Penguin, 2017).

1. Mother of Antagonism

1. Throughout this book, I use the term *demos* in contrast to the elite, as a means to refer to common and ordinary people—the working classes most broadly conceived. Though *demos* is now colloquially used to refer to the entire people of a polity, in its original political use, in ancient Greece, it was in fact a class category. See Aristotle, *The Politics*, transl. Benjamin Jowett, ed. Jonathan Barnes (Cambridge: Cambridge University Press, 1995).
2. André Gorz, *Strategy for Labor: A Radical Proposal* (Boston: Beacon Press, 1967), 8, 181.
3. China Miéville, *A Specter, Haunting: On the Communist Manifesto* (Chicago: Haymarket Books, 2022).
4. See David Collier, Jody Laporte and Jason Seawright, "Typologies: Forming Categories and Creating Categorical Variables," in *Oxford Handbook on Political Methodology* (Oxford: Oxford University Press, 2008).

5. What I offer is by no means the only word on levels of abstraction or how each should be defined. Antonio Gramsci adds an additional level of abstraction, the "situation," and theorizes conjunctures in a way that sharply departs from my use in this book. We might insert an even higher level of abstraction as well, to describe what all modes of production themselves have in common at the highest level of generality. For a useful review of the divergent uses of conjuncture in social theory, see Gillian Hart, "Modalities of Conjunctural Analysis: 'Seeing the Present Differently' through Global Lenses," *Antipode* 56, no. 1 (January 2024).

6. Nicos Poulantzas, *Political Power and Social Classes* (London: New Left Books, 1973), 15.

7. Philosophers Louis Althusser and Étienne Balibar termed this a "structure in dominance." See Etienne Balibar, "On the Basic Concepts of Historical Materialism," in Louis Althusser et al., *Reading Capital: The Complete Edition* (London: Verso, 2016), 365n5.

8. This is not to say that the power of capital cannot or even should not be theorized at the general level of abstraction. What matters is the purpose of that theorization. Werner Bonefield, Søren Mau, and William Clare Roberts all offer useful perspectives on the form that domination or economic power takes in the capitalist mode of production in general; William Clare Roberts, *Marx's Inferno: The Political Theory of Capital* (Princeton, NJ: Princeton University Press, 2017); Werner Bonefield, *A Critical Theory of Economic Compulsion: Wealth, Suffering, Negation* (New York: Routledge, 2023); Søren Mau, *Mute Compulsion: A Marxist Theory of the Economic Power of Capital* (London: Verso, 2023). They do not, however, derive ahistorical conclusions about emancipatory political strategy out of their theorizations, which is the principal theoretical danger here.

9. A similar move is made in Louis Althusser, *Machiavelli and Us* (London: Verso, 2000), 18. See also Louis Althusser, "Contradiction and Overdetermination," in *For Marx* (London: Verso, 2005). In *Machiavelli and Us*, Althusser reflects on the writings of the Florentine diplomat, commonly associated with the *real politic* of dusty international relations schools. Contrary to that view, Althusser argues that Machiavelli, in his classics *The Prince* and the *Discourses*, was principally a theorist of the conjuncture. As I show in the

penultimate chapter of this book, "Plebeian Recipes," Machiavelli also has much to teach about how to construct a democratic pool of finance.

10. David Gianatasio, "Spike Lee's New Ad Touts Crypto as the Great Social Equalizer," Muse by Clio, July 15, 2021, musebycl.io.

11. The work by Thomas Marois is an exception here (*Public Banks: Decarbonisation, Definancialisation and Democratisation* [Cambridge: Cambridge University Press, 2021]), as is Robert Meister's (*Justice Is an Option: A Democratic Theory of Finance for the Twenty-First Century* [Chicago: University of Chicago Press, 2020]).

12. Isabelle Ferreras, Julie Battilana, and Dominique Méda, *Democratize Work: The Case for Reorganizing the Economy* (Chicago: University of Chicago Press, 2022).

2. The Frankenstein Problem

1. André Gorz, *Strategy for Labor: A Radical Proposal* (Boston: Beacon Press, 1967), 8.

2. As Thomas Malthus wrote of the English Poor Laws, "A man who might not be deterred from going to the ale-house, from the consideration that upon his death, or sickness, he should leave his wife and family upon the parish, might yet hesitate in thus dissipating his earnings, if he were assured that, in either of these cases, his family must starve, or be left to the support of casual bounty." Thomas Malthus, *An Essay on the Principle of Population* (London: J. Johnson, 1798), 88.

3. This is paraphrased from Jon Elster, *Alexis de Tocqueville: The First Social Scientist* (Cambridge: Cambridge University Press, 2009), 155.

4. Poulantzas, *Political Power and Social Classes.*

5. Ralph Miliband, *The State in Capitalist Society* (London: Weidenfeld & Nicolson, 1969), 22; Paul Sweezy, *The Theory of Capitalist Development* (New York: Monthly Review Press, 1942).

6. Max Weber, *Economy and Society*, ed. Guenther Roth and Claus Wittich (Berkeley: University of California Press, 1978).

7. V. I. Lenin, *State and Revolution: Fully Annotated Edition* (Chicago: Haymarket Books, [1917] 2014).

8. Colin Barker, "The State as Capital," *International Socialism* 2, no. 1 (1978): 16–42.

9. As Poulantzas says, "The centralized unity of the State does not rest on a pyramid whose summit need only be occupied for effective control to be ensured." Nicos Poulantzas, *State, Power, Socialism* (London: New Left Books, 1978), 138.

10. The book is more a gesture toward certain insights than a comprehensive and internally coherent theory. Stuart Hall commented that "the book opens up a series of Pandora's boxes. Often, there is a too-swift attempt to secure their lids again, before their untamable genies escape. This produces a real theoretical unevenness in the book. Yet this unevenness also constitutes, by its reverse side, the stimulus of the book, its generative openness . . . He leaves us with a book which is, in many ways, clearly coming apart at the seams; where no single consistent theoretical framework is wide enough to embrace its internal diversity. It is *strikingly unfinished* . . . This is Poulantzas adventuring." Stuart Hall, "Nicos Poulantzas: *State, Power, Socialism,*" *New Left Review* 119 (1980): 68–9. And as Bob Jessop noted, *State, Power, Socialism* is "a provisional and transitional work." Bob Jessop, *Nicos Poulantzas: Marxist Theory and Political Strategy* (Basingstoke: Macmillan, 1985), 115.

11. Poulantzas's dual power characterization of Gramsci's state theory might be complicated by the recovery of Gramsci's concept of the integral state, which treats the state less as a citadel of capital and more like a dialectical unity between politics and civil society. See Peter D. Thomas, *Radical Politics: On the Causes of Contemporary Emancipation* (Oxford: Oxford University Press, 2023); Zachary Levenson, *Delivery as Dispossession: Land Occupation and Eviction in the Postapartheid City* (Oxford: Oxford University Press, 2022).

12. Poulantzas, *State, Power, Socialism*, 191.

13. Poulantzas does perform such an operation in two key texts, yet he fails to incorporate this into his general theory of capitalist states. Nicos Poulantzas, *The Crisis of the Dictatorships* (London: New Left, 1976); Nicos Poulantzas, *Fascism and Dictatorship* (London: New Left, 1974).

14. Nicos Poulantzas, "The Capitalist State: A Reply to Miliband and Laclau," *New Left Review* 95 (1976): 72.

15. Jessop, *Nicos Poulantzas*, 128–35.

16. Poulantzas, *State, Power, Socialism*, 256.

17. Ibid., 128.
18. Poulantzas, "The Capitalist State," 72.
19. Poulantzas, *State, Power, Socialism*, 132. This basic critique of relative autonomy is made powerfully by Bob Jessop in his intellectual biography, *Nicos Poulantzas*.
20. Terming it the "Frankenstein problem" was inspired by the sociologist Erik Olin Wright and can be found in his unpublished lecture notes on Claus Offe and the contradictory functionality of the state, some of which may be found at sscc.wisc.edu/soc/faculty/pages/ wright.
21. Erik Olin Wright, *How to Be an Anti-capitalist in the 21st Century* (London: Verso, 2019).
22. Claus Offe, *Contradictions of the Welfare State* (Cambridge, MA: MIT Press, 1984).
23. Ibid., 49.
24. This argument is made by James O'Connor in *The Fiscal Crisis of the State* (New York: St. Martin's Press, 1973).
25. Martijn Konings, "Contradictions of the Bailout State," in Vanessa Lemm and Miguel Vatter, eds., *The Viral Politics of Covid-19: Nature, Home, and Planetary Health* (New York: Palgrave Macmillan, 2022), 163–79.
26. Offe, *Contradictions of the Welfare State*, 50.
27. Offe, *Contradictions of the Welfare State*, 57–61.
28. Claus Offe and Helmut Wiesenthal, "Two Logics of Collective Action: Theoretical Notes on Social Class and Organizational Form," *Political Power and Social Theory* 1 (1980): 67–115.
29. C. Wright Mills, *The Power Elite* (Oxford: Oxford University Press, 1956); G. William Domhoff, *Who Rules America?* (New York: Prentice-Hall, 1967).
30. This is not to say that capitalists have homogenous interests. That they must also be "organized" via business associations and political parties into politics is a clear indication of their internal fault lines and potential points of conflict as a class. But capitalists are driven by a common goal—increasing profits. No such common goal defines membership in the working class.
31. A recent book that makes this theoretical error is Vivek Chibber, *The Class Matrix* (Cambridge, MA: Harvard University Press, 2022). For a systematic critique and alternative to the class abstractionist

perspective that I build upon here, see Michael A. McCarthy and Mathieu Hikaru Desan, "The Problem of Class Abstractionism," *Sociological Theory* 41, no. 1 (2023).

32. Göran Therborn, *The Ideology of Power and the Power of Ideology* (London: New Left Books, 1980), 18.

33. Matthew T. Huber, *Climate Change as Class War: Building Socialism on a Warming Planet* (London: Verso, 2022); Catherine Liu, *Virtue Hoarders: The Case against the Professional Managerial Class* (Minneapolis: University of Minnesota Press, 2021); Adaner Usmani and David Zachariah, "The Class Path to Racial Liberation," *Catalyst* 5, no. 3 (2021).

34. Gabriel Winant, "Professional Class Chasm," *N+1*, October 10, 2019; Erik Olin Wright, "Intellectuals and the Working Class," *Critical Sociology* 8, no. 1 (1978.): 5–18.

35. Erik Olin Wright, *Classes* (London: Verso, 1985), 9.

36. Erik Olin Wright, "Working-Class Power, Capitalist-Class Interests, and Class Compromise," *American Journal of Sociology* 105, no. 4 (2000): 957–1002.

37. Wright, *Classes*, 129; Erik Olin Wright, *The Debate on Classes* (London: Verso, 1989), 278.

38. Charmaine Chua, "Logistics," in Beverly Skeggs, Sarah Farris, and Alberto Toscano (eds.), *The Sage Handbook of Marxism* (London: Sage Publications, 2022), 1442–60.

39. Howard Botwinick, *Persistent Inequalities: Wage Disparity under Capitalist Competition* (Princeton, NJ: Princeton University Press, 1993).

40. Nicos Poulantzas, *The Poulantzas Reader: Marxism, Law, and the State*, ed. James Martin (London: Verso, 2008), 341.

41. Erik Olin Wright, *Envisioning Real Utopias* (London: Verso, 2010), 314.

42. In the same interview with Weber, Poulantzas suggested that he based his perspective on internal crises in the army, judiciary, and police (*The Poulantzas Reader*, 356). More important is his "second element" about introducing changes in the "structures of the state" (ibid.). He does not specify the precise conditions under which "structures of the state" are changed so as to produce a rupture, but in 1977 he suggested, again without elaboration, that the Common Programme being developed in France, which was adopted but then

subjected to a hard reversal under the socialist Mitterrand government, was precisely one such ruptural possibility.

43. Ilias Alami and Adam D. Dixon, *The Spectre of State Capitalism* (Oxford: Oxford University Press, 2024).

44. Poulantzas, *State, Power, Socialism*, 63.

45. Ellen Meiksins Wood, *Democracy against Capitalism: Renewing Historical Materialism* (Cambridge: Cambridge University Press, 1995); Ellen Meiksins Wood, *Empire of Capital* (London: Verso, 2003).

46. Nancy Fraser, *Cannibal Capitalism: How Our System Is Devouring Democracy, Care, and the Planet—and What We Can Do about It* (London: Verso, 2022).

3. A Primer

1. Aaron Benanav, *Automation and the Future of Work* (London: Verso, 2020); Robert Brenner, *The Economics of Global Turbulence* (London: Verso, 2006); Robert Brenner, "Escalating Plunder," *New Left Review* 123 (2000): 5–22; Cédric Durand, *Fictitious Capital: How Finance Is Appropriating Our Future* (London: Verso, 2014).

2. Gérard Duménil and Dominique Lévy, *Capital Resurgent: Roots of the Neoliberal Revolution*, trans. Derek Jeffers (Cambridge, MA: Harvard University Press, 2004); Katharina Pistor, *The Code of Capital: How the Law Creates Wealth and Inequality* (Princeton, NJ: Princeton University Press, 2019); Brett Christophers, *Our Lives in Their Portfolios: Why Asset Managers Own the World* (London: Verso, 2023).

3. Greta Krippner, *Capitalizing in Crisis* (Cambridge, MA: Harvard University Press, 2012).

4. As a measure of financial dominance, Brett Christophers has shown that value-added is not without its limitations. But the measure does point to profound organizational trends. Brett Christophers, "Making Finance Productive," *Economy and Society* 40, no. 1 (2011): 112–40.

5. Richard Davies, Peter Richardson, Vaiva Katinaite, and Mark Manning, "Evolution of the UK Banking System," *Bank of England Quarterly Bulletin*, Q4 2010.

6. Christophers, *Our Lives in Their Portfolios.*

7. Costas Lapavitsas, *Profiting without Producing: How Finance Exploits Us All* (London: Verso, 2014), 217.

8. Ibid., 219.

9. E. Stockhammer, "Financialization and the Slowdown of Accumulation," *Cambridge Journal of Economics* 28 (2004): 719–41; G. Krippner, *Capitalizing on Crisis* (Cambridge, MA: Harvard University Press, 2011).

10. H. Lin and D. Tomaskovic-Devey, "Financialization and US Income Inequality, 1970–2008," *American Journal of Sociology* 118 (2013): 1284–329; L. E. Davis, "The Financialization of the Nonfinancial Corporation in the Post-1970 U.S. Economy" (PhD diss., University of Massachusetts, Amherst, 2014).

11. Benjamin Braun and Daniela Gabor, "Central Banking, Shadow Banking, and Infrastructural Power," in Philip Mader, Daniel Mertens, and Natascha van der Zwan, eds., *The Routledge International Handbook of Financialization* (London: Routledge, 2020).

12. Adam Tooze, *Shutdown: How Covid Shook the World's Economy* (London: Penguin, 2021).

13. Lenore Palladino, "Financialization at Work: Shareholder Primacy and Stagnant Wages in the United States," *Competition and Change* 25, nos. 3–4 (2021): 382–400.

14. William Lazonick and Mary O'Sullivan, "Maximizing Shareholder Value: A New Ideology for Corporate Governance," *Economy and Society* 29, no. 1 (2000): 13–35.

15. C. Berry, *Pensions Imperiled: The Political Economy of Private Pensions Provision in the UK* (Oxford: Oxford University Press, 2020); Michael A. McCarthy, *Dismantling Solidarity: Capitalist Politics and American Pensions since the New Deal* (Ithaca, NY: Cornell University Press, 2017).

16. David H. Webber, *The Rise of the Working-Class Shareholder: Labor's Last Best Weapon* (Cambridge, MA: Harvard University Press, 2018).

17. Investment Company Institute, "Retirement Assets Total $39.9 Trillion in First Quarter 2024," press release, June 13, 2024, ici.org.

18. Mordor Intelligence, *United Kingdom Pension Fund Market Size and Share Analysis—Growth Trends and Forecasts (2024–2029)* (Hyderabad: Mordor Intelligence, 2024).

19. Teresa Ghilarducci, Joelle Saad Lessler, and Eloy Fisher, "The Macro-economic Stabilisation Effects of Social Security and 401(k) Plans," *Cambridge Journal of Economics* 36, no. 1 (2012): 237–51; Michael A. McCarthy, "Turning Labor into Capital: Pension Funds and the Corporate Control of Finance," *Politics and Society* 42, no. 4 (2014): 455–87; Michael A. McCarthy, *Dismantling Solidarity: Capitalist Politics and American Pensions since the New Deal* (Ithaca, NY: Cornell University Press, 2017).

20. Jeremy Rifkin and Randy Barber, *The North Will Rise Again: Pensions, Politics and Power in the 1980s* (Boston: Beacon Press, 1978), 100.

21. Neil Fligstein, *The Banks Did It: An Anatomy of the Financial Crisis* (Cambridge, MA: Harvard University Press, 2021); Adam Tooze, *Crashed: How a Decade of Crisis Changed the World* (New York: Viking, 2018).

22. William L. Silber, *Volcker: The Triumph of Persistence* (New York: Bloomsbury, 2012), 138.

23. Federal Reserve, "Record of Policy Actions of the Federal Open Market Committee," press release, September 23, 1977.

24. Milton Friedman, *The Counter-Revolution in Monetary Theory* (London: Institute of Economic Affairs, 1970).

25. Ho-fung Hung and Daniel Thompson, "Money Supply, Class Power, and Inflation: Monetarism Reassessed," *American Sociological Review* 81, no. 3 (2016): 447–66.

26. Paul A. Volcker, "Statement before the Committee on Banking, Finance, and Urban Affairs, U.S. House of Representatives, July 21, 1981," *Federal Reserve Bulletin* 614 (1981).

27. Paul A. Volcker, "Statement before the Joint Economic Committee of the U.S. Congress, January 26, 1982," *Federal Reserve Bulletin* 89 (1982).

28. Robert J. Samuelson, *The Great Inflation and Its Aftermath: The Past and Future of American Affluence* (New York: Random House, 2010), 110.

29. Gabriel Winant, *The Next Shift: The Fall of Industry and the Rise of Health Care in Rust Belt America* (Cambridge, MA: Harvard University Press, 2021).

30. Raymond Williams, *The Long Revolution* (New York: Columbia University Press, 1961), 48.

31. Kim Moody, *An Injury to All: The Decline of American Unionism* (London: Verso, 1988).

32. Andrew Elrod, "Stabilization Politics in the Twentieth-Century United States: Corporatism, Democracy, and Economic Planning, 1945–1980" (PhD diss., University of California, Santa Barbara, 2021).

33. Stuart Hall et al., *Policing the Crisis: Mugging, the State, and Law and Order* (London: Palgrave, 1978).

34. Leon Wansleben, *The Rise of Central Banks* (Cambridge, MA: Harvard University Press, 2023).

35. Tony Norfield, *The City: London and the Global Power of Finance* (London: Verso, 2016).

36. This has been described as "privatized Keynesianism." Colin Crouch, *The Strange Non-Death of Neo-Liberalism* (London: Polity Press, 2011).

37. Karen Dynan, "Changing Household Financial Opportunities and Economic Security," *Journal of Economic Perspectives* 23 (2009).

38. Daniel Harari, "Household Debt: Statistics and Impact on Economy," *House of Commons Briefing Paper* 7584, December 2018.

39. Susan Soederberg, *Debtfare States and the Poverty Industry: Money, Discipline and the Surplus Population* (Abington: Routledge, 2014).

40. Destin Jenkins, *The Bonds of Inequality: Debt and the Making of the American City* (Chicago: University of Chicago Press, 2021).

41. Keeanga-Yamahtta Taylor, *Race for Profit: How Banks and the Real Estate Industry Undermined Black Homeownership* (Chapel Hill: University of North Carolina Press, 2019), 11.

42. Lisa Adkins, Melinda Cooper, and Martijn Konings, *The Asset Economy* (London: Polity Press, 2020).

43. International Monetary Fund, "Household Debt to GDP for United States," Federal Reserve Bank of St. Louis, April 18, 2019.

44. Lapavitsas, *Profiting without Producing*.

45. Moritz Kuhn, Moritz Schularick, and Ulrike I. Steins, "Income and Wealth Inequality in American, 1949–2016," *Journal of Political Economy* 128, no. 9 (2020): 3469–519.

46. Federal Reserve, *2022 Survey of Consumer Finance* (Board of Governors of the Federal Reserve System, 2023).

47. Joseph Baines and Sandy Brian Hager, "COVID-19 and the Coming Corporate Debt Catastrophe," *Sandy Brian Hager* (blog), March 13, 2020, sbhager.com.

48. Joseph Baines and Sandy Brian Hager, "The Great Debt Divergence and Its Implications for the Covid-19 Crisis: Mapping Corporate Leverage as Power," *New Political Economy* 26, no. 5 (2021).

49. Serdar Çelik, Gül Demirtaş, and Mats Isaksson, *Corporate Bond Markets in a Time of Unconventional Monetary Policy* (Paris: OECD, 2019).

50. Board of Governors of the Federal Reserve System, "Financial Stability Report—May 2020," June 16, 2022, federalreserve.gov.

51. Teresa Ghilarducci, "The Recession Hurt Americans' Retirement Accounts More than Anybody Knew," *Atlantic*, October 15, 2015.

52. Teresa Ghilarducci, Joelle Saad-Lessler, and Eloy Fisher, "The Macroeconomic Stabilisation Effects of Social Security and 401(k) Plans," *Cambridge Journal of Economics* 36 (2012).

53. Hyman P. Minsky, *Stabilizing an Unstable Economy* (New York: McGraw-Hill, 2008 [1986]).

54. Brett Christophers, *The Price Is Wrong: Why Capitalism Won't Save the Planet* (London: Verso, 2024).

55. Stanley Reed, "Oil Giants Pump Their Way to Bumper Profits," *New York Times*, February 2, 2024.

56. Attracta Mooney, "The $9tn Question: How to Pay for the Green Transition," *Financial Times*, May 5, 2024.

57. Harriet Agnew, Adrienne Klasa, and Simon Mundy, "How ESG Investing Came to a Reckoning," *Financial Times*, June 6, 2022.

58. Will Schmitt, "Launches of ESG Funds Plummet as Investors Pull Back," *Financial Times*, January 9, 2024.

59. Patrick Tempe-West and Brook Masters, "JPMorgan and State Street Quit Climate Group as BlackRock Scales Back," *Financial Times*, February 15, 2024.

4. Financial Plunder

1. Joshua Cohen and Joel Rogers, *On Democracy* (New York: Penguin, 1983).

2. Göran Therborn, *What Does the Ruling Class Do When It Rules?* (London: New Left Books, 1978).

3. Elisabeth Jean Wood, *Forging Democracy from Below: Insurgent Transitions in South Africa and El Salvador* (Cambridge: Cambridge University Press, 2000).

4. Sam Ashman, Ben Fine, and Susan Newman, "Amnesty International? The Nature, Scale and Impact of Capital Flight from South Africa," *Journal of Southern African Studies* 37, no. 1 (March 2011).

5. Carles Boix, *Democracy and Redistribution* (Cambridge: Cambridge University Press, 2010), 41.

6. Ibid.

7. Quinn Slobodian, *Crack-Up Capitalism: Market Radicals and the Dream of a World without Democracy* (New York: Metropolitan Books, 2023).

8. Adam Smith, *The Wealth of Nations* (New York: Penguin Books, 1999).

9. Duane Swank, "Funding the Welfare State: Globalization and the Taxation of Business in Advanced Market Economies," *Political Studies* 46 (1998): 671–92; Alexander Hicks and Duane Swank, "Politics, Institutions and Social Welfare Spending in the Industrialized Democracies, 1960–1982," *American Political Science Review* 86 (1992): 658–74.

10. See Timothy Mitchell, *Carbon Democracy: Political Power in the Age of Coal* (London: Verso, 2011). Mitchell shows that coal concentrated production, which made energy chokepoints, created the possibility of more effective labor strikes and the basis for democratic-claim making by workers whereas the rise of oil led to a more diffuse and globally mobile production process, which disrupted this worker power by allowing oil companies to circumvent and avoid labor laws and democratic demands.

11. Victor Serge, *Year One of the Russian Revolution*, (London: Pluto Press, 1992).

12. W. E. B. Du Bois, *Black Reconstruction in America 1860–1880* (New York: Scribner Books, 1935).

13. Ibid., 30.

14. Adam Przeworski and John Sprague, *Paper Stones: A History of Electoral Socialism* (Chicago: University of Chicago Press, 1986).

15. Barbara Stallings, *Class Conflict and Economic Development in Chile, 1958–1973* (Stanford, CA: Stanford University Press, 1978), 35; Maurice Zeitlin and Richard Radcliff, *Landlords and Capitalists: The Dominant Class in Chile* (Princeton, NJ: Princeton University Press, 1988).

16. Stallings, *Class Conflict and Economic Development*, 43.

17. Richard Minns, *Take Over the City: The Case for Public Owner-ship of Financial Institutions* (London: Pluto Press, 1982), 57–60.

18. Peter A. Hall, *Governing the Economy: The Politics of State Intervention in Britain and France* (Oxford: Oxford University Press, 1986).

19. C. Wright Mills, *The Power Elite* (Oxford: Oxford University Press, 1956); G. William Domhoff, *The Power Elite and the State: How Policy Is Made in America* (New York: De Gruyter, 1990); G. William Domhoff and Michael J. Webber, *Class and Power in the New Deal: Corporate Moderates, Southern Democrats and the Liberal-Labor Coalition* (Stanford, CA: Stanford University Press, 2011).

20. Dan Clawson and Alan Neustadtl, "Interlocks, PACs and Corporate Conservatism," *American Journal of Sociology* 94, no. 4 (1989): 749–73.

21. Jacob S. Hacker and Paul Pierson, *Winner-Take-All Politics: How Washington Made the Rich Richer—and Turned Its Back on the Middle Class* (New York: Simon & Schuster, 2010).

22. Dan Clawson, Alan Neustadtl, and Mark Weller, *Dollars and Votes: How Business Campaign Contributions Subvert Democracy* (Philadelphia: Temple University Press, 1998); Thomas Ferguson, *Golden Rule: The Investment Theory of Party Competition and the Logic of Money-Driven Political Systems* (Chicago: University of Chicago Press, 1995); Martin Gilens, *Affluence and Influence: Economic Inequality and Political Power in America* (Princeton, NJ: Princeton University Press, 2012).

23. Claus Offe and Helmut Wiesenthal, "Two Logics of Collective Action: Theoretical Notes on Social Class and Organizational Form," *Political Power and Social Theory* 1, no. 1 (1980).

24. Nelson D. Schwartz, "Financial Leaders Expect Shift of Power after Elections," *New York Times*, November 1, 2010.

25. "Finance/Insurance/Real Estate Sector Summary," OpenSecrets, opensecrets.org.

26. Fred Block, "The Ruling Class Does Not Rule," *Socialist Revolution* 33 (May–June 1977); Charles Lindblom, *Politics and Markets: The World's Political-Economic Systems* (New York: Basic Books, 1977); Manolis Kalaitzake, "Structural Power without the Structure: A

Class-Centered Challenge to New Structural Power Formulations," *Politics and Society* 50, no. 4 (2022): 266–87.

27. Kevin Young, "Not by Structure Alone: Power, Prominence, and Agency in American Finance," *Business and Politics* 17, no. 3 (October 2015): 443–72, 448.

28. Nicos Poulantzas, *Political Power and Social Classes* (London: New Left Books, 1973); Nicos Poulantzas, *State, Power, Socialism* (London: New Left Books, 1978); Ralph Miliband, *Marxism and Politics* (Oxford: Oxford University Press, 1977).

29. Rogers and Cohen refer to this as the "demand constraint" (*On Democracy*).

30. Charles E. Lindblom, "The Market as Prison," *Journal of Politics* 44, no. 2 (1982): 324–36.

31. Jane F. McAlevey, *No Shortcuts: Organizing for Power in the New Gilded Age* (Oxford: Oxford University Press, 2016).

32. Kevin Young, Tarun Banerjee, and Michael Schwartz, *Levers of Power: How the 1% Rules and What the 99% Can Do about It* (London: Verso, 2018).

33. Cornelia Woll, *The Power of Inaction: Bank Bailouts in Comparison* (Ithaca, NY: Cornell University Press, 2014).

34. Jeffrey A. Winters, *Power in Motion: Capital Mobility and the Indonesian State* (Ithaca, NY: Cornell University Press, 1996).

35. Stephen R. Gill and David Law, "Global Hegemony and the Structural Power of Capital," *International Studies Quarterly* 33, no. 4 (December 1989): 475–99, 481.

36. James Meadway, *Why We Need a New Macroeconomic Strategy* (London: New Economics Foundation, 2013).

37. Hedge Clippers, "Hurricane Harvard and the Damage Done to Puerto Rico," Hedge Papers, no. 54, January 23, 2018, hedgeclippers.org.

38. Pepper D. Culpepper and Raphael Reinke, "Structural Power and Bank Bailouts in the United Kingdom and the United States," *Politics and Society* 42, no. 4 (2014). See also Woll, *The Power of Inaction*.

39. Michael Mann, "The Autonomous Power of the State: Its Origins, Mechanisms and Results," *European Journal of Sociology* 25, no. 2 (1984): 185–213, 208.

40. Ibid., 209.

41. Michael Mann, "Infrastructural Power Reconsidered," *Studies in Comparative International Development* 43 (2008).

42. Benjamin Braun, "Central Banking and the Infrastructural Power of Finance: The Case of ECB Support for Repo and Securitization Markets," *Socio-Economic Review* 18, no. 2 (April 2020); Marius R. Busemeyer and Kathleen Thelen, "Institutional Sources of Business Power," *World Politics* 72, no. 3 (2020): 448–80.

43. Benjamin Braun and Daniela Gabor, "Central Banking, Shadow Banking and Infrastructural Power," in Philip Mader, Daniel Mertens, and Natascha van der Zwan, eds., *The Routledge International Handbook of Financialization* (London: Routledge, 2020), 241–53.

44. Daniela Gabor, "A Step Too Far? The European Financial Transactions Tax on Shadow Banking," *Journal of European Public Policy* 23, no. 6 (2016).

45. "Nonfinancial Corporate Business; Debt Securities; Liability, Level," Federal Reserve Economic Data, fred.stlouisfed.org.

46. Bank of England Financial Policy Committee, "Financial Stability in Focus: The Corporate Sector and UK Financial Stability," October 2021; Bank of England, "The Impact of the Covid Pandemic on SME Indebtedness," November 2021.

47. Robin Wigglesworth, "Graphic: The New Corporate Debt Market," *Financial Times*, January 22, 2019.

48. Kevin Young and Stefano Pagliari, "Capital United? Business Unity in Regulatory Politics and the Special Place of Finance," *Regulation and Governance* 11, no. 1 (2017): 3–23; Kevin L. Young and Stefano Pagliari, "Lobbying to the Rhythm of Wall Street? Explaining the Political Advocacy of Non-financial Corporations over Financial Regulatory Policy," *Socio-Economic Review* 20, no. 2 (April 2022): 659–85.

49. Young and Pagliari ("Lobbying to the Rhythm of Wall Street?") argue that an even greater determinant of nonfinancial corporation activism on behalf of financial firms is the embeddedness in broader corporate networks, particularly business associations, which include other firms that are already advocating for finance. This underscores the way in which each of the forms of power explored here are intertwined with one another.

50. Peter Gowan, *The Global Gamble: Washington's Faustian Bid for World Dominance* (London: Verso, 1999).

51. Jerome Roos, *Why Not Default? The Political Economy of Sovereign Debt* (Princeton, NJ: Princeton University Press, 2019).

52. Ellen Meiksins Wood, *Empire of Capital* (London: Verso, 2005).

53. Benjamin J. Cohen, *Currency Power* (Princeton, NJ: Princeton University Press, 2015), 23; Jonathan Kirshner, *Currency and Coercion* (Princeton, NJ: Princeton University Press, 1997).

54. Cohen, *Currency Power*, 48.

55. Ibid., 55.

5. Mythologies

1. Ursula K. Le Guin, "97. Utopiyin, Utopiyang," *Ursula K. Le Guin* (blog), April 2015, ursulakleguin.com.

2. Robert J. Shiller, *Finance and the Good Society* (Princeton, NJ: Princeton University Press, 2013), 5.

3. Antonio Gramsci, *The Prison Notebooks* (New York: International Publishers, 1971), 275–6.

4. Stefan Eich, "Old Utopias, New Tax Havens: The Politics of Bitcoin in Historical Perspective," in Philipp Hacker, Ioannis Lianos, Georgios Dimitropoulos, and Stefan Eich, eds., *Regulating Blockchain: Techno-Social and Legal Challenges* (Oxford: Oxford University Press, 2019).

5. John Holloway, *Change the World without Taking Power: The Meaning of Revolution Today* (London: Pluto Press, 2002).

6. See David Golumbia, *The Politics of Bitcoin: Software as Right-Wing Extremism* (Minneapolis: University of Minnesota Press, 2016); Finn Brunton, *Digital Cash: The Unknown History of the Anarchists, Utopians, and Technologists Who Created Cryptocurrency* (Princeton, NJ: Princeton University Press, 2019).

7. Robert Hockett, "Money's Past Is Fintech's Future: Wildcat Crypto, the Digital Dollar, and Citizen Central Banking," *Stanford Journal of Blockchain Law and Policy*, June 28, 2019.

8. "El Salvador's Bitcoin Experiment Is Not Paying Off," *Economist*, November 17, 2022, economist.com.

9. Robert Hockett, "Finance Without Financiers," in Fred Block and Robert Hockett, eds., *Democratizing Finance: Restructuring Credit to Transform Society* (London: Verso, 2022), 23–79.

10. Brunton, *Digital Cash*, 151.

11. Laura Shin, *The Cryptopians: Idealism, Greed, Lies, and the Making of the First Big Cryptocurrency Craze* (New York: Public Affairs, 2022).

12. Nathan Schneider, "Crypto's Section 230: A Policy Platform for DAOs," Mirror, January 16, 2023, ntnsndr.mirror.xyz.

13. Kevin Owocki, *GreenPilled: How Crypto Can Regenerate the World* (San Francisco: Blurb Books, 2023), 11.

14. Ibid., 22.

15. Ibid., 41.

16. Josh Blaylock, "Anon vs Moloch: The Greatest LARP Has Begun," *GitCoin* 2 (2021).

17. "Slaying Moloch: Ameen Soleimani and Kevin Owocki," *Bankless* (podcast), episode 33, October 5, 2020, bankless.com.

18. Karl Marx, *Theories of Surplus Value* (Amherst, NY: Prometheus Books, 2000 [1863]), part 3, 592.

19. Richard A. Posner and E. Glen Weyl, *Radical Markets: Uprooting Capitalism and Democracy for a Just Society* (Princeton, NJ: Princeton University Press, 2019).

20. "Collective Decision Making with Matt Prewitt," *GreenPill* (podcast), episode 25, July 7, 2022.

21. Glen Weyl, Puja Ohlhaver, and Vitalik Buterin, "Decentralized Society: Finding Web3's Soul," ssrn.com, May 11, 2022.

22. "How Soulbound Tokens Can Make Gitcoin Grants More Pluralistic," Gitcoin, March 2022, gov.gitcoin.co.

23. "Fractal Sovereignty with Tracheopteryx," *GreenPill* (podcast), episode 5, March 17, 2022.

24. Marcell Mauss. *The Gift: Forms and Functions of Exchange in Archaic Societies* (New York: W. W. Norton, 2000).

25. Gail Weinstein, Steven Lofchie, and Jason Schwartz, "A Primer on DAOs," Harvard Law School Forum on Corporate Governance, September 17, 2022, corpgov.law.harvard.edu.

26. Igor Makarov and Antoinette Schoar, "Blockchain Analysis of the Bitcoin Market," National Bureau of Economic Research, working paper 29396, October 2021, nber.org.

27. Vitalik Buterin, "Governance, Part 2: Plutocracy Is Still Bad," *Vitalik Buterin's Website* (blog), March 28, 2018, vitalik.eth.limo.

28. Elizabeth Anderson, *Private Government: How Employers Rule Our Lives* (Princeton, NJ: Princeton University Press, 2019).

29. Will MacAskill, *Doing Good Better* (New York: Avery, 2015); Peter Singer, *The Most Good You Can Do* (New Haven, CT: Yale University Press, 2015).

30. Lana Swartz, *New Money: How Payment Became Social Media* (New Haven, CT: Yale University Press, 2020).

31. Anna Weichselbraun, "What's Governing Web3" (lecture, University of Southern California, Center of Science, Technology, and Public Life, February 1, 2023).

32. Randy Martin, *Financialization of Daily Life* (New York: Temple University Press, 2002).

33. Nicos Poulantzas, *State, Power, Socialism* (London: Verso Books, 1980), 63.

34. Ibid., 65.

35. Dylan Riley, *Microverses* (London: Verso, 2022).

6. Class Logics of Reform

1. Nina Bandelj, "Emotions in Economic Action and Interaction," *Theory and Society* 38, no. 4 (2009): 347–66.

2. Christian Olaf Christiansen, *Progressive Business: An Intellectual History of the Role of Business in American Society* (Oxford: Oxford University Press, 2016).

3. Larry Fink, "Larry Fink's 2018 Letter to CEOs: A Sense of Purpose," blackrock.com, January 12, 2018.

4. Eugene Fama, "Efficient Capital Markets: A Review of Theory and Empirical Work," *Journal of Finance* 25, no. 2 (1970).

5. Committee on Workers' Capital, *CWC Guidelines for the Evaluation of Workers' Human Rights and Labour Standards* (Vancouver: CWC, 2017), workerscapital.org.

6. Gunnar Friede, Timo Busch, and Alexander Bassen, "ESG and Financial Performance: Aggregated Evidence from More Than 2000 Empirical Studies," *Journal of Sustainable Finance and Investment* 5, no. 4 (2015).

7. David Wood, "Discussion Paper: Why and How Might Investors Respond to Economic Inequality?," Principles for Responsible Investment, November 2016, unpri.org.

8. David S. Lee and Alexandre Mas, "Long-Run Impacts of Unions on Firms: New Evidence from Financial Markets, 1961–1999," *Quarterly Journal of Economics* 127, no. 1 (2012).

9. Robert Smith, Simeon Kerr, and Joe Rennison, "Orders for First Saudi Aramco Bond Smash $100bn," *Financial Times*, April 9, 2019.

10. Adam Tooze, *Crashed: How a Decade of Crisis Changed the World* (New York: Viking, 2018).

11. Anat R. Admanti, "Toward a Better Financial System," Economics for Inclusive Prosperity, Policy Brief 2, February 2019.

12. Royal Commission into Misconduct in the Banking, Superannuation and Financial Services Industry, *Final Report*, Commonwealth of Australia, 2019, royalcommission.gov.au.

13. Mark Blyth, "The Politics of Compounding Bubbles: The Global Housing Bubble in Comparative Perspective," *Comparative European Politics* 6, no. 3 (2008): 387–406; Claudio Borio, "The Financial Cycle and Macroeconomics: What Have We Learnt?," Bank of International Settlements Working Paper no. 395 (2012).

14. Matthias Thiemann, "Macro-Prudential Regulation Post-Crisis and the Resilience of Financialization," in Philip Mader, Daniel Mertens, and Natascha van der Zwan, eds., *The Routledge International Handbook of Financialization* (London: Routledge, 2020), 468–81.

15. Thomas Herndon and Mark Paul, *A Public Banking Option as a Mode of Regulation for Financial Services in the United States* (Roosevelt Institute, 2018), rooseveltinstitute.org.

16. Christine Barry and Laurie Macfarlane, *A New Public Banking Ecosystem: A Report to the Labour Party* (Communication Workers Union and the Democracy Collaborative, 2019).

17. Robin Blackburn, "The Corbyn Project: Public Capital and Labour's New Deal," *New Left Review* 111 (May/June 2018): 14.

18. Lenore Palladino, "A Public Option for Asset Management in the United States," Roosevelt Institute, 2022.

19. Lenore Palladino, "Financialization at Work: Shareholder Primacy and Stagnant Wages in the United States," *Competition and Change* 25, nos. 3–4 (2021): 382–400.

20. Hannah Zhang, "China's Sovereign Wealth Funds: Too Big to Be Ignored," *Institutional Investor*, February 1, 2022; "Top 100 Largest Sovereign Wealth Fund Rankings by Total Assets," Sovereign Wealth Fund Institute, swfinstitute.org.

21. Patrick Mathurin, "Sovereign Wealth Funds Search for New Investments," *Financial Times*, August 18, 2018.

22. Matt Bruenig, *Social Wealth Fund for America* (People's Policy Project, 2018), 36–43.

23. Reda Cherif and Fuad Hasanov, "The Return of the Policy That Shall Not Be Named: Principles of Industrial Policy," International Monetary Fund Working Paper no. 2019/074, March 26, 2019.

24. Brad Plumer and Lisa Friedman, "A Swaggering Clean-Energy Pioneer, with $400 Billion to Hand Out," *New York Times*, May 11, 2023.

25. Lee Harris, "Who Will De-risk US Farming's Green Tech Breakthrough?," *Financial Times*, June 3, 2024.

26. Robert C. Hockett and Saule T. Omarova, "Private Wealth and Public Goods: A Case for a National Investment Authority," *Journal of Corporation Law* 43, no. 3 (2018): 437–90; Saule Omarova, "The National Investment Authority: A Blueprint," Berggruen Institute White Paper, March 23, 2022.

27. Angela Cummine, *Citizens' Wealth: Why (and How) Sovereign Funds Should Be Managed by the People for the People* (New Haven, CT: Yale University Press, 2016).

28. Michael Brennan, "Constructing the Democratic Public Bank: A Governance Proposal for Los Angeles," Democracy Collaborative, 2021, democracycollaborative.org; Thomas Marois, *Public Banks: Decarbonisation, Definancialisation and Democratisation* (Cambridge: Cambridge University Press, 2021); Michael A. McCarthy, "The Politics of Democratizing Finance: A Radical View," *Politics and Society* 47, no. 4 (2019): 611–33; Michael A. McCarthy, "Municipal Bank of LA: Democratic Governance Frameworks," Berggruen Institute / Jain Family Institute Working Paper, May 2023.

29. Marois, *Public Banks*, 206.

30. Mathew Lawrence and Loren King, "Examining the Inclusive Ownership Fund: Briefing Note," Common Wealth, November 13, 2019, common-wealth.org; Adrienne Buller and Mathew Lawrence, *Owning the Future: Power and Property in an Age of Crisis* (London: Verso, 2022).

31. Rajeev Syal, "Employees to Be Handed Stakes in Firms under Labour Plan," *Guardian*, September 24, 2018.

32. Rudolf Meidner, *Employee Investment Funds: An Approach to Collective Capital Formation* (London: Allen & Unwin, 1978).

33. Ministry of Finance, *Employee Investment Funds* (Stockholm: Ministry of Finance, 1984).

34. Philip Whyman, "Post-Keynesianism, Socialization of Investment and Swedish Wage-Earner Funds," *Cambridge Journal of Economics* 30, no. 1 (2006).

35. David Webber, *The Rise of the Working-Class Shareholder: Labor's Last Best Weapon* (Cambridge, MA: Harvard University Press, 2018).

36. Natascha van der Zwan, "Contentious Capital: The Politics of Pension Investment in the United States and Germany, 1974–2003" (PhD diss., New School for Social Research, New York, 2011).

37. Benjamin Braun and Daniela Gabor, "Central Banking, Shadow Banking and Infrastructure Power," in Philip Mader, Daniel Mertens, and Natascha van der Zwan, eds., *The Routledge International Handbook of Financialization* (London: Routledge, 2020), 241–53.

38. Matthew C. Klein, "Corbyn's 'People's QE' Could Actually Be a Decent Idea," *Financial Times*, August 6, 2015.

39. Fred Moseley, "The Bailout of the 'Too Big to Fail' Banks: Never Again," in Martin H. Wolfson and Gerald Epstein, eds., *The Handbook of the Political Economy of Financial Crisis* (New York: Oxford University Press, 2013), 624–44.

40. Gar Alperovitz, "Nationalize Banks That Overwhelm Regulation," *New York Times*, January 13, 2014; Thomas Hanna, *The Crisis Next Time: Planning for Public Ownership as an Alternative to Corporate Bank Bailouts* (Democracy Collaborative, 2018), democracycollaborative.org.

41. Mariana Mazzucato and Caetano Penna, "Beyond Market Failures: The Market Creating and Shaping Roles of State Investment Banks," Institute for New Economic Thinking Working Paper Series No. 7, 2014), available at ssrn.com.

42. Robert Pollin, "Tools for a New Economy: Proposals for a Financial Regulatory System," *Boston Review*, January/February 2009, 13.

43. Daniela Gabor, "The Wall Street Consensus," *Development and Change* 52, no. 3 (2021): 429–59.

44. Adrienne Buller, *The Value of a Whale* (Manchester: Manchester University Press, 2022), 150.

45. Emile Durkheim, *The Division of Labor in Society* (New York: Free Press, 1893).

46. Anya Degenshein, "The Object Economy: 'Alternative' Banking in Chicago," *Contexts* 19, no. 1 (2020): 18–23.

47. Laurie Macfarlane and Mariana Mazzucato, "State Investment Banks and Patient Finance: An International Comparison," UCL Institute for Innovation and Public Purpose, working paper 2018-01, 2018.

48. I owe the distinction between redistributive and hegemonic politics to Dylan Riley, who laid them out in a public lecture in Greece: Dylan Riley, "What Next? The End of Democratic Capitalism and the Tasks of the Left," livestreamed September 16, 2022, RosaLuxemburgStiftung AthensOffice, youtube.com.

49. Bob Jessop, *The Future of the Capitalist State* (Oxford: Polity Press, 2002).

50. Rune Møller Stahl, "Ruling the Interregnum: Politics and Ideology in Nonhegemonic Times," *Politics and Society* 47, no. 3 (2019): 333–60.

7. Minipublics

1. Robert A. Dahl, *Democracy and Its Critics* (New Haven, CT: Yale University Press, 1991), 119–31.

2. Carole Pateman, *Participation and Democratic Theory* (Cambridge: Cambridge University Press, 1970), 106.

3. Ibid., 108.

4. I offer this scheme for understanding democratic participation in a highly simplified way and paint in broad brush strokes in order to illustrate my main points. Archon Fung's work on "the democracy cube" includes a gradational scale for both dimensions and also offers up a third dimension on the authority and power of democratic participants (Archon Fung, "Varieties of Participation in Complex Governance," *Public Administration Review* 66 [2006]: 66–75). A fuller exploration of the kinds of democratic institutions that would best democratize financial flows would need a more fine-grained analysis along the lines that Fung offers. Here, however, I use these distinctions mainly as a heuristic to understand democratic participation in public finance in general terms.

5. Joseph Schumpeter, *Capitalism, Socialism and Democracy* (New York: Harper & Brothers, 1942), 242; his emphasis.

6. Ibid., 269.

7. Pateman, *Participation and Democratic Theory*, 104.

8. Fung, "Varieties of Participation in Complex Governance."

9. Ziva Kunda, "The Case for Motivated Reasoning," *Psychological Bulletin* 108, no. 3 (1990): 480–98.

10. Rune Slothuus and Claes H. de Vreese, "Political Parties, Motivated Reasoning, and Issue Framing Effects," *Journal of Politics* 72 (2010): 630–45; Ian Haney Lopez, *Merge Left: Fusing Race and Class, Winning Elections and Saving America* (New York: New Press, 2019).

11. Susan P. Shapiro, "Agency Theory," *Annual Review of Sociology* 31 (2005): 263–84.

12. Peter Drucker, *The Unseen Revolution* (New York: Butterworth-Heinemann, 1976).

13. Adolf Berle and Gardiner Means, *The Modern Corporation and Private Property* (New York: Transaction Publishers, 1932).

14. Pepper D. Culpepper, *Quiet Politics* (Cambridge: Cambridge University Press, 2012).

15. Martin Gilens, *Affluence and Influence: Economic Inequality and Political Power in America* (Princeton, NJ: Princeton University Press, 2012).

16. Bernard Manin, *The Principles of Representative Government* (Cambridge: Cambridge University Press, 1997), 23.

17. Gianpaolo Baiocchi and Ernesto Ganuza, "Participatory Budgeting as if Emancipation Mattered," *Politics and Society* 42, no. 1 (2014): 29–50.

18. Archon Fung and Erik Olin Wright, "Thinking about Empowered Participatory Governance," in Archon Fung and Erik Olin Wright, eds., *Deepening Democracy: Institutional Innovations and Empowered Participatory Governance* (London: Verso, 2003), 11.

19. John Gastil, *Democracy in Small Groups: Participation, Decision Making, and Communication* (Philadelphia: New Society Publishers, 1993).

20. Helene Landemore, *Open Democracy: Reinventing Popular Rule for the 21st Century* (Princeton, NJ: Princeton University Press, 2020).

21. Bernard Manin, Elly Stein, and Jane Mansbridge, "On Legitimacy and Political Deliberation," *Political Theory* 15, no. 3 (1987): 338–68.

22. Gianpaolo Baiocchi and Ernesto Ganuza, *Popular Democracy: The Paradox of Participation* (Palo Alto, CA: Stanford University Press, 2017).

23. Josiah Ober, *The Athenian Revolution: Essays on Ancient Greek Democracy and Political Theory* (Princeton, NJ: Princeton University Press, 1996), 32–52.
24. G. E. M. de Ste. Croix, *The Class Struggle in the Ancient Greek World* (Ithaca, NY: Cornell University Press, 1981), 289.
25. Aristotle, *The Athenian Constitution* (New York: Penguin, 1984), 96.
26. James S. Fishkin, *Democracy When the People Are Thinking: Revitalizing Our Politics Through Public Deliberation* (Oxford: Oxford University Press, 2018).
27. Aristotle, *Athenian Constitution*, 108.
28. Ibid., 80.
29. Perry Anderson, *Passages from Antiquity to Feudalism* (London: New Left Books, 1974).
30. Andrew Lintott, *The Constitution of the Roman Republic* (Oxford: Oxford University Press, 1999), 50.
31. Yves Winter, "Plebeian Politics: Machiavelli and the Ciompi Uprising," *Political Theory* 40, no. 6 (2012): 736–66.
32. Bernard Manin, *The Principles of Representative Government* (Cambridge: Cambridge University Press, 1997), 54.
33. John M. Najemy, *Corporatism and Consensus in Florentine Electoral Politics, 1280–1400* (Chapel Hill: University of North Carolina Press, 1982).
34. Frederic C. Lane, *Venice: A Maritime Republic* (Baltimore, MD: Johns Hopkins University Press, 1973), 110.
35. Alex Guerrero, "Against Elections: The Lottocratic Alternative," *Philosophy and Public Affairs* 42 (2014): 135–78; David Van Reybrouck, *Against Elections: The Case for Democracy* (London: Bodley Head, 2016).
36. John Gastil and Erik Olin Wright, *Legislature by Lot: Transformative Designs for Deliberative Governance* (London: Verso, 2019); Landemore, *Open Democracy*; John P. McCormick, *Machiavellian Democracy* (Cambridge: Cambridge University Press, 2011).
37. Mark E. Warren and John Gastil, "Can Deliberative Minipublics Address the Cognitive Challenges of Democratic Citizenship?," *Journal of Politics* 77, no. 2 (2015): 562–74; David M. Estlund, *Democratic Authority: A Philosophical Framework* (Princeton, NJ: Princeton University Press, 2007).
38. Slothuus and de Vreese, "Political Parties, Motivated Reasoning."

39. Kristinn Már and John Gastil, "Tracing the Boundaries of Motivated Reasoning: How Deliberative Minipublics Can Improve Voter Knowledge," *Political Psychology* 41, no. 1 (2020): 107–27.

40. Lu Hong and Scott E. Page, "Groups of Diverse Problem Solvers Can Outperform Groups of High-Ability Problem Solvers," *Proceedings of the National Academy of Sciences* 101, no. 46 (2004): 16385–9.

41. Audre Lorde, *The Master's Tools Will Never Dismantle the Master's House* (New York: Penguin, 2017).

42. Helene Landemore, *Democratic Reason* (Princeton, NJ: Princeton University Press, 2012), 90.

43. Arash Abizadeh, "Representation, Bicameralism, Political Equality, and Sortition: Reconstituting the Second Chamber as a Randomly Selected Assembly," *Perspectives on Politics*, January 10, 2020.

44. Aristotle, *The Politics and the Constitution of Athens* (Cambridge: Cambridge University Press, 1984), 88.

45. Alex Zakaras, "Lot and Democratic Representation," *Constellations* 17 (2010): 455–71.

46. OECD, *Innovative Citizen Participation and New Democratic Institutions: Catching the Deliberative Wave* (OECD, 2020).

47. Christoph Niessen and Min Reuchamps, *Designing a Permanent Deliberative Citizens Assembly: The Ostbelgien Modell in Belgium* (Canberra: Centre for Deliberative Democracy and Global Governance, 2019).

48. Claudia Chwalisz, "A Movement That's Quietly Reshaping Democracy for the Better," *Noema Magazine*, May 12, 2022.

8. Plebeian Recipes

1. Karl Marx, *Capital*, vol. 1 (London: Penguin, 1976), 99.

2. Ibid.

3. In *The German Ideology*, Marx and Engels also wrote, "Communism is for us not a state of affairs which is to be established, an ideal to which reality [will] have to adjust itself. We call communism the real movement which abolishes the present state of things. The conditions of this movement result from the premises now in existence." Karl Marx and Friedrich Engels, *The German Ideology* (New York: Prometheus Books, 1998), 57.

4. Robert E. Goodin, "Enfranchising All Affected Interests, and Its Alternatives," *Philosophy and Public Affairs* (2007): 40–68, 40.
5. Ibid., 43.
6. Joseph Schumpeter, *Capitalism, Socialism and Democracy* (New York: Harper & Brothers, 1942), 244.
7. Robert Dahl, *After the Revolution?* (New Haven, CT: Yale University Press, 1990), 64.
8. For an elaboration of this narrower view see Archon Fung, "The Principle of Affected Interests and Inclusion in Democratic Governance," in Jack Nagel and Rogers Smith, eds., *Representation: Elections and Beyond* (Philadelphia: University of Pennsylvania Press, 2013), 236–68, 247.
9. Ibid., 253.
10. Ibid., 254.
11. Johannes Althusius, *Politica Methodice Digesta* (Cambridge, MA: Harvard University Press, 1932).
12. Jonathan S. Blake and Nils Gilman, *Children of a Modest Star: Governance for a Planetary Age* (Stanford, CA: Stanford University Press, 2024).
13. See Camila Vergara's discussion of the debate between Rosa Luxemburg and V. I. Lenin in Camila Vergara, *Systemic Corruption: Constitutional Ideas for an Anti-oligarchic Republic* (Princeton, NJ: Princeton University Press, 2020), 175–81.
14. Elinour Ostrom, *Governing the Commons: The Evolution of Institutions for Collective Action* (Cambridge: Cambridge University Press, 1990).
15. Carl Schmitt, *The Concept of the Political* (Chicago: University of Chicago Press, 2007).
16. Ernesto Laclau, *On Populist Reason* (London: Verso, 2017), 83.
17. Ibid.
18. Chantal Mouffe, *The Return of the Political* (London: Verso, 1993), 6.
19. Chantal Mouffe, *The Democratic Paradox* (London: Verso, 2005).
20. Chantal Mouffe, *Agonistics: Thinking the World Politically* (London: Verso, 2013), 3.
21. Gordon Arlen, "Aristotle and the Problem of Oligarchic Harm: Insights for Democracy," *European Journal of Political Theory* 18 (2019): 393–414; McCormick, *Machiavellian Democracy*; Andreas Møller Mulvad and Rune Møller Stahl, "Civilizing Left Populism:

Towards a Theory of Plebeian Democracy," *Constellations* 26 (2019): 591–606; Vergara, *Systemic Corruption*.

22. James Green, *Shadow of Unfairness: A Plebeian Theory of Liberal Democracy* (Oxford: Oxford University Press, 2016), 9.

23. Niccolo Machiavelli, *Discourses on Livy* (Chicago: University of Chicago Press, 1998), Book 1, Chapter 5, 31–2.

24. McCormick, *Machiavellian Democracy*, 106.

25. Vergara, *Systemic Corruption*, 242.

26. Niccolo Machiavelli, *Florentine Histories* (Princeton, NJ: Princeton University Press, 1988), 122–3.

27. McCormick, *Machiavellian Democracy*.

28. Ibid., 184.

29. Vergara, *Systemic Corruption*, 227, 244.

30. Ibid., 245.

31. Ibid., 12.

32. Mulvad and Stahl, "Civilizing Left Populism," 589.

33. Vincent Harting, "An Egalitarian Case for Class-Specific Political Institutions," *Political Theory* (2023).

34. Camila Vergara, "Towards Material Anti-oligarchic Constitutionalism," *Revus* 46 (2022).

35. Democratic finance should also be financially sustainable. The technical aspects of financing a public financial institution, such as a bank, is beyond the purview of this book. But it is clear that such reproduction does not require an orientation toward maximizing returns on investments. Financing is always a *political* question. If deemed socially useful by our demos, loss-making programs can be offset through public subsidies. There is simply no reason to think that democratic finance has to be profitable in order to be durable. Thomas Marois, *Public Banks: Decarbonisation, Definancialisation and Democratisation* (Cambridge: Cambridge University Press, 2021), 226.

36. Ibid., 232.

37. Dean Baker, "Reining in Wall Street to Benefit All Americans: The Case for a Financial Transactions Tax," Century Foundation, 2016, tcf.org.

38. I am indebted to work by Michael Brennan at the Democracy Collaborative in elaborating on the ways sortition might be used in a bank, institutionally. See "Constructing the Democratic Public

Bank: A Governance Proposal for Los Angeles," Democracy Collaborative, 2021, democracycollaborative.org.

39. "Itinerant Citizen Assembly of Bogota," LATINNO, latinno.net.

40. Helene Landemore, *Open Democracy* (Princeton, NJ: Princeton University Press, 2020), 185.

41. "Standing Citizens' Assembly in Paris," Bürgerrat, October 17, 2021, buergerrat.de.

42. Parlament der Deutschsprachigen Gemeinschaft Belgiens, Bürgerdialog website, buergerdialog.be/en.

43. Erik Olin Wright, *Class Structure and Income Determination* (New York: Academic Press, 1979).

9. Democracy on Fridays

1. Rudolf Hilferding, *Finance Capital: A Study in the Latest Phase of Capitalist Development* (London: Routledge, 2007), 235.

2. György Lukács, *History and Class Consciousness* (Boston: MIT Press, 1972), 101.

3. Halah Ahmad, Jack Landry, Mirada Strominger, and Paul Williams, *Municipal Bank of LA: Housing Solutions and Portfolio Options* (New York: Jain Family Institute and Berggruen Institute, 2023).

4. Kali Akuno and Matt Meyer, eds., *Jackson Rising Redux: Lessons on Building the Future in the Present* (London: PM Press, 2023).

5. Halah Ahmad et al., *Municipal Bank of LA: Financial Justice Portfolio Options* (New York: Jain Family Institute and Berggruen Institute, 2023).

6. Adrienne Buller and Mathew Lawrence, *Owning the Future: Power and Property in an Age of Crisis* (London: Verso, 2022); Kate Aronoff, Alyssa Battistoni, and Daniel Aldana Cohen, *A Planet to Win: Why We Need a Green New Deal* (London: Verso, 2019).

7. Yakov Feygin, Michael A. McCarthy, and Leila Lorenzo, *Coordinating the Supply Side: Creating a Systemic Industrial Policy for the 21st Century* (New York: Berggruen Institute, 2023).

8. Cited in Stephen Jay Gould, *Leonardo's Mountain of Clams and the Diet of Worms* (New York: Three Rivers Press, 1998), 172.

9. Ibid., 175.

Index

O
Ocasio-Cortez, Alexandria, xiii, 147
Occupy Wall Street, 7, 125, 170
OECD (Organisation for Economic Co-operation and Development), 57, 69, 80, 81, 183
Offe, Claus, 35–6, 221n20
oligarchy, against, 181–2
Omarova, Saule, 145
"110 Propositions," 95
On Populist Reason (Laclau), 191
Orçamento Participativo reform, 170
Organisation for Economic Co-operation and Development (OECD), 57, 69, 80, 81, 183
O'Sullivan, Mary, 62
Overton window, 179
ownership society, 4–5, 78
ownership structure, speed of transformation of, 58
ownership transfer, enlarging democratic economy through, 195–7
Owocki, Kevin, *Greenpilled: How Crypto Can Regenerate the World*, 120

P
Palladino, Lenore, 61–2, 143
Paris Citizens' Assembly, 183
Participation and Democratic Theory (Pateman), 162
participatory budgetary experiments, 170
Pateman, Carole, 163–5
    Participation and Democratic Theory, 162
PBLA (Public Bank LA), xiii, 146
pension funds, 64
People's Assembly, 199, 201, 202, 205

People's Investment Board, 202–3
People's QE program, 149–50
People's Research Juries, 201–2
People's Review Board, 202–3
"People's Tribunate," 193–4
Personal Responsibility and Work Opportunity Act (1996), 77
plebeian republicans, 192, 194
policy reform, modes of, 15
Political Power and Social Classes (Poulantzas), 31–2
politics
    democratic ruptures and class, 45
    finance as political projects, 65–76
    forms of political leverage, 10
    political domination, 85–7
    political organization of capitalists, 39–40
    political organization of workers, 40–4
    Poulantzas on political theorists, 30
    working-class, 41–2
The Politics (Aristotle), 181–2
Pollin, Robert, 151
Popular Unity coalition, 92–3, 94, 95
Porto Alegre, 170
positive externalities, 128, 188
Positive Money, 149
Posner, Richard, *Radical Markets*, 123
postal banking, 208
Post Bank, 142
Poulantzas, Nicos
    about, 220n9, 220n11, 220n13, 222–3n42
    on abstractionism, 32–3
    on class functionalist theory, 31–2
    on deep social-structural inequalities, 130
    on democratic ruptures, 45–6